## Praise for *Readings Against Type*

I think of Albert Mobilio as a flâneur of culture. To follow the path of his criticism down alleyways and boulevards is to be immersed in the sights, sounds, and feel of literature and art. I've long been in awe of the breadth of his interests and the depth of his empathetic imagination, and this collection, a series of amiable detours ranging from road atlases to asemic writing to the art of list making, doesn't disappoint. His language, too, is a marvel—tactile, dazzling, and ripe, like fruit at the peak of summer. —Nicole Rudick, *What Is Now Known Was Once Only Imagined: An (Auto)biography of Niki de Saint Phalle*

Each piece in this book distills intently focused fascination, whether with maps, magic, cemeteries, aerial surveillance, collages of found objects, or how cities and landscapes change over time. Wherever he directs his gaze Albert Mobilio teases out unexpected perspectives, by turns playful or macabre or ironic or sublime. Tiny objects or odd hobbies may be tokens of cataclysm or prescient intuition. Glimpses discerned in a snapshot or a stretch of desert engender metaphors that blossom into narratives. A word-centered artwork by Ed Ruscha evokes "a bathroom graffito on a doomed U-boat," a falcon traces "the inseam of the void." Among the places on a West Virginia road map Mobilio finds "incantatory music" and in the argot of Mafia wiretaps "a poetry of the oblique." In the lives and works of artists (Harry Smith, Weegee, Frédéric Bruly Bouabré, Vivian Maier, and many others) he is alert to endlessly suggestive processes, and from what might seem random detritus (lists, manuals, hoarded mementos) he elicits hidden histories whose implications spread out in all directions. *Readings Against Type* is like a steamer trunk overflowing with the evidence of many lives and many places: at once memoir and urban chronicle and meditation on art, and, not least, acknowledgment of how mysteriously all its elements interconnect. —Geoffrey O'Brien, *Arabian Nights of 1934*

In *Readings Against Type* Albert Mobilio maps cultural curiosities like few others. Whether making sense of Gertrude Stein's sentences, reading travel guides and how-to books as literature, musing on a museum devoted to one man, or glossing photographs of men's footwear on city sidewalks, his sharp prose illuminates cultural artifacts that favor odd angles of approach. Read these pocket-size pieces of the planet for a keener sense of where we've been—and where we might be headed. —Louis Bury, *Exercises in Criticism*

# Readings Against Type

## *Essays and Reviews*

# *Readings Against Type*

## *Essays and Reviews*

Albert Mobilio

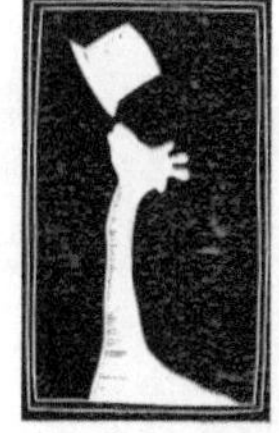

MadHat Press
Cheshire, Massachusetts

MadHat Press
MadHat Incorporated
PO Box 422, Cheshire, MA 01225



The Library of Congress has assigned
this edition a Control Number of
2025943984

ISBN 978-1-968422-01-1 (paperback)

Cover art and design by Marc Vincenz
Book design by MadHat Press

www.madhat-press.com

First Printing
Printed in the United States of America

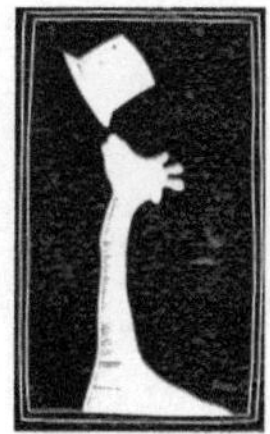

# Table of Contents

## On Camera

# Introduction

A book critic faces certain complications. When writers write about writing they are conducting a form of self-interrogation. That is to say, in the truest sense, reviewers review themselves. This isn't the case for most cultural critics: movie critics don't often make films; music critics aren't composing string quartets. Their vigorously expressed opinions won't swing back to bite them in the ass the way they surely could for a reviewer who critiques a novelist's, say, overwrought metaphors. A potential letter to the editor might cause that critic to think twice about the suitability of any metaphors they deploy in their review. Yet criticism should be daring, extravagant even. A heightened sense of style and literary self-consciousness can free a critic from such constraints; you read them not because of the subject at hand but because of their voice.

I wrote for several New York-based publications, including *Bookforum* (for which I served as an editor for a dozen years), *Hyperallergic* (where I have also worked as an editor), *The Village Voice*, *Tin House*, and *Harper's* at a time when cultural studies had come into vogue and subjects fit for close reading expanded well beyond traditional bounds. I sought out subjects not obviously literary or even, well, primarily understood as books. For instance, for the *Voice Literary Supplement* I wrote a short essay about the remote control as the very embodiment of the postmodern aesthetic.

The readership for these publications included many academics, to be sure, but probably a larger number were grad school dropouts (like myself) and eccentric enthusiasts who were acutely knowledgeable about an array of intellectual fascinations rather than in possession of scholarly depth about a few. This audience read across disciplines, disdained them; they were as keen on 1950s physique magazines as they were on Thomas Bernhard. My contributions to these publications aimed to reflect the moment's recombinatory aesthetic as well as a sense of play. Paramount was a sense of discovery about interpretative possibilities. In this vibrantly heterodox milieu, critics questioned not only the reading experience but the notion of what, in fact, can be read.

As a working critic, I reviewed books about the invention of longitude, Thomas Edison, groupies, bioterrorism, tattooing, rafting down the Colorado, the Empire State building, Vince Lombardi, and the First World War. Primarily, though, I wrote about fiction by authors ranging from Stephen Crane to Lydia Davis, Ivy Compton Burnett to William Gass. But the reviews and essays assembled here were driven by more eccentric fascinations.

**Collectors:** These pieces address collectors, their collections, lists, and compilations, treating them as legible archives—be it Joe Brainard's lists of memories, Umberto Eco's lists of lists, Harry Smith's paper airplanes and string art, or Tony Oursler's compendium of spiritualist paraphernalia. The key essay here is devoted to Christian Sanderson, a Pennsylvania schoolteacher born in 1882, whose life is meticulously preserved in his home, now a museum, in Chadds Ford. His obsession with his personal history led him to save and annotate nearly every object he encountered: the rack on which his father hung his hat; the burnt matches from a decades-old birthday party. "Peep Show," an essay on New York's Museum of Sex, explores whether or not "sex" as a category is both too broad and too evanescent (what to make of the dress Xaviera Hollander wore for the cover of her book *Letters to the Happy Hooker?*) to be presented in a museum. "What Writers Talk About" ranges over volumes of collected interviews with Mark Twain, Theodore Dreiser, Jack Kerouac, and others to begin to define the genre conventions of the author interview, as well as the evolution of that practice across many decades.

**Unreadables:** A favorite quote of mine comes from Gertrude Stein, who, upon arriving in America in 1934, was questioned by a reporter who asked, "Why don't you write the way people read?" Her deft reply: "Why don't you read the way I write?" Stein, who indeed was and is still considered unreadable, sought to "make it new" in a way markedly different from other Modernists. "The Lost Generator" argues that, instead of texts thick with literary allusions, Stein offered readers an open-ended game in which interpretations were presumed to be private and thus always in flux. Similarly, Renee Gladman's drawn sentences dismantle, I suggest, recognizable literary forms to move between figurative and abstract elements. "The Bookness of Not-Books" addresses the "unreadability" of artist's books; "In a Word," the asemic texts of Jackson Mac Low; and "Collected Letters" examines how Ed Ruscha's depictions of words and phrases lend them a distinct tactility. An essay on Ray Johnson's use of correspondence ("Post Modern") and the mechanics of mail shows how he both undermined and enhanced the structures of interpersonal communication. Serving as a kind of companion piece, "Correspondence School," an essay on the history of letter-writing manuals, ponders the formulaic essence of letters. Two essays published in *Harper's* ("Made Men of Letters" and "The Criminal Within") delve into sub-genres (informational guides on, for instance, bomb-making and corpse disposal, and a piece on the myth of the unlimited exercise of power in Mafia tales) not typically thought to merit readerly consideration. And "Nonsense and Sensibility" reveals how Glen Baxter's koan-like cartoons occupy the space between image and text, between perplexity and the mundane to create a locale where uncertainty emerges as weird and weirdness recedes into uncertainty. The narrative conjuring provided by cartography is explored in two pieces: "On the Road," a review of the *1998 National Geographic Road Atlas*, and "Off the Map," a personal meditation on the talismanic power of maps.

**On Camera:** Writing about art allows a book critic to avoid the self-referential bind. But more particularly, I am drawn to photography's opportunities to read provocatively, to view its most essential power as storytelling. Because of its vexed relationship to factuality and its routine deployment for documentary purposes, this is an art whose social implications require narrative rather than solely formalist interpretation. "A Boy's Own Story" details how Gordon Parks, the famed African American photographer of civil rights struggles, was sent by *Life Magazine* to a favela in Rio de Janeiro in 1961 to document the extreme poverty there. His empathic portraits of a young boy changed the child's life for good (he was brought briefly to the US, where his asthma was cured) and bad (he has spent the rest of his life distraught over missing his time in America). "Night and the City" reflects on the effect of Weegee's post-war images on our understanding of New York. Lastly, both Vivian Maier and Saul Leiter employed obscure angles and subjects to explore the interior world of public space.

# Collectors

# For Keeps:
# The Christian C. Sanderson Museum

Chris Sanderson saved almost everything he touched. He saved the toy trains from his childhood in the 1880s. He saved the slate board on which he did his lessons as a boy. He saved dance cards from a barn dance in 1906. The pencil he used to vote for Alf Landon in 1936. A rock from the hill where he served as an air-raid spotter in World War II. The burnt matches that lit a candle commemorating what would have been his late father's eighty-fifth birthday. A piece of the flagpole from the school where he taught. He also saved anything anyone gave him: a vial of melted ice from the South Pole; sawdust from a Billy Sunday revival meeting; a small wheel from a zeppelin shot down in England in 1916; a hyena's head; a hangman's noose; and a cup once hidden in a well by the great-great-grandfather of a friend. Sanderson saved everything and anything—from the shawl his mother wrapped him in the day he was born to a lock of George Washington's hair—filling his farmhouse in Chadds Ford, Pennsylvania, with the flotsam and jetsam of his most intimate life, as well as that of distant times and locales. He carefully tagged nearly all of these items with handwritten notes specifying dates and contexts ("Tissue paper from box of Indian clubs"). From childhood onward, as his well-preserved stuffed animals attest, Sanderson was a zealous, perhaps obsessed, collector. For most of his eighty-four years (he died in 1966), he pursued a somewhat quixotic goal: to memorialize himself as the subject of his very own museum; that is, to become the archaeologist and curator of his own life.

There are no marble steps or columns at the Christian C. Sanderson Museum; it is the early-nineteenth-century farmhouse where Sanderson lived for most of his life. Although the two-story, wood-frame structure sits only a hundred yards from busy Route 100 as it passes through Chadds Ford, visitors are infrequent. Still, those who come to visit the nearby homes of Andrew and N. C. Wyeth, as well as the Brandywine Battlefield, where Washington was defeated in the largest land battle of the Revolutionary War, sometimes find themselves standing on the front porch peering through the screen door. They are usually greeted by Thomas R. Thompson, a one-time friend of Sanderson's, who oversees the eight-room museum and has made a valiant attempt at archiving the thousands of letters and notes (over a ton in weight) Sanderson left stacked in dusty piles around the house. "After Chris died, you could hardly move in here," Thompson says. "He was quite the pack rat." The understatement is almost comical. A photo of Sanderson's bed shows that he slept on barely a third of the mattress, the remainder being buried in books and papers. This and other photos of Sanderson's rooms taken before they were cleaned up recall stories about other lifelong hoarders—for instance, Harlem's Collyer brothers, who packed their Fifth Avenue brownstone with 136 tons of stuff (including fourteen grand pianos, the chassis of a Model T Ford, an X-ray machine). In 1947, when one brother was killed by a falling bundle of newspapers, his blind and paralyzed sibling, unable to make his way through the labyrinth, starved to death. But Sanderson wasn't pathological; the tenor of his collecting mania was domestic and pedagogical, not rabid.

Every day, we make dozens of decisions about what things we want to keep and what things should be discarded. We sit in judgment over our material domain: the postcard from an old friend that's been on the kitchen counter for a month, toss it; the set of unidentifiable keys, keep them just in case; assorted Post-Its with various numbers and illegible names, keep for now; a coffee mug given by office mates, goodbye. It's an unending and often perplexing chore. Most decisions we make automatically, appraising the relative utility of things—does it work? do I need it?—but other decisions are more fraught. I have a birthday card signed by my mother. Generally, I would keep these cards for what I believed to be a respectful period of about a month and then consign them to the trash (with a small but nonetheless manageable pang). There's nothing special about the inscription on the card I have kept for several years, except that she wrote the words "Your loving mother and father" two weeks before she died. I keep the card, for what reason, I'm not sure. It's standard-issue Hallmark, individuated only by a dash of her penmanship, but I cannot bring myself to throw it away; the pang is not manageable. Sanderson, it's clear, couldn't endure even the hint of such a pang.

The personal objects he saved are familiar to us; they are things we also may have saved: Easter eggs, family photos, pressed leaves, pencil boxes, China plates, baby toys, train schedules. Such things pass through our hands, acquiring a brief significance, and then they somehow disappear. Who still has the pencil box they clutched on their first day of school? Or the train schedule they used when they left home to live somewhere else? There was a moment when that printed piece of paper was important to us, then it wasn't; it became disposable. But if saved, of course, such a schedule might gain talismanic power. We would consider it an object of importance in our story. If there were a museum devoted solely to your life, it would be there, under glass, perhaps with a Sanderson-like annotation: "Train schedule with 9:16 express circled."

Sanderson keenly anticipated his longing for his own past, and he hoarded against the prospect of being alone, the dispersal of his possessions. The odder, less obviously evocative objects that he saved attest plaintively to this fear of loss. These items are so embedded with narrative that they acquire the kinetic quality of *tableau vivant*. There's a hat rack with his father's hat still hanging on a knob—the father hung it there but never retrieved it; he died some days later in 1898. It's easy to imagine Sanderson ensuring that the hat remained at the precise angle it was left. There is a nail (yes, a solitary nail) whose significance is detailed in the accompanying note: "A very precious Relic and keepsake. The nail from the middle of the front room ceiling... from here hung our paper, etc., for parties." *Very precious* are words you see over and over, neatly penciled on cards attached to the most quotidian things. There are several packets of "precious" burnt matches; their notes recall the occasion of their use while also invoking a lost parent: "Matches used to light candles by dad's pictures and flowers ... the day he would have been 85." The poignancy of these charred wooden sticks wrapped in wax paper is sharpened by the inventiveness of the aesthetic conceit. The matches are a commemoration of a commemorative act—the kind of self-reflexive, postmodern gesture you would expect from, say, Jasper Johns, not a rural schoolteacher in the 1940s. The artist Sanderson most readily evokes is Joseph Cornell; both men were entranced by the intricate sentimentality that ephemera can generate.

One of the most touching relics is a handmade Christmas star tied to a dry evergreen branch. The star was tied to the top of the tree by Sanderson's mother in 1943, just weeks before she died. What is of value here is, of course, the actual knot. Sanderson preserved his mother's act of tying it. Did he believe that something of her inner being, the domestic events of that day, were caught up in its loops? It's hard to say. But this desiccated pine branch and yellowed star joined by some rough twine pierces deeply as a reminder of how intimately things cohabit with us; how they are almost phantom limbs. This knot is a fetish object, the repository of desire and belief. Still, we tie knots every day. We hang jackets on hooks. We comb our hair. Yet we don't deliberately save the knotted shoelaces of our children or the combs threaded with our spouse's hair. To do so would be to welcome and appease an unbearable apprehension of loss.

No doubt, Sanderson was quite the odd duck. (In a photo from Thompson's biography, *Chris,* he is seen "playing with one of his rats.") Yet he was also a schoolteacher, square-dance fiddler, amateur historian, and expert Indian club juggler, in short, the kind of quaint figure (he played Rip Van Winkle in town pageants and, of course, saved locks of his fake beard) who populates the small towns of an idealized American past. Indeed, in a painting by his friend Andrew Wyeth, Sanderson, with his angular face, big ears, and bookish mien, looks a little like Ichabod Crane. A devoted son who never married and lived with his mother until she died, Sanderson (bachelor scoutmaster and pack rat eccentric) would probably arouse suspicion these days. But life in the early part of the last century meant he could leave a note on his open front door reading, "Walk in yell upstairs (not well.)" It was also a time when many Americans shared Sanderson's straightforward, if not naïve, enthusiasm for American history: historical commemorations engaged whole communities, and figures like Lincoln and Washington were held in uncomplicated reverence.

But Sanderson's fascination with history is marked by an idiosyncratic passion that can't simply be attributed to patriotism. He gathered up anything with even the slightest trace of historical value (restaurant place mats with maps of Gettysburg, presidential campaign buttons, a bit of the plane that crashed into the Empire State Building), and he also created his own artifacts. An inveterate attendee of public celebrations and memorial ceremonies (he was in Washington, D.C., for every inauguration from Theodore Roosevelt's to Lyndon Johnson's), he recorded his attendance in hundreds of notes which employed the officialese of government documents: "It is now 11 p.m. May 31, 1926. Have just returned to my boarding house at Roselle, Delaware. Today I attended the opening of the Sesquicentennial, 150th anniversary of the Declaration of Independence." Pressed in the folds of the note might be the flower or ribbon he wore on his coat, or the bill from the boardinghouse. He drew public history into the realm of his private myth just as he enlarged his private myth to embrace history. From his years living in the house that was Washington's headquarters for the Battle of Brandywine, Sanderson saved some charred wood, which he duly noted was the "remains of a fireplace log used Christmas Eve 1919." Through the mundane experience of warming up at a fire, Sanderson connected to the first president, the blackened log a token of their intimacy across the centuries at the same hearth. He also collected the detritus of battlefields—spent shells, aircraft pieces, flag shards, bomb fragments. If there's something decidedly inglorious about this assemblage of metal scraps (an anti-war activist could hardly devise a more grim depiction of battle as mere detonation), that surely wasn't Sanderson's intent. For him, the burnt, broken odds and ends of the past—rather than, for instance, a mint-condition uniform—offered the surest conduits into history's inner drama. They are as small (and as *used*) as the soldiers they equipped, and thus bear witness to human scale on the larger stage.

In the spring of 1968, when Robert Kennedy's funeral train passed through my town on its way to Washington, D.C., I was one of the many kids who—in the hope of fabricating instant historical treasure—set coins on the railroad track. Not being much of a pack rat myself, I've long since lost the tongue-shaped pennies the train left behind. But standing in Sanderson's house surrounded by a congeries of similar cultural debris, I wonder what relationship, if any, those flattened bits of copper bore to Kennedy or the event of his assassination. Certainly, thinking about them evokes little about the microhistory. (Televised images hold sway there.) Rather, what I mostly recall about the day was pressing my parents—who were not Kennedy enthusiasts—to hurry to the station as the car radio tracked the train's approach. I may have vivid memories of the flag-draped coffin and Ted Kennedy waving from the back of the train, but the history I would want to remember more clearly—which I simply cannot—is what my parents said, how we got along, if my mother wore a dress for the occasion, and what exactly I was thinking as I stood between them, the bell clanging as the big engine slowed for the crowd. All of that's gone. If I had saved those coins, noted the date and time the train passed, could they now conjure for me—like Proust's madeleine—some fresh habitation of my own lost time?

What is perhaps the most curious and affecting item in the house evidences Sanderson's talent for synthesizing public and private narrative, as well as devising fetish objects meant to ward off impending loss. It is a 1940 photo taken by Sanderson of his mother on the anniversary of Lincoln's assassination. Curled on her side, clutching a handkerchief in one hand, the other hand tucked under her head, Hanna Sanderson mournfully contemplates a portrait of Lincoln draped with a small American flag. A note written by Mrs. Sanderson decodes the dramatic scene: She had been nine years old, "sick with some childish ailment," on the morning of April 15, 1865, when her father returned from the village post office with news of Lincoln's death. And now:

"Today, April 15 between 9 and 9:30 a.m., Christie took my picture as I lay on that same sofa and at the same end as on that distressing day 75 years ago." Private grief at public tragedy is memorialized in a photo that commemorates their intertwined nature. As with all of Sanderson's mementos, emotion is particularized. Important to both mother and son is the fact that she lies "at the same end" of the couch (probably holding the same handkerchief). The theatricality of the enterprise, with its attendant suggestion of the ersatz, is redeemed by this fervor for exactitude, for particularity. Sanderson's emotional precision—his knowing sense of what Stendhal called the "small truths" (*les petits faits vrais*)—animates his keepsakes with visceral tension. As the image of this elderly woman posing as a child eerily recollects one death, it also prophesizes another. On the wall close to the photo are two other images—Sanderson's photo of his mother on her deathbed two years later, a nineteenth-century American flag draping her body, and Andrew Wyeth's painting, based on that photo, titled *Christmas Morning*. Mortality, with its sly insinuations into the everyday laid bare—the hat you hang tomorrow you may never touch again—haunts this house and invests a burnt match, a nail, and some knotted twine with a lyric melancholy. Things can, indeed, be "very precious."

It's a kind of magical thinking—ancient and vigorously abiding—to believe that something of ourselves, those we love, and those we esteem inheres in mere objects. This wishful desire to memorialize flesh within the inanimate is our hedge against separateness from others and the body's frailty. (The lowly candle that lit your first birthday cake could easily outlast your great-grandchildren.) From museums to monuments, from attics to family scrapbooks, the sum of consecrated things is vast, and the number of candidates even greater. My son's crowded room needs clearing, but he claims every broken toy to be "special" to him. And, truly, many are special to me, too. In this way, a world of would-be relics presses in upon us: an unplayable album, Jimi Hendrix's *Axis: Bold as Love*, the cover of which you once fell into headlong, being stoned for the first time; an unwearable hand-me-down tie of your father's; or a headless action figure all vie for canonization, for their place on some shelf. Sanderson could not resist their clamorous demand. Objects spoke insistently to him of their power to mitigate loss, to salvage something durable in the face of unrelenting decay. That's why his memorabilia collection may amuse, transfix, and even unnerve us, but ultimately it is a source of formidable sorrow. It's not just the sadness that so readily springs from Sanderson's poignant, evocative *objets*. Surpassing that feeling is a nagging sense of waste that mounts to heart-withering distress over this life spent on the verge of mourning. Within all these strangely sacred things resides a too-familiar kernel of fear. It went unresisted by Sanderson until it overwhelmed his being, until he became his own archaeologist or, put another way, the exhumer of his own grave. Of course, we all must shore up some fragments against the ruins. They will prove the necessary charms that one day will summon our long-lost selves. My son can keep his headless Batman and three-wheeled race car. But he also needs to learn to let go of some "special" things; he needs to learn that the pang is manageable.

*Tin House*, Winter 2003.

# Peepshows: Museums Want to Sex You Up

A recent headline of the dog-bites-man variety appeared in *The New York Times* announcing, "Sex Museum Reports Profitability." The director of New York City's newly opened Museum of Sex, Daniel Gluck, "a former computer entrepreneur, painter, and sculptor," was pleased to report that attendance—even with an admission ticket costing seventeen dollars—was running more than 50 percent ahead of projections. It's hard, though, to imagine that this museum's backers seriously fretted—like, let's say, the trustees of the Museum of Numismatics—over whether the public would come out to take a look. Institutions up to their ears in Giottos and Cézannes may be compelled to wear ever more user-friendly faces, but one might safely guess that a joint with nothing more than a roof and a sign saying MUSEUM OF SEX could draw a crowd (not only of paying customers but reporters and TV news crews) without much effort. After all, as carny barkers, movie moguls, and every publisher since Caxton knows, there's nothing quite so user-friendly as sex. And so it's gone for the Museum of Sex, which offers not only a roof but is, in fact, a clean, well-lighted place with prerecorded tour guides. After the predictable spate of media coverage, the curious (including me) flocked to its lower–Fifth Avenue address, cash in hand, ready for our dose of carnal culture.

To say it was not all I expected is, of course, the required coda—"Before, a joy propos'd, behind, a dream," as Shakespeare put it—for long-hoped-for trysts and stolen peeks, or visits to sex museums. It would be hard to say just what I did expect; at the coin museum, you're sure to see coins, but how do you get sex on a wall or under glass? The typical museum displays the consequences of expressive acts—paintings, quilts, or matchstick bridges—so, to pursue the analogy between artistic creation and sexual consummation, would a sex museum show images of infants, hang rumpled sheets, or post guilty confessions? Such objects are surely the result of sex. Or consider a Museum of Natural History approach, featuring anthropologically accurate dioramas of human specimens—"Elderly Scottish heterosexual couple petting to orgasm, 1963," for instance—engaged in all manner of sex. Then again, why not recruit real people? Variants of that show played on 42nd Street for decades. Sex is an activity, not an artifact; the problem for curators of a sex museum is that they are limited to choosing among tangible items that facilitate rather than embody that act. Those things which might be said to be sexual artifacts, whether they are pornographic images, hootchy-kootchy dances, or cock rings, might best be described as products of anticipating sex; they spring from longing, lust, seduction, and fantasy, in short, from the "joy propos'd." (Or denied, as the case may be.)

The current show at the Museum of Sex, titled *NYC Sex: How New York City Transformed Sex in America,* attempts to position the city as the vanguard locale of sexual culture in America. The argument is hardly an adventurous one; making the case instead for Pittsburgh would have been hailed as a curator's tour de force. Given the cosmopolitan and essentially liberal nature of the city, there is a surfeit of sex-related material with some New York connection—from nineteenth-century brothel guides to *Screw* magazine, from Evelyn Nesbit to Annie Sprinkle. The show handily exploits New York's sexual equivalent of the Yankees roster: Mae West, Irving Klaw, the Village People, Margaret Sanger, Xaviera Hollander, Minsky's Burlesque, Gypsy Rose Lee, Paul Cadmus, Plato's Retreat, Linda Lovelace, the Anvil, and ACT UP. Even when it comes to repression, the city has in Anthony Comstock the benchmark for bluenoses.

Of course, it's the vintage material—films of shimmy dancers, Tijuana bibles, French postcards, etc.—with its reassuring note of *plus ça change* that most delights. We can read selected pages from *Guide to the Harem,* an 1855 Zagat survey for the city's houses of prostitution, and sample an old-timey climate of intertwined snobbery and sexual hypocrisy which thrives equally well today in both the *New Yorker* and *Maxim*. The best sort of young gentleman might visit Miss Jenny Grey's establishment at 27 Mercer Street, where he would find his pretensions well flattered: "Her young ladies are invariably selected for their personal charms and conversational attainments. Among them is Belle Seymour, a perfect Joan of Arc." The same gentleman—when not looking for quite so saintly an encounter—might peek in at Miss Smith's on Leonard Street since "[t]he girls that peddle peanuts and candy attend here, and all the drunken trulls of the city congregate with them." The quaintly euphemistic tone—"The hours fly by with startling rapidity"—reminds us of what a long way, baby, we've come only to end up with a similar nudge-nudge, wink-wink language for sex talk, albeit one which enables talk show hosts to joke about knee pads and oral exams.

Much of the more recent sexual bric-a-brac is probably quite familiar to anyone who hasn't spent the past twenty years on an Amish farm. If you struck a piñata labeled THE SEXUAL REVOLUTION, this is what would spill out: peep-show coins, sex toys, porn movie posters, dirty magazines, lesbian pulp novels, Gil Elvgren's cheesecake art, Robert Mapplethorpe's bull-whip-in-the-bum "Self Portrait" and more photos—lots of photos—of antiporn protesters, topless bar hawkers, Plato's Retreat revelers, and the Gay Pride Parade. Slightly more rarified items like John Coutts's S&M drawings from his magazine *Bizarre,* Thomas Painter's 1950s photos of hustlers and sailors, or Charles Guyette's custom-designed bondage outfits might be news to brunch-club members down from Westchester, but overall there's not much here—thanks to pop culture's hunger for the naughty—that hasn't been seen many times before. Even the more "underground" material has long been available in dozens of books, chiefly those published by the German publisher Taschen. A stop at the "sex table" at the Strand Bookstore will acquaint you with much of what the museum has on hand and is an acceptable alternative for the budget-conscious.

An alternative mode of presentation—a coffee table book or a documentary film—would have been quite adequate, since the show offers very little that can't be fully comprehended as a reproduction; it's hardly essential to view original prints of Charles Guyette's photos of bound breasts. And those items sparking the most curiosity are the least well served by being set behind glass. Two pages from Denny F. Pace's "Handbook of Vice Control," published in 1971, give cops the clues to ferreting out "toilet snipes" in men's washrooms. There are photos of "footsie" being played between stalls and instructions on how to identify homosexuals: "Wears extreme clothing styles—e.g., an old man in a purple Nehru suit or a tight-fitting outfit that outlines his private parts." The handbook itself belongs in an archive of sex history, but its pages would reach the largest audience and be most easily enjoyed as, perhaps, postcard reproductions to be sold in the same campy trinket shops currently selling postcard reproductions of lesbian pulp novel covers. At the museum, those novels have been encased and carefully mounted like Etruscan pottery shards.

No doubt sensitive to its surfeit of printed material, the show's curators have sought out artifacts like the dress Xaviera Hollander wore for the cover photo of her 1973 book *Letters to the Happy Hooker*. Leaving aside the fact that this "artifact" doesn't get us very far from the printing press, its value within New York's sex history is comically slight. Another mildly ridiculous attempt to imitate a traditional museum greets you as you enter the exhibit, much as Perseus does at the Metropolitan Museum. It's a life-size, white bas-relief sculpture of the murdered body of Helen Jewett, a prostitute who was butchered and set aflame in what became nineteenth-century New York's most famous sex crime. Jewett's story, and the story of the trial of the man accused of killing her, are compelling ones (and they are well told in a recent book by Patricia Cline Cohen), but this blanched sculpture neither shocks nor informs. Rather, it evidences just how anxious this sex museum is about the "displayability" of its subject.

The exhibition is arranged chronologically—one moves from the ground floor's dark old days of sexual repression upstairs to the glam-spangled era of bondage and drag queens—and thus invites observations of a sociological cast. When we hear an audiotape featuring the transcript of the 1903 court proceedings which followed a police raid on a men's bathhouse, we are meant to be amused by the clinical language—"made indecent motions with his hand while holding said penis"—and thus, I suppose, more keenly appreciate the social maturity and expressive freedom marked by, say, the Village People, whose tunes play ceaselessly further on in the show. Likewise, the ground floor's medical specimens (there's a baleful face, its nose eaten away by syphilis) and turn-of-the-century abortion tools appear to give way to a less fraught domain of Alberto Vargas portraits and the Happy Hooker. The tale of sexuality's relentless march from the back alleys to the nightly news is approvingly told with attention to detours such as Mayor La Guardia's closing of burlesque houses, Anthony Comstock's banning of contraceptive material in the mail, and a 1965 antipornography film made by a religious group which all, in turn, actually amplify the approbative tone. Regardless of how you feel about this—and I am certainly glad I live in the era of condom ads and belly shirts rather than enforced anti-sodomy laws and illegal abortions—the museum's attempt to contextualize sex within an uplifting cultural narrative is a gambit with a long pedigree.

Last fall, the Brooklyn Museum of Art presented "Exposed: The Victorian Nude," an exhibition organized by the Tate in London. Many of the painters and sculptors featured in that show—William Etty, Edward John Poynter, George Frederic Watts, William Mulready, and Lawrence Alma-Tadema—were among the most popular and controversial painters of their day. Nonetheless, their lavish, idealistic, and earnestly narrative imagery has long languished in ill repute. Even now, when almost every aesthetic moment has its champions—if for no other reason than the general critical disposition to contrarianism—this assemblage of salon paintings caused one New York critic to begin his review with the statement, "I hate this art." It's hard to imagine what about the show could inspire such ardent disinclination: the paintings are beautifully made, and their luxuriant corporeality is so vivid that the urge to reach out and touch must be resisted. True, for contemporary viewers, much of the imagery is kitsch—an awful lot of naked women lounge on divans, wrestle with serpents, and prepare for their baths—yet the great biblical tales, legends, and classical myths were routinely pressed into service as fig leaves for these otherwise lascivious bodies. As a result, many of these paintings fairly well burst from their frames with vigorous storytelling.

The Victorian audience could accept the full-frontal depiction of a woman's body if the body, for instance, belonged to the lovely Andromeda as she awaited, chained to a rock, her sacrifice to the sea monster. In Edward John Poynter's painting of this scene, she writhes ever so slightly, her eyes closed and lips slightly parted, seemingly unaware of her dire straits. Perhaps she knows that Perseus will soon appear to save the day, or perhaps she simply likes being bound and naked. Viewers of this painting in 1870 surely would have known her fate, being in full possession of all the details of the ancient story. For them, knowledge of the narrative pretext—despite the image's unavoidable sexuality—served as a dispensation from the sin of voyeuristic lust. The flagrant eroticism could be understood as a necessary detail—her scant clothing clenched in the monster's teeth merely confirmed the peril—in a salutary heroic quest; no doubt, it was experienced somewhat differently. Since this dispensation required enough schooling to know your Ovid, it also handily confirmed the Victorian aesthete's social status, a status which helped preserve their dignity while staring eye level at bare pudenda. If their loins stirred, it was merely one of intellect's many delights.

Compare, for instance, possible reactions to the Betty Page photos at the Museum of Sex, which depict the '50s raven-haired temptress engaged in various girl-girl activities like spanking, wrestling, and bondage. These images cannot be situated in any storyline other than the process of their production—for instance, we can muse over photographer Irving Klaw's insight into nascent fetish communities—and the obsessions of their consumers. The imagery—and this was and is surely a chief part of its allure—is self-evident and requires no foreknowledge or interpretation, only a taste for garter belts, ropes, and Betty. Indeed, this lack of "socially redeeming value," or in other words, narrative, is precisely what a judge or censor might cite to classify it as pornographic. Betty's pictures are designed to deliver their sexual frisson immediately, and no care has been taken to invoke Greek philosophies of the beautiful or tragic tales of doomed princesses; the photos are candid about their use as spurs to sexual desire.

In Herbert Schmalz's 1888 painting titled *Faithful unto Death,* we view several enticing young women bound to posts on the coliseum floor awaiting the lions as thousands of Romans watch from above. One woman clasps her hands in prayer, another hangs her head as if ashamed; the women are arrayed in various unmistakably erotic postures and are bound by straps artfully placed to accentuate their nakedness. (A critic at the time noted that the straps "cut into the soft flesh" with a realism that could only have been achieved if "Mr. Schmalz had a post erected in his studio and bound the girl exactly as represented.") Of course, this painting, quite popular as a reproduction in its day and later an influence on Cecil B. DeMille's film *The Sign of the Cross,* is far from candid. Its wealth of outré sexual content—bondage, torture, the bones strewn about the women's feet, the bare-chested enslaved African who lashes one girl to her pillar, not to mention the charged intermingling of voyeurism and exhibitionism—has been placed within a story, a heroic story of Christian faith, no less.

Initially, it would seem the Museum of Sex presents such things as the Betty Page photos as a way of highlighting their purely sexual nature, their candor. But, as you move through the museum and its array of increasingly explicit images, you discover that a narrative has been imposed on the images and objects, and this narrative is the story of society's gradual acceptance of sexual expression. (In his introduction to the catalog, museum director Gluck pointedly claims lineage with Magnus Hirschfeld's Institut für Sexualwissenschaft and he notes how that collection was destroyed by the Nazis in 1933.) Acceptance does hit the wall when it comes to children and sex. The museum scrupulously steers away from this radioactive topic—and, given the recent arrest of Paul Reubens, "Pee-wee Herman," for some pictures of children in his vast vintage porn collection, who can blame them. On the other hand, the Victorian show, reflecting the expressive freedoms allowed by that era's intricate hypocrisies, presents several explicit images of naked, sometimes coyly erotic, children. Still, the upbeat message-of-tolerance narrative is surely, in its broadest strokes, mainly true, but what remains intriguing is the Museum's felt need to recapitulate Victorian "fig leafing" by contextualizing its materials within a triumphant tale of human betterment. Justifying sexual content with an uplifting narrative is now, over a hundred and fifty years later, again employed to transmute tits and ass into something grander, something more acceptable.

A video display features several screens simultaneously running tape loops from porn films starring Vanessa del Rio. As you stand with other museumgoers, all heads cocked to dutifully listen to the tour-guide recording, and watch oh-so-living-color movies showing, variously, a close-up of double penetration, a close-up of a penis ejaculating on del Rio's vagina, and several men masturbating on her breasts and face, you may find it hard to get in the spirit of things. I mean, you can't get more ... well, candid, and on the one, two, or forty-seven occasions I've seen such movies before, I must confess I chose to be alone, not in the company of half a dozen strangers. But my discomfort is readily addressed by the voice in my ear: Vanessa del Rio, with scholarly verve, describes how these movies were made—"On my first film I actually blew the cameraman. That's how hot it was"—and their role in the overall history of porn films in New York. She talks about an actress's requisite "abandonment" and explains, regarding a scene in which she contends with several men, that eight is "the max for a gang bang. Anything above that is just ridiculous." Her reasonable, if not solicitous, tone of voice and sage advice assure this little group whose eyes are fixed on del Rio's most accommodating orifices that we are not, after all, voyeurs, that there's nothing stimulating about these scenes, that we are merely sampling a well-annotated bit of social history.

In his essay in the catalog accompanying *NYC Sex*, Grady T. Turner writes, "The history of sex in New York has been formed by the actions of those who, by chance or design, came into conflict with prevailing attitudes about sexual conduct or propriety." This includes not only the famous sex-biz names mentioned earlier but "scores of others that fill the arrest ledgers of the New York Society for the Suppression of Vice." In this formulation, the routine, under-the-covers copulation which has peopled the planet to the tune of several billion is hardly considered sex, or at least part of sexual history. Indeed, any sex that hasn't taken place on a stage or in a movie, or resulted in a reform movement is relegated here to background noise, constituting the dull throb of "prevailing attitudes." Apparently, mere sex is too mundane for the Museum of Sex. Not only is it problematic to "show" but it is, in a fundamental way, narrative resistant. People have lusted and fucked the same way for ages—the actual desires, acts, and emotions are a human constant. (This fact enabled Victorian artists to win ardent fans in their day even though they presented "ancient" sex.) For public display, sex, which is essentially ephemeral, must be mixed with plot. Story is the amber, so to speak, that captures and stabilizes what's otherwise transitory. One especially affecting micro-tale can be found in the displayed diary pages of Donnie Reynolds. In 1990 he recounted an anonymous sexual encounter: "His name was Bill. He was sweet. I am worried that I might have given him T. B. When I left I felt so dead." The sentiment—much sharper than mere post-coital sadness—is an ominous one: the following entries track Reynolds' career as an AIDS activist. Yet Reynolds's despair is buoyed up by the surrounding artifacts from ACT UP and thus secured within a story of self-empowerment and political resistance. Personal despondency in the wake of unfettered sexual license apparently is just a speed bump in the museum's mission to celebrate "spectacular" sex in NYC.

If there's cause for disappointment at the Museum of Sex, it's not because they've turned to storytelling to lend the heft of significance to strippers' costumes and filmed orgasms; they had little choice. Instead, it's because the museum has chosen such a thin and predictable tale of reassurance to shepherd us through the nasty bits: It's getting better, this show tells us. We're getting better. Freer. More human. It is a message so self-ennobling, so self-congratulatory that you can imagine it making a Victorian audience blush from modesty.

*Tin House*, Spring 2003.

# Diamonds in the Rough: On Havelock Ellis

In 1898, English bookseller George Bedborough was arrested for selling *Sexual Inversion*, the first volume of Havelock Ellis's epic work *Studies in the Psychology of Sex*. A physician, psychologist, and social reformer, Ellis began his career as a teacher but later trained in medicine. His fascination with sex and his focus on what was then regarded as deviancy came to mark his wide-ranging investigation of sexual behaviors. Today, *Sexual Inversion* is regarded as the original English textbook on homosexuality. (Ellis was one of the first authors to present same-sex attraction as an innate condition rather than a disorder.) Other volumes followed, with chapter titles such as "The Evolution of Modesty," "Love and Pain," "The Phenomena of Sexual Periodicity," "The Origins of the Kiss," and "The Mechanism of Detumescence."

I was barely aware of Ellis's career when I came across a mid-1940s compendium of the multivolume *Studies* in a used bookstore on Cape Cod. I may have recognized Ellis in the frontispiece photo—the wavy mane of white hair, the profound beard—but I confess I had often confused him with Richard Freiherr von Krafft-Ebing, the Austro-German psychiatrist and author of *Psychopathia Sexualis*. After all, both were pioneer sexologists with names that sound like law firms.

I began to read the chapter titled "Auto-Erotism," perhaps a bit of happenstance or perhaps the pages just fell open where they were most used to falling. My eye, long trained to locate the libidinous, hit upon the case study of a woman, "age 31, in good health, with, however, a somewhat hysterical excess of energy," according to Ellis. She recounts a discovery: "After some manipulation, I succeeded in awakening what had before been unconscious and unknown. I purposely allowed the habit to grow upon me, and one night—for I always operated on myself before going to sleep, never in the morning—I obtained considerable pleasurable satisfaction, but the following day my conscience awoke." The matter-of-factness, the certainty of feeling, and, most of all, the oddly technical language drew me in. The use of the term *operated,* a word both intimate and antiseptic, fascinated me. The clinical diction struck a powerful chord, evoking my first-ever encounters with sexual knowledge in encyclopedias and medical books read covertly at the library when I was an eight-year-old who thought kissing yucky. Anatomical designations such as *frenulum, corpus cavernosum,* and *fallopian* had then seemed like elements of some secret incantation, a spell cast only by adults when they were alone together. Sex, this parochial schoolboy believed, must be Latinate, polysyllabic, and at least as ritualistic as High Mass. Those literary explorations are as charged with nostalgic delight as actual adolescent crushes. I bought the book.

Ellis can be numbered among those adventurous scientists whose compulsion to study sexuality is likely to have found its spark in very personal questions. Alfred Kinsey's exhaustive tabulation of libidinal experience was an attempt to understand his own proclivities to sadomasochism and homosexuality; evidence abounds of Freud's cocaine addiction, misogyny, and homosexual tendencies; and, Ellis, who was married for decades to an openly lesbian woman, was a virgin suffering from impotence until the age of sixty, when he discovered that watching a woman urinate (he dubbed the fetish "undinism") proved sufficiently arousing. A work in the Renaissance tradition of a commonplace book, *Studies* brings together selections from hundreds of other texts dating from antiquity to the early twentieth century to report on sexual habits from around the globe. Ellis, who began his career writing literary criticism, knew he needed more than scholarship, hence the case studies, first-person accounts he garnered from medical interviews and correspondence with patients and other doctors. The process was hardly systematic. We are introduced to a subject who "belongs to a large family having some neurotic members," and Jules, "aged 22, of good heredity on his father's side, but bad on that of his mother, who is highly hysterical, while his grandmother was very impulsive and sometimes pursued other women with a knife." Instead of appearing as carefully documented participants in a regulated assessment, these folks could be the dramatis personae for a novel whose theme is desire and its discontents. At least, that's how I choose to read them.

Ellis narrates his subjects' sexual histories in prose that aims for professional distance while observing Victorian proprieties of a sort. The precise and technical vocabulary, the fastidiousness about sociological factors, the occasional phrasings lifted from domestic dramas all combine for a disquietingly erotic effect. In "Love and Pain," we meet the married woman "of good social position" who, via "external friction and pressure," finds she's able to "produce an orgasm almost without effort by calling up the image of any man who had struck her fancy. She has often done so while seated talking to such a man, even when he is almost a stranger; in doing it, she says, a tightening of the muscles of the thighs and the slightest movement are sufficient. Ugly men (if not deformed), as well as men with the reputation of being *roués*, greatly excite her sexually, more especially if of good social position, though this is not essential."

It's not hard to imagine this case as a subtextual gloss on some intimate yet chastely rendered scene in a nineteenth-century novel, say, Dorothea Brooke with Will Ladislaw in George Eliot's *Middlemarch*. I have always suspected that Dorothea's self-righteous self-denial throughout the novel possessed more than a hint of libidinal stricture. Since, in terms of class and emotional disposition, the case-study subject and Eliot's heroine aren't very dissimilar, I'm willing to venture a guess about how Dorothea might have manifested her repression. However fanciful the speculation, I don't think the urge behind it is without warrant; Ellis sure sounds like a novelist at times. Narrative grace notes—"if not deformed," "though this is not essential"—add nuance to this "character" probably more than they might enlighten another physician seeking insight about psychosexual disorders. But the mechanical imagery and mode of laboratory observation work with and play against the writerly flourishes. The tension between propriety, control, and factual rigor and the impulse to embellish, to bring forward a human story, is a textual embodiment of the struggle that characterizes our attempts both to understand and to take pleasure in the body.

While some of Ellis's case studies form pocket-size narratives with dramatic arcs and character development, other reports take a more enumerative turn. This following list not only offers a survey of the marriage bed at the turn of the century but also constitutes a précis of a dozen current TV soap-opera plots:

> An American physician in the State of Connecticut sends me the following notes concerning a series of 13 married women.... They are in every way respectable and moral women: Mrs. A says that her husband does not give her sufficient sexual attention, as he fears they will have more children than he can properly care for. Mrs. B always enjoys intercourse; so does Mrs. C. Mrs. D is easily excited and fond of sexual attention. Mrs. E likes intercourse if her husband is careful not to hurt her. Mrs. F never had any sexual desire until after second marriage, but it is now very urgent at times. Mrs. G is not easily excited, but has never objected to her husband's attention. Mrs. H would prefer to have her husband exhibit more attention. Mrs. I never refused her husband, but he does not trouble her much. Mrs. J thinks that three or four times a week is satisfactory, but would not object to nightly intercourse. Mrs. K does not think her husband could give her more than she would like. Mrs. L would prefer to live with a woman if it were not for sexual intercourse. Mrs. M, aged 40, says that her husband, aged 65, insists upon intercourse three times a night, and that he keeps her tired and disgusted. She each time has at least one orgasm, and would not object to reasonable attention.

With Whitmanesque verve, the list marches forward through these marriages, some sad, others surprisingly (given our assumptions about the amorous lives of late Victorians) quite heartening. Mrs. J.

longs for more; Mrs. F. made a good second match; Mrs. M. just wants her husband to be reasonable, but, disgusted though she is, she's still managing "at least one orgasm" every time they have intercourse. Brief and elegantly pointed, each one-sentence biography is a kernel ready to burst with intimate particulars. The dispassionate notation simultaneously hints at and tamps down the elaborative possibilities.

Phyllis Grosskurth, Ellis's biographer, finds the psychologist's terminology "ponderous." In *Havelock Ellis: A Biography,* she calls the *Studies* "dull reading" and wonders how they could have ever "have been judged 'dirty.'" It's true that the material Ellis gathers is poorly organized, presented repetitively, and footnoted and sourced without a thought to narrative flow, but the case studies stand apart. Real voices—assured, attentive—arise, and they are propelled by the familiar rhythms of storytelling. Again, there's a productive tension at play: describing the mechanics of sex required strict candor from individuals (and Ellis) whose natural inclination was circumlocution and euphemism. In one of my favorite tales, a young man recalls his introduction to same-sex contact: "At 7 years of age, while staying in the country, a very good-looking groom, about 25 years of age, misbehaved himself with me.... While doing so he produced my penis and also his own, which was in full erection. He tried in every way to excite my feelings, in vain. For him, the occasion terminated in an ejaculation.... From that day I hated the groom and I felt a sort of guilt as if I'd 'lost something.'" Pathos undergirds impersonal diction; the result is the crossbreed of a sex manual with D.H. Lawrence, with a tincture of confessional memoir. The gap, though, between sex and sex writing in these vignettes is so wide as to be irrelevant. No one is trying to depict emotion and excitement; they mainly want to get the geography right and to do so clearly. These are mannerly operating instructions for bodies tumescent, bodies in collision.

The poet Jonathan Williams was also a fan of *Studies,* of what he called its "frank courtly narratives." In composing his book *The Loco Logodaedalist,* Williams laid cutout sheets on the English physician's pages to create found poems, almost all of which are cause for serendipitous delight, but "History VI" effectively captures Ellis at his strangely sensual, earnestly accurate best: "about 16 lying on the grass in the sunshine his hand / with all his might / opened, exposed manipulated / the other's / to this day a telescope / excites me / They grew up normal men." Taken together, the testimonies gathered by Ellis remind us that desire and compulsion have been ever intertwined and, as such, all too normal, lubriciously so.

*Tin House*, Winter 2012.

# Weird Séance: Tony Oursler's Compendium of the Paranormal Reveals a Twilight World

They saw dead people. They heard them too. When summoned, dead people rang bells, wrote on slates, and levitated tables. Sometimes their faces hovered in the air. The dead made this commotion for their parents, children, siblings, and friends at the behest of gifted individuals capable of readily communing with the world beyond. If the movement associated with this phenomenon, known as spiritualism—which was popular to varying degrees from the mid-nineteenth to the early twentieth century—now appears a quaint relic of a benighted past, we should consider the vigorous currency of aura reading, crystal healing, and psychic consultations. These descendants of spiritualism testify to the ongoing human desire for an eternal force that operates outside the mortal limits of the body.

Of course, many of spiritualism's practitioners—known as "mediums," "psychics," or "conjurers"—preyed on those in mourning, duping grief-stricken family members into believing they could communicate with lost loved ones. The especially cruel nature of the fraud provoked many skeptics and debunkers, including Charles Fulton Oursler (1893–1952), the grandfather of multimedia and installation artist Tony Oursler. An author of mystery and detective novels, Fulton Oursler (as he was known) waged battle alongside Harry Houdini against spiritualist practice, exposing its tricks and deceptions. Tony

Oursler's fascination with the eventful life of his grandfather—he was a polymath and agnostic, and his novel *The Greatest Story Ever Told* was adapted for the screen—is focused particularly on Fulton Oursler's skeptical crusade, which is copiously evidenced by the 2,500 assorted photos, books, pamphlets, and objects the younger Oursler has collected over nearly twenty years. Both the show at MoMA and the portion of that archive that has been sequenced by the artist and published as *Imponderable* offer a dialectical view into a twilight world both distant and familiar, an archaic domain (there's a printing plate for a late-eighteenth-century manual on how to cast spells believed to have been compiled by Moses) and one whose UFO and séance photos could be lifted from sci-fi and horror films. Oursler's visual narrative animates the tension and mutual dependence between faith and science and, more crucially, between the longing for mystery and the need to understand.

The two images on the book's first page encapsulate these paradoxes: A sepia-tinted photo of the Temple of the Sibyl at Tivoli, outside Rome, is juxtaposed with a schematic published in 1824 by Dr. Samuel Hibbert-Ware in a book investigating ghostly apparitions. His table purports to "measure the faintness or vividness of ideas, sensations, and emotions when one is experiencing a hallucination." The sixth-century-BCE philosopher Heraclitus described sibyls as speaking with "frenzied mouth uttering things not to be laughed at." So the female oracles and prophets who were worshipped at the temple in the photograph very likely behaved in ways that Dr. Hibbert sought to explain millennia later. His chart suggests that supernatural phenomena have physiological and psychological causes. While phantasms bequeathed by gods may turn out to be nothing more than the products of a high fever, the doctor's precise-looking graph probably isn't quite credible either by current medical standards. But solely in aesthetic terms, the decaying grandeur of the temple and its evocation of visionary rites make a more persuasive argument for the mythology that inspired its construction than Hibbert's dull grid does for the scientific method.

With *Imponderable*—in addition to the book, Oursler released a film by this title in 2016, and his archive was recently the subject of a traveling museum show—Oursler engages a creative mode heralded by Hal Foster in his 2004 essay "An Archival Impulse" and recently showcased by the New Museum's exhibition "The Keeper," which treats materials collected and organized by artists as artworks. Archival artists, Foster writes, "seek to make historical information, often lost or displaced, physically present." He cites the work of Thomas Hirschhorn, whose installations, or "monuments," devoted to philosophers such as Spinoza and Gramsci present sociology texts, pornography, and art reproductions. Hirschhorn's expressed desire to "connect what cannot be connected" also describes Oursler's intention—to thread together various histories (ancient, photographic, pop-cultural, occult, criminal, and familial) in order to breed multiple (and even contradictory) comprehensions.

In book form, *Imponderable* grants Oursler some control over his tale; for instance, materials are sequenced somewhat chronologically. At the museum exhibition, one wanders from vitrine to wall display, depending on what catches the eye. However it is viewed, the archive is experienced as immersive and integrative. Even as its materials range across time and continents: for instance, the cranial theme (Robert Fludd's hand-drawn diagram of the mind, a decorated Tibetan skull, a production still from Georges Méliès's *La source enchantée* featuring the disembodied head of an actress, and a selection of "thought photographs" that are allegedly mental images burned onto paper) is readily apparent. Less so may be the connection between those images and, for example, a *SoHo News* cover shot of Kathy Boudin, a photo capturing the air around the muzzle of a discharged gun taken at four-millionths of a second, newspaper snaps of a nude man arrested at a convenience store, a postcard of an "image of Christ" as discerned in a rock formation in Minnesota, and a photo of "Monkey Trial" defendant John Scopes. One's progress through the pages slows to accommodate micro-eddies of meaning and then speeds up as connections jump like electrical charges, from Wilhelm Reich to Houdini, from dream drawings by Federico Fellini to the drawings of Augustin Lesage, an early-twentieth-century coal miner whose pen was directed by spirit voices. Typically, the structure of an archive connotes an orderly inclusiveness, but voraciousness marks Oursler's; he's creating an inhabitable atmosphere (screenings of the film version of the show even offer sensory effects such as smells and vibrations under the seats) that mimics the mind's buzzing confusion—its combinations, collisions, revisions, and intuitive feats. His archive's coherence is its persuasive performance of incoherence.

But Oursler's tale of spiritualism—its occult antecedents, powerful presence in American and Victorian culture, and the controversy its paranormal claims generated—is straightforward enough. Grounded in his grandfather's rationalist quest, Oursler's image trove reveals how various charlatans attempted to use the products of science (principally photography) to validate the supposed mystical truth of their histrionics. The faked images of spirit photography, in which the ghost-white bodies of the deceased loom in darkened rooms, or billows of ectoplasm pour from a medium's mouth, were deployed as conclusive evidence by spiritualism's true believers. No less than the creator of the deductively inclined Sherlock Holmes was taken in by this gimmickry; Oursler includes the images of sprites that Arthur Conan Doyle professed to be real in his book *The Coming of the Fairies*. Spirit photographers were intrepid innovators—two Scottish brothers devised "a new kind of spirit writing" by wrapping photographic plates in black paper on which the dead then supposedly scribbled. These "skotographs" were delicately beautiful and anticipated the visual poetry of asemic writing—still, that didn't prevent the brothers' arrest when undercover police discovered that the images were manipulated. Of course, debunkers employed the same technology to unmask frauds. A Chicago medium who made use of a "spirit horn," through which she claimed the Native American chief Black Hawk whispered, was exposed when a journalist's camera caught her in the darkened room with the horn to her lips. Technology could abet both deception and detection.

The scholarly zeal evidenced by this archive suggests that Oursler recognizes the stakes in this battle over truth. By concluding with several pages devoted to UFO sightings, he connects current contestation over outlandish government conspiracy theories to the passions once generated over talking ghosts. Still, he delights in the entertainment value found in the cage matches that pitted skeptics against believers. A luridly illustrated 1920s poster has it both ways, as it invites the audience to witness "FAKE MEDIUMS EXPOSED" and "See How Spook Crooks Fool Their Victims" while "solemnly" warning that "during séances almost anything is liable to happen." The hair-raising brew of grief, fraud, the uncanny, and the cops proved irresistible to showbiz. Houdini's much-celebrated debunking efforts were both grandiose and logically purposeful. To prove that it was medium Margery Crandon, and not a ghost, ringing the bell during her séances, Houdini built a cabinet with "extra hasps and staples" to contain all but her head. That the box looked more like a torture device from his escape act than an instrument of scientific experimentation was no accident. Spiritualists took a revenge of sorts, if only on Houdini's wife, by relaying messages from her husband after he died in 1926.

The archive—diversely sourced but deeply interconnected, provocative but hardly polemical—makes it difficult to know what Oursler thinks about any of its particulars or even the big eschatological questions; after all, the title of the project is *Imponderable*. His inclusion of Kirlian photos—images that appear to document the "coronal energies" that emanate from objects—done by his friend David Bowie might indicate an actual belief in auras, admiration for the rock star, or simply an aesthetic attraction to the pictures. At least half the items in the volume could be separated from their archival context and still warrant attention as artworks: The photo depicting several bare-chested young men in various states of slack repose under the ministrations of a hypnotist brings to mind Diane Arbus's portrayals of patients in mental institutions; another in which a medium's hands float against darkness, poised as if preparing to crawl toward the viewer, recalls Albrecht Dürer's *Hand of God the Father*; a "thought photograph" from 1950 could easily be mistaken for one of Alberto Burri's *Combustione Plastica* (plastic combustions). Perhaps there is no portal between the mortal world and the spiritual realm, if such a locale even exists. Oursler's archive merely invites us to brood over the myriad ways humans have thought and acted on their wish for, or denial of, the supernatural. But experience *within* this prodigious assemblage of scientific documents, posters, pop-culture curiosities, obscure engravings, newspaper ads, doctored photos, and so much more proves a different permeability—one between high and low culture, between the found and forgotten, and between the art of fraud and the truth of art.

*Bookforum,* Summer 2017.

# Some Trick:
# A New Volume Surveys the Art of Magic

The gold- and silver-colored crucifix that hung opposite my childhood bed was only one of many that adorned the walls of my home, my school, and, of course, the church I attended. On early-summer mornings, the bright, filigreed metal caught the rays that leaked around a too-narrow window shade, and the dying Christ glowed as if electrified. At age eight, I understood the principle of reflected light but didn't yet grasp the concept of an afterimage—the result of photoreceptors retaining an impression after the eye is closed or upon looking away from the object. After waking one morning, I allowed my gaze to linger awhile on the shiny thing, and when I rose I found I couldn't rid my vision of its specter: A cross hovered just in front of me as I stood in the bathroom, and it grew even more vibrant when I closed my eyes. Years of parochial school and a diet of religious movies about Bernadette of Lourdes and the children of Fátima had primed an acceptance of the miraculous. So, try as I might to blink away the apparition, I began to believe I'd been chosen for a visitation from the Lord.

That this spark of faith flickered for even a few minutes before I dismissed the idea (and turned to training an errant cowlick in the mirror) always struck me, from my adult vantage, as a wondrous thing. While, in subsequent years, spirituality, the supernatural, and magic have failed to gain much purchase with me, that morning I did thrill to a sliver of the otherworldly. The prospect of departing from dreary material reality for airier, more malleable territories animates most spiritual beliefs and, of course, most art. Magic is one entertainment designed to ignite wonder and possibility—a deck of cards transformed to all clubs speaks to the same human need for joy and transcendence as an appearance of the True Cross above the commode. For *The Spectacle of Illusion,* Matthew L. Tompkins has compiled a trove of posters, photos, and illustrations from magical, psychic, and spiritualist practices over the past two centuries that evidences both the strong lure of enchantments and the meticulousness of their deceptions. The assemblage also proves intriguing as it unintentionally suggests a kinship between some portion of twentieth-century art and magic and the occult. Their imagistic vocabulary, one that articulates the fluidity of bodies and the transformational nature of objects, finds parallel expression in the work of artists from Max Ernst and Dorothea Tanning to Louise Bourgeois and Jean-Michel Basquiat.

The twined phenomena of spiritualism and mesmerism thrived during a period—the mid-to-late nineteenth century—when photography might have been deployed to challenge practitioners' claims of mind reading and communication with the dead. But almost immediately, magicians and fraudsters put the technology to use to promote and validate their shady arts. While the earnest theatricality that characterizes depictions of séances and hypnotized subjects now registers as camp, nineteenth-century viewers were likely less jaded about the portrayal of strong emotion, as well as the presumed authenticity of photographic images. A pair of photos from 1866 portrays German magician Jacoby-Harms contemplating floating objects—a violin, tambourine, and drum, in one; a skull, in the other. In both, a disembodied hand gestures reassuringly. The conjurer has fallen to the floor in response to the hovering instruments; in contrast, he regards the skull matter-of-factly. These images doubtless served to excite as well as soothe: the spirit world might not be subject to known physical laws, but its emissaries meant no harm. In the nineteenth century, there would have been few reference points for such gravity-less domains, yet a few decades later, they would become common visual tropes in, say, the work of Chagall and Dalí, as evocations of intense inwardness and dreams, both elements on a continuum with the mystical.

By trafficking in a common longing for connection to something larger than the self (and our fear of mortality), illusionists probed the psychological undercurrents of their audiences—and those audiences, in turn, responded to the proposition that they possessed a deeper inner life than they were aware of, one capable of communion with a shared yet unseen realm. No doubt this is why Freud employed hypnosis early in his career as a means of accessing the unconscious. Had he discovered the all too tangible evidence of psychosexual stages demonstrated by a photo from the turn-of-the-century manual *Practical Lessons in Hypnotism,* he might not have abandoned the practice. In this image, a hypnotist stands behind a pair of beguiled children, a boy reclining in a girl's lap, and places his hands as if in benediction over their heads. The caption reads, "The young gentleman believes himself to be once again a nursing infant while the young lady thinks she is a nurse in a foundling asylum." Hypnotists claimed to offer previously unimagined views of primal states, and manuals promised "methods for curing your own ailments without either drugs, doctors, expense or exposure," as well as a means of transferring a healing "magnetic fluid" from practitioner to patient. One photo of a man unbothered by a needle piercing his tongue testifies to the power to transcend pain itself.

One of the odder phenomena documented in *The Spectacle of Illusion* is the supposed "ejaculation" of ectoplasm—a fluidlike substance that hardened as it poured from the nose or mouth of a medium during a séance. Photos of these emanations were posited as proof of spiritual energies acting on the body. Mediums were typically shown unconscious, head thrown back and face covered in a ragged mass of cheesecloth or gauze that they had hidden on their person before the ceremony. Harry Price, a paranormal investigator, discovered that one famous medium active in the 1930s and '40s, Helen Duncan, was able to ingest the cloth before the séance and regurgitate it, to dramatic effect. Duncan also concealed the material in a "variety of her bodily orifices." One photo shows a voluminous rope of ectoplasm flowing from her mouth to the floor, which leads one to wonder about the capacity of those hiding spots. In many images of mediums—most of whom were women—there is a strong sexual implication; the unruly body is revealed as being subject to forces greater than its ability to control. Such imagery could never have been cast as explicitly erotic, yet to audiences then, the intimation would have been undeniable, though disguised as a quasi-religious manifestation. In a series of photos taken of medium Mina Crandon, this sexual undertone advances to what could be constructed as a representation of childbirth. Crandon reclines motionless as a disembodied hand appears to emerge from between her legs (retrieved by her husband, who was always at her side during this demonstration). The scene's provocativeness remains undiminished by the likelihood that the "hand" was a lump of animal liver. However fraudulent these performances, they nevertheless show the female body as vulnerable and disruptively corporeal in ways that anticipate the work of Carolee Schneemann (think *Interior Scroll*), Marina Abramović, and Ana Mendieta.

Throughout this volume, bodies in thrall to magicians or the supernatural are often asleep or almost comically passive, given the dire circumstances. In a full-color German poster from 1923, the tuxedo-clad magician holds a vividly serrated saw while his assistant, a woman wearing only a slip, lies peacefully on a table. In the smaller inset image, the saw cuts deep into her stomach, yet she retains an implausible equanimity. A poster advertising the magician Harry Kellar's most famous trick depicts the levitation of a supine "Hindu princess" who also appears to be lost among blissful dreams. The psychosexual import of these images—male mastery over acquiescent women—is not dissimilar from the power dynamic between artist and model, in which the artist has complete control over the model's representation. The radical reconfiguration of female figures by painters like Picasso and de Kooning might be compared to the effects achieved by the popular "Zig-Zag Girl" illusion. A "lovely assistant" is placed in a vertical cabinet with only her head and left foot visible; the middle of the cabinet—her torso, according to the schematic body painted on the exterior—is pulled away to reveal a gap. Where has everything but her head, shoulders, and legs gone? Variations on the trick feature sections of the cabinet (and the assistant's body) being rearranged like Legos. The plasticity of the body, of the self, isn't restricted to women: Posters show Kellar decapitating himself—his halo-ringed head rising from his starched collar. And stills from an 1898 Georges Méliès short film titled "The Four Troublesome Heads" make use of trick photography to show the director performing the same self-separation three times and then placing the heads on a table to sing along as he strums a guitar.

The French filmmaker's humorous nonchalance contrasts markedly with the serious countenances worn by most of the supernatural world's ministers and acolytes. The mediums and mesmerists, magicians and crystal-gazers all appear burdened by their visions and powers. And perhaps they should be. The desire to believe in something more than what's visible and tangible is undeniably tenacious, and these would-be wizards and conjurers are teasing that desire as much as any artist or cleric. A trick that allows the dead to speak—or a painting like Tanning's *Fish Out of Water,* in which a woman communes with a trout—entices us with the possible comprehension of the unknown. That cross that hung before my eyes can be readily explained; less so the excitement I felt when I believed I was seeing what shouldn't be seen.

*Bookforum,* Summer 2019.

# Frédéric Bruly Bouabré: World Unbound

One day in March 1948, a twenty-five-year-old clerk in the French colonial administration in Ivory Coast experienced a transformative vision. He reported that the sky opened and "seven colored suns described a circle of beauty around their 'Mother-Sun'" and that he was then called upon to be "the Revealer." This divine command would set Frédéric Bruly Bouabré on an investigative path deep into the folklore, language, and religion of his people, the Bété, an undertaking that produced voluminous texts and thousands of drawings, all aimed at elucidating his cultural heritage as the foundation of a universal cosmology. A current show at the Museum of Modern Art presents two artistic series—"Alphabet Bété" (1990–1991) and "Knowledge of the World" (1987–2008)—whose titles proclaim their vast ambition. Each of the 449 colored-pencil and ballpoint-pen drawings on cardboard that constitute "Alphabet Bété" illustrates a single monosyllable in the Bété language. The enumerated images depict familiar activities (lighting a fire, chopping down a tree, rowing a boat, copulation) and common objects (chair, leaf, snake, spear) that illustrate the handprinted syllable. Undoubtedly, some linguistic proficiency would enrich the connection between, say, a saw and the syllable "si = ci," but the relationships still prove enticingly cryptic for the uninitiated. Thirty similarly devised drawings comprise "Knowledge of the World," an encyclopedia-like attempt to document the range of human experience, from being disfigured in a war to seeing a butterfly, from "une divine signature" to wine gourds.

The taxonomic scope of these projects, especially the "Alphabet," predicates a large number of images, many with only minor variations from the others. The distinction between two sequential pieces—*Fé* and *Fê*—is represented by the difference between a female figure with an axe chopping two logs and the same figure, same posture, chopping at the air. These near repetitions, along with Bouabré's consistent palette of soft greens and yellows, establish an almost incantatory rhythm that rewards viewing multiple pictures at once. Immersion is invited, and the resulting effect is akin to listening to poetic declamation.

Francophone Bouabré annotates many drawings with a description that often extends around the full margin of the rectangle. The caption "*Le symbole de la sublime navigation á partir de l'empire des morts*" (The symbol of the sublime navigation from the empire of the dead) surrounds a solitary figure in a comma-shaped vessel. Reading the sideways and upside-down text requires an angled attention that might lead the viewer to suspect it's a ploy to encourage closer engagement with the artwork. But Bouabré's intent is far from canny; rather, he explicitly seeks to explain his depictions. In a film on display at MoMA, he declares, "Writing is what immortalizes. Writing fights against forgetting." The endeavor is Blakean—to reveal the world in a grain of Bété sand—and the artist's unflaggingly inventive imagination is well suited to the task.

*Bookforum,* Summer 2022.

# Enumeration Sensation: Umberto Eco's Book of Lists

Middle of the night, and your head teems with half-formed thoughts: Did I pay the car insurance? Where did I park the car? Is my favorite dress shirt at the dry cleaners? What time's the wedding this Saturday? Need a map of Vermont to get there. Should I frame my vintage maps one of these days? Maybe start with that bird's-eye view of New Amsterdam, or the blue-tinted mariner's chart.... How stop this ceaseless ticker tape? The mind's associative reflex is as rapid as it is circuitous; myriad things and things-to-do always unspooling in the brainpan. If you get out of bed, though, and grab a pen, you can at least slow it down by making a list. You can rank items in importance, annotate, categorize, and subcategorize—in short, you can give some material shape and make order of what Henry James dubbed "the great blooming, buzzing confusion" of the world. So somewhere between penciling "Pick up prescription" and "Live a more examined life," a portion of calm might be found.

The notion that unwieldy consciousness might best be tamed by enumerative form has beguiled more than a few writers and artists. Umberto Eco, in *The Infinity of Lists: An Illustrated Essay,* recounts his fascination with lists, lists of lists, and the infinite regress of the adding up and counting down any- and everything. In compiling this roster—a sort of metacollection—Eco ranges widely through Western civilization to include lists verbal (from Homer to Pynchon) and visual (from a fifth-century Greek shield to an installation by Christian Boltanski). Like any good cataloguer, Eco subdivides: His two big kinds of lists are those that evidence the "poetics of 'everything included' and the poetics of the 'etcetera.'" The first aims for completeness and closure (provisionally so); the latter takes its cue from the mind's perpetual-motion association machine. It's the difference between a New York telephone directory and, say, Jacques Collin de Plancy's nineteenth-century *Dictionnaire infernal*, which offers a census of demons ("Aamon, Abigor, Abracace, Adramelech ... Xafan, Zagam, Zaleos, Zebos, Zepar"). The phone book includes the more or less fixed number of names of actual phone owners; the roster of devils is limited only by the imagination's disinclination to invent more.

List making is therapeutic: Either tack—"etcetera" or "included"—offers some measure of respite from the "blooming and buzzing." It's easy to imagine that, when an endless chain of fiends swirled through his midnight mind, Collin de Plancy quieted his jitters by filling out his roster. In less dire circumstances, many prospective parents no doubt cope with prebirth worries by creating lists of baby names. But lists are not only tools to quell anxiety; they are just as often celebratory. Eco treats us to choice samples from the usual literary suspects, epic enumerators like Joyce, Cervantes, Borges, Calvino, and Whitman. The selection from Proust—biographies note that he lulled himself to sleep by perusing railway timetables—handily captures the joy to be taken in prolific accounting, in this case of small French towns:

> I compare and contrast them; how was one to choose, any more than between individual people, who are not interchangeable, between Bayeux, so lofty in its noble coronet of rusty lace, whose highest point caught the light of the old gold of its second syllable; Vitre, whose acute accent barred its ancient glass with wooden lozenges; gentle Lamballe, whose whiteness ranged from egg-shell yellow to a pearly grey; Coutances, a Norman Cathedral, which its final consonants, rich and yellowing, crowned with a tower of butter; Lannion with the rumble and buzz, in the silence of its village street, of the fly on the wheel of the coach ...

This single sentence speeds along, trainlike, through many more locales while improbably seizing at every pointillist detail. Even while caught up in Proust's propulsive naming, we are also made mindful of, if not stalled outright by, the dilemma—"how to choose"—that serves as a kind of muse's invocation at the start of this litany. Indeed, the list maker often is compelled to acknowledge that each accounting predicates an uncountable number of shadow lists, alternative choices abounding. Such recording seeks order even as the process implies the chaos of ever-lengthening inventories—thus the "infinity" of lists.

If the list maker's first task is to choose, the next might be to make more from those choices than mere addition: A list can tell a story. What Eco dubs the "rhetoric of enumeration," we might understand as the drama that flows from rhythmic excitation. In *Leaves of Grass*, Whitman's incantatory compilations rise to crescendos and fall back to rumination, taking accurate measure of the pulsing landscapes the poet feels compelled to swallow whole. Eco cites one Georg Philipp Harsdörfer, whose seventeenth-century treatise on linguistics at times exemplifies the list as an undeterred refinement of a single property. Harsdörfer wrings from his premise—to sing the praises of German—every last metaphoric turn:

> [German] speaks with the tongues of nature.... It thunders with the heavens, flashes with the swift clouds, glitters like hail, whistles with the wind, foams with the waves, clatters like locks, resounds with the air, detonates with cannons, roars like a lion, lows like the ox, snarls like the bear, bells like the deer ...

As the similes grow wilder and wilder, less and less tethered to any comprehensible comparison, the rhetoric of the list qua list supersedes its ostensible point; quickly, readers are tapping their feet ("caws like the crow"!), having pretty much forgotten about an actual language and what it sounds like. The list instead becomes a self-enacting tale about the meaninglessness of words, all the while praising speech as inexpressively expressive.

Repetition drives any good list; it is the engine that gives shape to the compulsive psychology behind the mnemonic chants of poets and bookies, manic prophets and neurotics. No matter how epic the scope of inclusion or diverse the items inventoried, a locution, assiduously repeated, binds it all, makes a wholeness out of particularity. Eco offers a snippet from the *Carmina Burana* in which humankind is revealed as both multifarious and monomaniacal:

> The mistress and the master drink
> the soldier and the cleric drink
> that man and that woman drink
> the servant drinks with the maid
> the white man drinks, so does the black
> the stay-at-home drinks, so does the wanderer
> the fool drinks, so does the scholar.

A list is an intimation of totality; a simulacrum of knowing much, of knowing the right much. We select our ten best big-band recordings, all-time basketball starting fives, mysteries to read this summer; add up the people we slept with or people we wished we had; index our movie-memorabilia collection; count our blessings; itemize reasons for not getting out of bed. We jot these accounts on envelopes, store them on hard drives, murmur them under our breath as we ride home from work—it's no accident that many prayers are nothing more than lists.

Eco is especially fond of lists that take visual form, and he includes many, such as medieval mosaics that assemble masses of angels; the congeries of Joseph Cornell; and Max Ernst's painting, *33 Little Girls Chasing Butterflies* (1958), a detonation of bright shards scattering to the corners of the canvas. But it is Giuseppe Arcimboldo's *Spring* (1573) that most strongly evokes not just the visualization of a list but the core predicament of the enterprise. Arcimboldo painted a series of portraits making use of fruits, vegetables, or flowers as anatomical elements. In the case of *Spring*, he musters a veritable encyclopedia of flora to fill out and color the face and upper body of a young aristocratic woman. Her head can be understood as a compendium of flowers—their names and lore, their very stems and petals. Truly blooming and buzzing, she looks more than a little perplexed. The lady is in need of pen and paper so she can begin to make sense of herself: daisies, nightshades, daffodils, thyme, anemones, azaleas, irises, bloodroot, cornflowers, etcetera. She's in need of a list. To make order. To understand what's on her mind.

*Bookforum*, December–January 2010.

# Past Forward: Joe Brainard Made His Memories Yours

Joe Brainard achieved a singular position in the poetry world before his death from AIDS-induced pneumonia in 1994. An artist identified with a rarefied strain of Pop Art, he was also a poet affiliated with the so-called New York School, a loose collection of wry Francophiles who could be readily described in the mid-'60s as avant-garde without anyone wincing at the designation. Ensconced in the circumscribed world of highbrow, camp-inflected culture, Brainard penned *I Remember*—a litany of self-regard whose formal rigor sharpens the kind of intimacies that invite readers to feel like co-conspirators. The multi-book work escaped New York's narrow precincts to reach a wide (for modern verse) and enthusiastic readership as it brought the genre of the list poem to a kind of perfection. Along with Ginsberg's more famous "Howl," *I Remember* is the post-1950 poem people who don't read poetry might know. That major effort, along with other poems, prose pieces, and drawings done over Brainard's three-decade career, has been gathered in one volume by the Library of America. Smartly edited by his lifelong friend Ron Padgett, the collection demonstrates that this unlikely success was no fluke.

Brainard arrived in New York in 1960, along with fellow Tulsa teens Padgett and Dick Gallup; another Oklahoma pal, Ted Berrigan, soon joined them. He began writing poems, making art, and meeting the people—Frank O'Hara, Andy Warhol—who would prove influential in both endeavors. Having settled on the Lower East Side, Brainard began producing collages, drawings, and paintings, appropriating images and texts from popular culture and the city's street life. In a 1977 interview with poet Tim Dlugos (included in this volume), he recounts being inspired to make altarpieces by the "Puerto Rican religious ... junk" he found on display in bodegas. This would prove to be a signature gesture—assimilate, repurpose, and subvert—that would eventually play out, for instance, in an extensive series of collages devoted to the comic-strip character Nancy, in which the spiky-haired imp can be found hiding in the "basket" of a sailor's pants or spouting non sequiturs while caught in flagrante delicto. Brainard liked to help the pure products of America go even crazier.

If O'Hara was, in the words of critic Marjorie Perloff, a poet among painters, Brainard worked with equal vigor on both teams. His visual and verbal art cross-pollinated, and this was never more evident than in *I Remember*. Initially published in several editions (*I Remember, I Remember More, More I Remember More*) by the small press Angel Hair, this serial work has been collected to form an epic chant. Like some liturgical rite that emphasizes its trance-inducing music, the 130-page poem rings out with a series of simple declarative statements, each beginning "I remember." But the length and repetition hardly ever cause our reading to drag. *I Remember* speeds along, a broken-field, decidedly unchronological dash through the poet's life that manages to feel both condensed and expansive at the same time: "I remember chalk," an observation elemental and universal, is closely followed by the more discursive and personal "I remember how much I tried to like Van Gogh. And how much, finally, I did like him. And how much, now, I can't stand him."

Drawing on his Dadaist and Surrealist experiments in art and infusing their juxtapositional impulses with his own calculated offhandedness, Brainard gave birth to a wholly original (and, despite its numerous homages and exemplary employ in a thousand creative-writing classes, near-inimitable) form: the collage memoir. To note *I Remember*'s utter freshness when it began appearing in the early '70s isn't to discount its antecedents: There's Whitman's dithyrambic listing (in his introduction, Paul Auster enumerates Brainard's myriad topics—

more than a hundred entries for "The Body," fifty for "Holidays," and "Movies, Movie Stars, T.V., and Pop Music" scoring several dozen); Proust's obsessional verve for detail ("I remember the very thin pages and red edges of hymn books"); and Christopher Smart's call-and-response patterning in "Jubilate Agno," in which every line starts with either "Let" or "For." Brainard joined these formal approaches to his quicksilver and utterly congenial sensibility; the poetic thrill in *I Remember* derives not from inventive imagery or linguistic sport, but rather from the piquant, piercing evocation of Brainard's charm. He routinely renovates sentimentality with the slightly perverse and still ends up landing sweetly: "I remember playing doctor with Joyce Vantries. I remember her soft white belly. Her large navel. And her little slit between her legs. I remember rubbing my ear against it." Or he elevates confessional intimacy to self-dramatizing: "I remember, eating out alone in restaurants, trying to look like I have a lot on my mind. (Primarily a matter of subtle mouth and eyebrow contortions.)" Cultural history is digested and crystallized: "I remember movies in school about kids that drink and take drugs and then they have a car wreck and one girl gets killed." Even though Brainard performs Brainard with great élan, the show never feels ego-driven; his poems could be transcriptions from a late-night talk with a close friend who wanders through matters both striking and banal with equal aplomb, refusing to recognize the difference, but not for a moment failing to entertain you. Brainard was a master of life's micro-comedies, the unheard laughter that courses through any truly alert consciousness.

If there is a unifying theme that emerges from the poem, it might be the fluidity of the self—the posited truth that our memories, beliefs, and feelings are always in flux and thus ever redefining who and what we are. In the Dlugos interview, Brainard talked about the composition of *I Remember*: "I have a terrible memory.... But then I began to realize that beyond that point, there is another level of knowledge that could be triggered off." The deliberateness of the enterprise, this "triggering," may seem an odd source for a poem that flows with the insouciance of conversation, but this is the crux of Brainard's art—the meticulous construction of naturalness:

> I remember the first erection I distinctly remember having. It was by the side of a public swimming pool. I was sunning on my back on a towel. I didn't know what to do, except turn over, so I turned over. But it wouldn't go away. I got a terrible sunburn. So bad that I had to go see a doctor. I remember how much wearing a shirt hurt.

This casual recollection (which slyly embeds a parable of sexual guilt and punishment—is this the other "level of knowledge"?) registers ingenuously. The speaker is familiar, and the anecdote is, too. The next entries shift sharply:

> I remember the organ music from *As the World Turns.*
> I remember white buck shoes with thick pink rubber soles.

Here the lens tightens focus—even as it verges on camp. The details—the cheesy theme from a daytime soap opera and the pavement-eye view of footwear—sit in pointed juxtaposition to the "authentic" memory of adolescent distress. Skillfully mixing tones and points of view, Brainard mimics the randomness of perception, as well as the unpredictability of emotional associations. The reader continues to zig with his zags, as these lines are followed by "I remember living rooms all one color." We move in a blink from sexual secrets to pop-culture ephemera to sociological précis—the material is always kept in contrapuntal balance. Many entries begin, "I remember thinking ..." or "I remember a story ..." or "a daydream." Memories of memories send us spiraling down the rabbit hole: It's not just that we are always remembering, Brainard is saying, but that we are always remembering that we remembered.

Weighty as that idea is, it treads lightly through the poem. Brainard's comedic touch—a deadpan wit that veers toward sincerity rather than sarcasm—marks all of his writing. Reliant on nuances of tone and inflection, it is the kind of graceful, openhearted humor that barely claims its laughter upon reading, yet you recall and recount to others weeks later. In full, the prose poem titled "Ron Padgett":

> Ron Padgett is a poet. He has always been a poet and he always will be a poet. I don't know how a poet becomes a poet. And I don't

> think anyone else does either. It is something deep and mysterious inside a person that cannot be explained. It is something that no one understands. It is something that no one will ever understand. I asked Ron Padgett once how it came about that he was a poet, and he said, "I don't know. It is something deep and mysterious inside of me that cannot be explained."

Traditional tools are at work—alliteration, repetition, formalized diction—while the parodic intent is deftly turned. The coterie-style joke is on aesthetic theorizing and essentialist creeds (O'Hara's "Why I Am Not a Painter" is close kin here), but it's precisely this earnest intellectualism that sparks Brainard's deeper jest. This is a poet who candidly reports to Dlugos that the poetry of longtime friend John Ashbery is, "you know, over my head.... My mind wanders off." His sophistication was his simplicity.

*The Collected Writings* makes its case—Brainard surely belongs in this canonical series, in no small part because he represents that peculiarly American aspiration to self-mythologize in the face of an otherwise relentlessly quotidian world. But this is done gently, with affection and a profound sense of commonality with his readers. Sounding playful, sometimes naive notes, Brainard nevertheless advances a serious cause—the enlargement of the self to include all friends, family, movie stars, old high school teachers, anonymous subway riders, great artists, decisive moments, embarrassing scenes, hidden truths, celebrated falsehoods, and Dinah Shore. The welcome sign hung over this concoction of reference and remembering reads "Joe." Brainard's artistry can appear as plain as that name, yet all the while giving subtle, human-pitched voice to the many selves swirling beneath.

*Bookforum*, April 2012.

# Art House:
# On "John Ashbery Collects"

So, just what is the "thingness of the thing" that Heidegger was talking about? The phrase's riddlesome poetry could easily have been penned by John Ashbery, instead of the aloof German phenomenologist. Is Heidegger suggesting that material things possess an essence, an abstract quality that both defines and constitutes, say, a shoe—its shoeness? Perhaps, but Ashbery, in fact, offers a more straightforward assessment of the unseeable stuff that makes stuff what it is in the opening lines of "Grand Galop": "All things seem the mention of themselves." Such are my thoughts as I roam the rooms of Ashbery's Hudson, New York, home ... well, only to the degree that the galleries at Loretta Howard, in Chelsea, have been decorated with trompe l'oeil drawings—wainscoting, doorways, mantels—to look like the rooms of the poet's well-appointed nineteenth-century house. Thoughtfully curated by Loretta Howard Gallery and poets Adam Fitzgerald and Emily Skillings, the show offers a selection of Ashbery's own paintings, prints, collages, bric-a-brac, and furniture; it's all cozily arranged to conjure as much domestic atmosphere as might be had in a gallery space. Kitschy figurines, VHS tapes (Daffy Duck and Jack Benny among them), bawdy toys, and hand-painted plates line the shelves of cabinets and bookcases that could have been lifted whole from Ashbery's parlor. Other items, like the French Provincial chairs and Oriental rugs, have been. They complement a piano drawn on a wall on which are hung several selections of early twentieth-century sheet music ("Mr. and Mrs. Is the Name," "Flirtation Walk"), that have been placed as if resting on the instrument's music desk.

Alongside such homey items (the cartoons playing on the TV jangle in a familiar way with the filigree wallpaper designs) are pieces by many of the poet's friends and artistic confederates, such as Joan Mitchell, Fairfield Porter, Larry Rivers, Trevor Winkfield, Jess, Alex Katz, Jane Freilicher, and Willem de Kooning. There's a gemütlich vibe, equal parts wry and melancholic, generated by this assemblage of things cultural that ably recalls the mood and manner of Ashbery's writing. To elucidate this point, the curators include wall text featuring apt passages of his verse that treat the world, if not the mind, as a congeries of curios, a kind of Cornell box. Of course, the show includes a few of those; given that his poems are populated by Popeye, Henry Darger, Chopin, *Faust*, Parmigianino, and a myriad of other arcane references, it's no surprise that Ashbery is a devotee of Cornell's eclectic connoisseurship. Both share an affinity for the *metaphysique d'ephemera*, an aesthetic that elevates the trivial to the transcendent.

Porter's well-known portrait of Ashbery—it graces the cover of his first Library of America volume—depicts him in his late twenties, his face in profile, his seated figure slightly off-center and recessed in the frame. Painted around the time Ashbery published his first book, *Some Trees*, the portrait is classical in composition, restrained in palette. Porter's muted tones and contemplative regard reveal Ashbery's observational mien—he's not looking at the viewer but outside the picture, somewhere we can't see. It is as if Porter caught the poetic persona behind the opening lines of "The Instruction Manual" from that first book:

> As I sit looking out of a window of the building
> I wish I did not have to write the instruction manual on the uses of a new
> metal.
> I look down into the street and see people, each walking with an inner peace,
> And envy them—they are so far away from me!

The show suggests that there are different kinds of collectors. Unlike those detailed in Werner Muensterberger's *Collecting: An Unruly Passion*, Ashbery isn't an obsessive—a Robert Opie–type who acquires a museum's worth of supermarket goods—but rather appears to be someone who simply arrives at the objects he collects; they are ready to be plucked up from his path as he makes his way among friends, passing fancies, nostalgic affections, and sundry oddities. Instead of the scholarly verve driving many collectors, something like the associative logic that arranges the images in his poems determines Ashbery's acquisitions. These objects—not individually, but collectively—evoke the multifariousness of consciousness, instead of its brooding, innermost zones.

Or so I speculate. Because, after all, what do I know about how Ashbery came to own the things he owns? I do know that this show could be the prop room for his verse, a place where totems of high and low, irony and utter seriousness await staging. To be sure, such connections constitute, for me, the great drama of the poems. And those points of contact spark in conversation with Ashbery, too. I visited the house in Hudson many years ago and was duly enchanted by its grandeur, the movie-set staircase (there's a painting of it and other interiors by Archie Rand in the show) with its polished banisters. In an upstairs room, John Yau, Joseph Donahue, David Kermani, Ashbery, and I watched a TV show featuring old B-movies that had been overdubbed with wisecracking, deliberately anachronistic dialogue. Ashbery was heading to New York the next day for the big 1986 PEN Congress, and someone asked him what he thought of the controversy roiling around one of the invitees, then–Secretary of State George Shultz. "Well," he offered, "I've always liked *Peanuts*." Between the TV show and Ashbery's ongoing commentary, I felt sure the materials for a poem were gathering within him as he sat there on the couch.

To scan these rooms is to carom among minute but vibrant worlds of sensibility—from the Utagawa Kunisada woodblock prints, with their floral-draped and delicate maidens, to Shirley Goldfarb's painterly detonation, titled *Storm*; from Jane Freilicher's still life *Peonies* to Henry Darger's collage of military figures; from Mark Tobey's airy brushwork in *World Dust* to Joe Brainard's palpably dense collage *Madonna*; from ceramic cocker spaniels to a video cassette of Fritz Lang's *The Spiders*. The ricochets impact gently (after all, there are even antimacassars on the chairs in this comfy home), but no less bracingly. It's the sly jolt that arises from untested circuits, fresh neural pathways flashing to life. Another bit from "Grand Galop" comes to me—"For things can harden meaningfully in the moment of indecision"—and I remember that night in Hudson years ago: among these things, amid their thingness, I realize that I'm standing inside one of Ashbery's poems.

*Paris Review Daily*, October 22, 2013.

# Soon There Was Nothing Left: A Posthumous Volume from John Ashbery Troubles the Line between Finished and Incomplete

What does the characterization *unfinished* mean when describing a poem? Some things merit the adjective—a chair with three legs, a portrait with a swath of raw canvas where facial features should be, a song cut short just before its crescendo. Such cessations can be plainly seen or felt. But unless a line stops in mid-thought, a poem doesn't immediately appear truncated. Take the famous example of Samuel Coleridge's "Kubla Khan." We only know it's a fragment because the author explained upon its publication that the interruption of an annoying visitor prevented him from fully recounting his dream vision (rather than having nodded out on opium). In the case of a more modern specimen—a free-form poem that traffics in ambiguity of purpose and effect—any degree of incompletion will be somewhat camouflaged by that aesthetic disposition. To be sure, fragmentation, lacunae, and open-endedness have been central to the modernist and post-modern enterprises. A seemingly unfinished work may be so, or appear to be so intentionally—that being the point of the poem. The mood of the ongoing moment tilts against the totalizing impulse; our emblematic punctuation is the ellipsis rather than the period. The once necessary sense of an ending has given way to the notion that thinking has merely come to rest for a brief spell.

Perhaps more than any other poet of the post-war period and beyond, John Ashbery gave voice to rumination's off-handed, recursive, and ever-expansive circuits. Beginning in his early volumes, *Some Trees* (1956), *The Tennis Court Oath* (1962), and *The Double Dream of Spring* (1970), he tested the conventional limits of how a poem might start. He often begins in medias res with what feels like a snatch of overheard conversation, as in "A White Paper," which casually opens, "And if he thought that / All was foreign—." Many of his poems also conclude without quite concluding; the many pages of "Europe," for example, cease with the unpunctuated line "the breath." Poems from this period, during the late 1950s to the mid-'60s and continuing well through the book-length poems of the later decades, seem to emerge from an animated discourse already in progress. In a 1981 interview with Richard Kostelanetz, Ashbery described his creative process: "I have a feeling that in my mind is an underground stream, if you will, that I can have access to if I want. I want the poetry to come out as freshly and as unplanned as possible." In another interview in 1984, he directly addressed the issue of resolution: "I don't look on poems as closed works. I feel they're going on all the time in my head, and I occasionally snip off a length."

The five long poems in *Parallel Movement of the Hands,* a volume expertly edited and introduced by the poet Emily Skillings, who was also Ashbery's long-time assistant, offer an opportunity to assess what, if any, difference exists between the "finished" poem that resists closure and a work that the poet himself deemed incomplete. As Skillings relates, Ashbery continued writing up to a week before he died, at age 90, in 2017. Such industry is further evidenced by the two dozen-plus original collections (not including compilations) he produced over his lifetime, 11 of which he published after turning 70. The underground stream was a torrent. Her account of Ashbery's revision process and how he selected poems for inclusion in a book (he gave them grades of A, B, or even C, often sharing them with fellow poet John Yau for his rating) provides a glimpse of the craft behind work that was sometimes criticized as being composed extempore. She demonstrates an equal measure of care transcribing text from manuscript pages:

when confronted with the typescript's obvious error "on the point ot hopening," she chooses "of opening" rather than "of happening" owing to "the organization of the keyboard and that the entire word is contained within the misspelling." Because the spider king, who appears earlier in the line, is said to "unhitch himself to plummet directly into our daily affairs," Skillings surmises he is likely "falling through the dilations in space and reality created by events." Alert to ways in which the literal and figurative are hardly separable for this poet, she aptly dubs such a problem "a particularly Ashberian conundrum."

Ashbery frequently wrote long poems—"Litany" from *As We Know* (1979) and the titular poem from *Self-Portrait in a Convex Mirror* (1975) are among the most well-known—and book-length works such as *Flow Chart* (1991) and *Girls on the Run* (1999). Each of the essayistic prose poems in *Three Poems* (1972) immerses the reader in the experience of consciousness, with the rigor of their logical analyses neatly balanced by a wry and knowing tone. The expansive nature of the form allowed him to roam among multiple historical moments, to deploy his abundant cultural vocabulary, and unhurriedly explore a variety of dictions. Ashbery's instinct for close and digressive examination of minute changes in our mental climate equipped him for extended outings that sustain attention by the sheer force of their stamina.

Four of the five works that Skillings gathers—"The History of Photography," "The Art of Finger Dexterity," "21 Variations on My Room," and "The Kane Richmond Project"—were written during the '90s and early 2000s; the fifth, a prose poem titled "Sacred and Profane Dances," is undated. That Ashbery had these several extended works underway simultaneously not only testifies to his unflagging fealty to the long poem form but to his extravagantly varied powers of invention and intelligence. Composer Carl Czerny's book of piano exercises, published in 1839, provides individual poem titles ("Maximum Velocity in Arpeggios," "Delicacy in Skips and Staccatos"), as well as the overall title for "The Art of Finger Dexterity"; allusions to images created by Eugène Atget, Adolph de Meyer, Charles Nègre, and others are threaded through "The History of Photography"; "The Kane Richmond Project" draws on long-forgotten serial cliffhangers from the late '30s and early

'40s starring the dashing actor Kane Richmond. Even as the references that undergird these projects range from the reassuringly familiar to the dauntingly obscure, as is typical with Ashbery, they characterize a rarefied mental atmosphere, one in which the poet's droll self-awareness deflates what otherwise might be pretension.

"The History of Photography" isn't quite a history. Or at least not obviously so. Instead, over the course of the poem's six numbered sections, we seem to travel among vaguely recognizable, half-remembered images, entering their narrative possibilities briefly and then moving on to the next. Of course, *seem* is the operative word. Where we are in place and time, and just what is happening, is purposefully indeterminate. Is a single image being described, a composite of many, or perhaps something like the essence of any photograph? Likely all of these. But chiefly, Ashbery enacts a photograph's ability to simultaneously spark intimate personal associations even as it offers a portal to another world, unfamiliar yet alluring. Innumerable photos throughout history depict an old man leaving someplace; does it matter if we know which one may be the poet's departure point?

> Now the old man takes his leave.
> Courtesy wrenched from confusion douses
> the reproach of his having here. We all imbibe
> the new freshness like a straw, a stem
> takes us from there to there, like heaven.

Factual clarity emerges at intervals. Without naming Louis Daguerre, Ashbery ventriloquizes him as he takes *Boulevard du Temple,* a momentous photo from 1838:

> The first person to be photographed was a man
> having his boots cleaned. There were others
> in the same street, but they moved and became
> invisible. How calm I am!

Other photographers are mentioned directly ("Mapplethorpe the dissenting penis"; "Muybridge's hopping / woman—"), and sprinkled about are observations that remind us of Ashbery's longstanding role as an art critic:

The first photographers
who got it right knew what they were doing.
Then a second generation came along, happy to play
in the ruts already carved, to flood them and conceal them under
flowers.

While the history in "The History of Photography" peeks its head out just enough to keep the reader alert to clues to specific images, the poem doesn't rely on successful identifications. The fact of the world being recorded via an admixture of light and chemicals for nearly two centuries subsumes any single photo—the snapshot lost in a drawer, the iconic image on a t-shirt—within an amorphous and intensely personal archive. This is the history Ashbery illuminates.

All of the poems in this volume extend a career-long meditation on what it means to make or experience art. Even—in the case of "The Art of Finger Dexterity"—practicing to make art. Ashbery once told an interviewer that Czerny's book of exercises "was written to torture piano students ... It's mostly silly little tunes ornamented in a very complicated way to stretch the fingers to the limits of their endurance." (Skillings, who witnessed the poem's composition in 2007, notes that Ashbery recalled to her playing Czerny's *Études* as a child.) The 28 poems gathered under this title are short—some are only several lines; one reads in its entirety, "O happy something"—and fittingly gymnastic in their verbal shifts. This brevity is matched by most of their line lengths. Taking a structural cue from the composer, Ashbery compacts complication to "dismangling" effect: these poems hug the corners as they pivot from, say, brooding mood to comedic fillip as, for instance, in "Changing Fingers on the Same Key":

Orderly soul, looking for a way in telling
us about dismangling—in a book?—
the way in is reversed now.
You bungle candor in issuing
an edition with notes—
what manner can they confine,
what new subjects elide
whose wan exegesis never tattled?

Fine with me, guv'nor.
I *love* it.

Ashbery isn't so much ornamenting "silly tunes" as he is sounding out tonal variations with an ear attentive to colloquial speech. It is hard not to believe that the expressions "you do you" and "haters gonna hate" have infiltrated "Delicacy in Skips and Staccatos" to reside cheek by jowl with Jaspers Johns's dictum about artmaking, "Do something to it. Do something else to it." A snippet of delighted French rounds off the impersonations:

People,
    half-hurled,
you gonna know.
You gonna do.
You do something else.
*Mais non, je t'adore.*

When the breezy loquacity tightens and turns epigrammatic ("Trespass in shade," "Soon there was nothing left," "The wind blows where it wants," or "O my truth"), such terse declarative statements are all the more invigorating because of the change-up. The 45-year gap between the two works notwithstanding, the cryptic angularity of "The Art of Finger Dexterity" shares kinship with *The Tennis Court Oath*, a book often regarded as one of Ashbery's most challenging. While even fans concede this opacity (in a favorable *New York Times* profile from 1976, Kostelanetz described the poetry as "extremely difficult, if not often impenetrable"), Ashbery nevertheless earned a lifetime of accolades and acceptance. The acclaim didn't influence his intentions; he always wrote in accordance with the aesthetic expressed in his 1995 Robert Frost Medal address. "With a poem," Ashbery said, "there is nothing to explain ... because the act of writing the poem was an explanation of something that had occurred to the poet."

Perhaps intended to be part of longer works, the volume's relatively shorter pieces—"Sacred and Profane Dances" and "21 Variations on My Room"—are more suggestive of possibilities than realized visions. "Sacred and Profane Dances" does, though, broaden our awareness of Ashbery's cultural scope as he unexpectedly assumes the role of biblical exegete exploring the Parable of the Ten Virgins from the Gospel of Matthew. The numbered stanzas in "21 Variations on My Room" leave off at 18, giving the clearest indication of being unfinished. But Skillings suggests it may be a portion of the collection's most sustained and unitary piece, "The Kane Richmond Project," an enterprise that returns the poet to what his readers will recognize as familiar ground—the domain of old and esoteric movies. "Film," Ashbery asserted in a 2007 interview, "has been a major influence on me. I think it's probably been more influential than visual art." The first piece in this book-length effort, "Spy Smasher," shares its title with the 1942 serial in which Richmond plays a cape-wearing avenger who battles Nazis. The opening line installs us in what might be a seat in a "decrepit cinema" (a description from "The Phantom Agents," included in Ashbery's 1992 collection *Hotel Lautréamont*), and we are plunged into a world of proliferating plot complications: "A hundred major developments— / that's what I think about...." Action unspools as a "Man wanders along a ledge," "old lovers fall apart," "tall ships ... / pass obviously on their way to something," and it's all "more than Mary could stand." Descriptions of the characters' hectic doings are collaged with snatches of Tom Swift and Hardy Boys books—the stuff of childhood filtered through an idiosyncratic sensibility that delights in disjuncture and improbability:

> Kane was a righteous dude, heat-packing
> Cared not for right or wrong,
> rode east, rode west. "Home's best," he smiled.
> But indeed, where was home? Some place
> under the sky's petals, attuned to harmony?
> He preferred the poetry of Charlotte Mew to that of Nathalia Crane,
> sang in the shower while the radio poured discord
> about not believing in the Bible, or in hell, more precisely.

Of course—in this poem titled "The President's Dream"—Ashbery *would* meld a kid's assessment of Kane's manliness with a recondite reference to a pair of female poets. Hierarchies of all sorts, whether cultural or linguistic, dissolve in a narrative flow that combines and recombines source materials with assured equanimity; this is a voice that slides with ease among sentimental, analytical, and ironic registers, rarely snagging on an unforeseen bend. The very fluency of the "underground stream" persuades the reader of the rightness of what otherwise might strike us as awkward or indecipherable.

In his foreword, the poet and novelist Ben Lerner thoughtfully addresses the question of the "unfinished" and recounts an anecdote about an Ashbery appearance at St. Mark's Poetry Project in 1971. About to read his epic prose poem "The System," the poet realized he didn't have the last page. He reassured the audience: "If you feel like leaving at any point, it won't really matter. You will have had the experience.... I am disturbed that it's incomplete, but maybe that's good." This wasn't glibness, but rather a fitting expression of his approach to composition and to interpretation; both processes are marked by provisionality and the poet's control over either is fluid and changeable. As Skillings discloses, "a poem that was an A on Tuesday could be downgraded to a B or even C by Friday." During the week, did that poem appear more or less finished to its author? By what measurement do we as readers make that judgment? This isn't to cast all evaluations as hopelessly subjective and therefore moot. It's simply to recognize that barring the fact of that missing last page, or the author's declaration about the state of the work, determinations about what's done and *done* are variable. Depending, maybe, on the day of the week.

One of the treats contained in *Parallel Movement of the Hands* is its selection of typed manuscript pages that include Ashbery's handwritten revisions. On the second of two poems titled "Parallel Movement of the Hands," we can discern a small yet significant change in the lines "pulling your house / and delusions with it into the stream." On the typescript, the word "delusions" has been written next to the crossed-out word "decisions." The substitution is provocative. Every word in a poem requires decision, but whether that decision is correct may be a delusion the author indulges if for no other reason than to move on to the next word, the next line. Ashbery recognized the porous border between decision and delusion, between finality and its seeming appearance. This collection of unfinished works allows readers to tread that border as well.

*Poetry Foundation,* June 2021.

# Unpopular Mechanics: Two Photographers Search the Archives for the Hidden Story of Post-War America

Children's picture books are often our first acquaintance with storytelling. In a board book devoted, say, to trucks, what appears to an adult to be a series of discrete images will, for a preverbal child, provide a narrative: Embedded in the facing images of a pickup and a monster truck is likely a tale of growth and diminishment, or maybe simplification and elaboration. Of course, this is a rough surmise; we can't be sure exactly what's going on inside the kid's head. But we can assume a basic human impulse to look for order and imbue it with meaning. In 1977, Larry Sultan and Mike Mandel, both recent photography graduates of the San Francisco Art Institute, published a project that might test this assumption. The artists assembled a volume of fifty photographs plucked from myriad government and private archives and published it as a limited edition titled *Evidence*. While the book figures significantly in the populous domain that includes, for examples, Richard Prince, Barbara Kruger, John Baldessari, and Sherrie Levine, its out-of-print status meant it was more talked about than read. This reprint provides a timely reminder of its place not only in the history of contemporary photography but also in the development of appropriation art.

The corpus of images that Mandel and Sultan collected was in one sense random, but in another not so. A good number of the dozens of institutions that permitted them access to their files were located in California, many in what would become Silicon Valley: police and fire departments, the United States Forest Service and United States Geological Survey, the Army Corps of Engineers—all rich repositories. They also visited tech-oriented corporations and educational institutions, including Itek, Lockheed, Stanford's W. W. Hansen Laboratory of Physics, and United Technologies. Indeed, the list overall is a roll call for constituents of the postwar technocracy. It's no surprise, then, that for viewers who came of age in that era, the white shirts, skinny ties, dials, wires, and detonations will be quite familiar from weekly readers in school, *Life* and *Look* magazines, and the pages of *Popular Mechanics*. (Born in 1946 and 1950, respectively, Sultan and Mandel grew up in the suburbs of the San Fernando Valley, California.) But even as these photos serviceably record the moment between the clank of World War II machinery and the sibilant hum of digital technology, they also, individually and in aggregate, tilt strongly against that documentary role.

In the early '70s, both collaborators were pressing at the boundaries between conceptual art and photography: Mandel published *Myself: Timed Exposures*, a collection of ad hoc self-portraits taken in various incongruous locales; the underwater photos that comprised Sultan's series "Swimmers" defamiliarized the ubiquitous SoCal swimming-pool experience by featuring partial, distorted, and consequently otherworldly bodies. Both artists had come under the influence of photography guru Minor White, an advocate of indeterminacy, as well as imbibing the general atmosphere of appropriation and repurposing created by fellow Californians such as Ed Ruscha, Jess, and Bruce Conner. Their first collaborative book, as described in this volume's essay by Sandra S. Phillips, contained "drawings and rather lowbrow photographic illustrations lifted from cheap ads or instructional manuals, the sort found on the back of comic books." The leap from these sources to the archives of, for instance, the Los Angeles Department of Water and Power or the National Semiconductor Corporation, is a big one in terms of social imprimatur. But for Sultan and Mandel, these were simply other—albeit more organized—troves that could be subject to the same techniques of selection, juxtaposition, and sequence.

Just a few years before *Evidence*'s publication, Michael Lesy employed precisely those methods to pioneer the photographer's role as a curator of extant images with his 1973 book *Wisconsin Death Trip*. Lesy drew mostly from a single turn-of-the-nineteenth-century photographer as his source and included contemporaneous newspaper accounts to provide context for his grim portrait of Midwestern rural life. The intensity of the visual focus on the terrain and its people generated enormous emotional power—Lesy's volume is a landmark work of artfully rendered historical narrative. In contrast, Sultan and Mandel's project aimed to tell an allusive, darkly comic story, one that resembles experimental fiction (think Donald Barthelme) more than any documentary effort.

*Evidence*'s first photo—bare footprints striding across the page, as if into the book—seems perhaps too obvious as an introduction. Yet upon closer inspection, it's apparent that one set of footprints is reversed, and both sets are too widely spaced to be attributed to a person's natural gait, thus raising some questions: How did these footprints come to be? Are they an effort to dissemble? The mystery deepens when we notice a pencil placed strategically parallel to one of the prints. While the image recalls those taken at archaeological digs that show some primitive paw mark with a pencil used to denote scale, it also suggests fraud or, at the very least, the uncertainty of not only measurement but of knowing just what's being measured. The next two pages—a bas-relief-style cast of a hand accompanied by a ruler, and a faded group photo seemingly discarded on a dirty, ergonomically designed Eames chair—may extend this theme of how a body fits in the world, but do so elliptically.

Sultan and Mandel quite purposefully eschewed captions. We're on our own in guessing what that metal connector-type device is doing strewn, as it appears, in a desert landscape. And since none of the photos are credited to their source, it can't be known if, for instance, that photo of those footprints emerged from the files of the Medical Illustration Department at the University of California, Davis, or the Federal Power Commission. That lack of provenance amplifies the enigmatic quality of individual images as well as the rich ambiguities between them. The rather banal photo of an arm with a gloved hand holding a looped length of rope could be the demonstration of a rescue technique if drawn from the Burbank Fire Department; yet, if we believe it has been culled from the Bureau of Prisons, it might look more like a noose. The image's relation to the corpus of sources, and to the other images (the rope photo is followed by a picture of a large, vaguely mammalian foam-like entity nonchalantly stored in what could be a laboratory), activates a sense of indeterminacy and suggests a provocative array of possibilities and potential connections.

What betrays the photos' origins in corporate and governmental file cabinets is their shared artlessness. They were taken for documentary purposes by employees of the various agencies and offices enumerated in the book's first pages; they are, in a very real sense, work product. Their bland functionality, though, is itself a source of intrigue. A disquieting apprehension attends Sultan and Mandel's choices, as if each image were an outtake from just before or just after some exciting tale's climax. For instance, a man in office attire is seen at the bottom of a deep concrete shaft; he's making his way across a pile of rubble carrying a large box. Are we witnessing the aftermath of a collapse or the outset of construction? What is the well-dressed man there to do? And what is in his box—much bigger than a briefcase but not big enough for construction tools? The levels of improbability and strangeness are high enough to pique curiosity but hardly reach Diane Arbus territory. In all likelihood, the man is an engineer, his box contains some kind of measuring equipment, and the purpose of the photo was to document the state of the rubble for some white-shirted fellow higher up in the food chain.

There are many such photos here: Another image presents a similarly dressed man wearing knee-high boots and standing in a tunnel in ankle-deep water. He's there, we can again guess, to testify to the depth of water. These workplace photos were, after all, evidence. They were part of a process of analysis, assessment, or remedy. In this sense, they depict the very essence of the postwar technocracy's approach to remaking the world. While Sultan and Mandel's assemblage tells this story, it also critiques—and even undermines—the assumptions and certainties that undergirded that era's exuberant confidence in the scientific method and technological advancement. The figures (mostly men, often viewed only partially or from a distance) who contend with a world of experiments and devices, from wires and pulleys to hard hats and explosions, are not merely anonymous but appear as appendages to the stuff they calibrate and manipulate. One pair of photos in particular epitomizes this unsettling relationship: In the first, the head of a deceased and weirdly hirsute man is being pushed by a gloved hand into some kind of leather bag. This image is followed by an outstretched arm, a wristwatch in prominent view, holding a ruler in place, its angle ascendant. The visual mirroring—two living hands, one concealing the dead, the other carefully planning some future ascent—catalyzes a library's worth of Faustian brooding on the deployment of knowledge in the battle against mortality. By skillfully arranging scenes drawn from the bureaucratic periphery of the Cold War period, Sultan and Mandel conjure the spectacle of the mundane as well as the percolating dread that infused that time. Our current moment isn't dissimilar, and *Evidence* encourages us to close-read its pages to discover its many unnerving and pertinent provocations.

*Bookforum*, April–May 2017.

# Quote Unquote; Or, You Can Say That Again

To quote or not to quote, that's the question. "Classical quotation," may be, as Samuel Johnson put it, "the *parole* of literary men all over the world," but the no less imperial Gertrude Stein, whose fame rests largely upon her *bons mots*, warned that "remarks are not literature." Of course, most of us don't want to make literature, we're just hoping to sound a little brighter than we are, raise a laugh, maybe cadge a phone number for a prospective date. Some received wisdom can come in handy, but only if you get it right. "Famous remarks," Simeon Strunsky, a long-ago *New York Times* columnist, wrote, "are very seldom quoted correctly." True enough. When it can be hard enough to recall what the lunatic on the bus was screaming this morning, a glib quip gone wrong—"Like wanton boys to the gods, they play with us for their sport"—will surely remind your friends that stupid is as stupid does. Quotable Emerson was blunt on the subject: "I hate quotation. Tell me what you know." But just what do we empirically know? What haven't you taken from someone else's text, and they, in turn, from someone else? Churchill understood this modern dilemma and prescribed a quick get-smart program: "It is a good thing for an uneducated man to read books of quotations." No doubt someone who took this advice has cornered you in the kitchen at a party. The poet Edward Young had them in mind when he wrote, "Some for renown on scraps of learning dote, / And think they grow immortal as they quote." Of course, any writer anxious to meet a deadline (*moi?*) and spare themselves the chore of making their own sentences knows it's always best to quote, quote against the setting of the type.

To quote wisely, with precision and sophistication, a keen memory and a book of quotations are musts. While recall power isn't easily purchased, there are over two dozen quote collections in print. (To judge by this surplus, you'd think we were a nation of *Masterpiece Theater* refugees, dispensing Disraeli to tollbooth clerks.) Fatter by nearly a thousand pages than any of the handy volumes of after-dinner remarks, abridged student editions, and paperbacks that mine light ores like humor or literature, are *Bartlett's Familiar Quotations* and the *Oxford Dictionary of Quotations*, the canonical lords of the biz. Their girth reflects their impossible task—to record and index every memorable bit of human utterance from Archilochus to Eldridge Cleaver. In John Bartlett's first try in 1855, the book was mostly drawn from the Bible and Shakespeare, with a heavy dash of assorted Big Brits and a pinch of Yankees. Although the Bible and the Bard still hold page-count sway in both books, other continents and centuries are beginning to get their due.

Within the past year, both of these hardbound veterans have gone into new editions—*Oxford*, its fourth, and *Bartlett's*, its sweet sixteenth. Since the previous editions, 1979 and 1989, the multicultural and canon debates have gotten underway, and these standard reference works now show faint signs of cultural renovation. In the preface to the *Oxford Dictionary*, editor Angela Partington points with pride to the inclusion of "previously neglected authors, especially early women poets." And Justin Kaplan, Bartlett's general editor, sounds a pitchman's note when he announces, "over fifty new quotations that come directly from the movies," plus "Jimi Hendrix, Elvis Presley, Bruce Springsteen, Chuck Berry, the Doors, [and] Jack Dempsey."

In a recent *New Criterion* piece titled "Affirmative Action Bartlett's," John Simon sniffs over the "demotic" readership Kaplan seems to have in mind. He complains that including pop-music lyrics and ad slogans means "Stanley Kunitz shrinks from twenty-one entries to eight." Putting aside Simon's tiresome contempt for pop culture, he does have half a point. Although designed in part as dictionaries, quote compilations also serve as anthologies. Their indexes give access to all quotes containing, for example, the word *winter*. Every editor will include "the winter of our discontent," but novelist Richard Condon's equally memorable title, *Winter Kills*, is up for grabs. Thus, all these books are prey to some complaint of exclusion. I could easily sacrifice all of Kunitz for a smidgen of Charles Olson, Robert Creeley, or Frank O'Hara, all major American poets unrepresented here. Trying to squeeze the vast, mercurial realm of mass culture in among Thomas Aquinas and Annie Dillard may be a foolish enterprise that trims back quotes unavailable elsewhere while providing us with what is already too familiar. How necessary are citations for catch phrases like "Say it with flowers," Helen Reddy's "I am woman," or Zippy the Pinhead's "Are we having fun yet?"?

It's painfully clear that the editors, who are more accustomed to sorting through the likes of Robert Herrick than Hendrix, are out of their depth when panning for gold in pop's muddy waters. For instance, Jimi (or James Marshall, as we're reminded) appears in *Bartlett's* with the full stanza from "Purple Haze" that ends with "Scuse me while I kiss the sky," while *Oxford* inexplicably provides only the first two lines—"Purple haze is in my brain / Lately things don't seem the same." Although they remind us that LSD had brand names, just like detergent, these lines are bland; whatever poetry is to be found in the song lies in Hendrix's polite request to treat himself to a transcendental kiss. *Bartlett's*, too, culls flat, generic snips from Bob Marley's infectious, patois-soaked lyrics. Still, if I'd done the selection, I might have embarrassed myself. Paging through *The New Penguin Dictionary of Quotations*, I discovered under the eighteenth-century English poet William Cowper what I'd always thought was one of the Rastaman's choicer lines—"Can a woman's tender care / Cease towards the child she bare?" The canon works in mysterious ways.

Quotation is both a ritual act and rhetorical gimmick. It's an invocation of a higher power, an authority more apt, more persuasive, more credible than the speaker; a quote can indicate deference and respect for the wordcraft of others. But more often, it's intellectual larceny that allows us to steal another mind's thunder while being praised for having the taste and savvy to do so. "Thieves respect property," G. K. Chesterton writes. "They merely wish the property to become their property that they may more perfectly respect it." When you read that line, you might begin to think that I've read Chesterton, think perhaps I've read not just him but other English Catholics, such as Evelyn Waugh and Hilaire Belloc, people with whom you are only vaguely acquainted. Did you miss something? How did these writers escape your notice? They may be minor, but they are, after all, real English Authors. So, while you brood over your botched education, I can tear ahead while making little sense, and you won't notice. Nice trick, right? Quotation clarifies and connects for some, but mystifies and excludes for others. *Bartlett's* and *The Oxford Dictionary* serve as the secret code books containing passwords.

No one sits down to read a dictionary of quotes straight through. Usually, the hunt for something specific—what's that about the mills of the gods grinding fine?—cracks the book, but from there it's easy to get hooked on an irresistible trip crisscrossing centuries, dashing through whole epochs of thought as if they were so many matchbook-cover messages. Consider Virginia Woolf. *Oxford* offers 13 entries, *Bartlett's* 12, and *Penguin* 11. Subtracting the surprisingly small overlap leaves nearly 30 bite-sized samples of Woolf's pithy wit to be devoured while someone puts you on call waiting. Of course, this isn't reading Woolf, but rather an appetite-whetting skim in which one quick taste—"So that is marriage, Lily thought, a man and a woman looking at a girl throwing a ball"—might prompt a sit-down dinner with *To the Lighthouse*. However, the net effect of picking at these feasts can be somewhat dispiriting; nothing will make it clearer how little you've actually read. Take heart, though—at least you will be prepared to ace some outdated cultural-literacy test.

When editors narrow the chronological focus, as Tony Augarde has done in *The Oxford Dictionary of Modern Quotations*, overall familiarity picks up. These are our neighbors, so to speak—Susan Sontag, Zsa Zsa Gabor, Langston Hughes, and Richard Nixon. Augarde ably condenses the twentieth century into an epic *Our Town* in which everyone from Dean Acheson to Frank Zappa steps forward to comment on the modern condition. "That men do not learn very much from the lessons of history is the most important of all lessons that history has to teach," observes Aldous Huxley, taking in the big picture. On personal politics, Doris Lessing heralds the triumph of the self ("There's only one real sin, and that is to persuade oneself that the second-best is anything but the second-best"), while Mae West nods to an age of moral ambiguity ("Between two evils, I always pick the one I never tried before"). Grazing the pages reveals most contemporary quotes to be almost telegraphic in their brevity. No long discursive stanzas from the poets; instead, we have "faces in the crowd; / Petals on a wet, black bough." Indeed, *The Oxford Modern* reads like an accelerated version of the bigger quote books. It's an express train, seat belts unfastened, on our century's bumpy ride.

Narrowing the scope ever further is *Simpson's Contemporary Quotations,* which advertises "The Most Notable Quotes Since 1950." Much less attentive to traditional literary sources, James B. Simpson closely tracks the mass media. He provides thousands of quotes from anonymous scribes and talking heads, their words lifted from television interviews, newspapers, magazines, billboards, and congressional hearings. You may not recognize specific lines, but you know you've heard something close before. "I see all those Solomons out there," Phil Donahue is immortalized as saying, "I can't wait to hear your wisdom." What use a workaday quote like this might be is doubtful, but when it's taken together with less than trenchant soundbites from the likes of Linda Ellerbee, Russell Baker, and Morley Safer, a fairly accurate echo of the mass media drone emerges.

Some of these semiprecious jewels might get kicked upstairs into *Bartlett's,* or maybe lodged resolutely in the collective memory. If not, they will probably disappear with the paper they're printed on. Many quotes are called, but few are chosen. The ones that enter the language, either spoken or written, tend to slip their owner's leash and even lose their identity as quotes. A study of *Bartlett's* and *The Oxford Dictionary,* especially the pre-20th-century sources, reveals hundreds of familiar phrases and expressions most of us would be hard-pressed to trace back to their origins. Who coined commonplaces like "Eureka!," "Cruel necessity," "I see all the birds are flown," "Death will have his day," "New wine into old bottles," and "All this and heaven too"? We certainly don't cite Archimedes, Oliver Cromwell, Charles I, Shakespeare, Saint Matthew, and Philip Henry every time we air them out. They are alive in ordinary sentences, unfootnoted, yet still at work, lending some small grandeur to simple talk. Although the apparent task of quotation books is to apportion credit, what they chiefly end up doing is impressing upon us that words are not property—they are, as Samuel Butler said, "but wind," and just as we draw them in, we have to breathe them out. With style, of course, and quotation marks.

*Village Voice Literary Supplement,* June 1993.

# On the Record: The Talk Writers Talk

When did what writers say in interviews become at least as important as what they actually write? If readers once pried at their paragraphs looking for revelations, they are now more likely to graze their quips in some magazine feature like "Twenty Questions" in the *New York Times Magazine*. Gertrude Stein—herself no mean quipster—rebuked Ernest Hemingway by saying, "Remarks are not literature," but like many such *bons mots*, hers doesn't quite hold up. The author interview, which has truly come into its own in the last century (in antebellum America, newspaper interviews were reserved chiefly for convicted criminals), might be best thought of as a literary genre, with its tone, rhythm, and themes all as intentionally crafted as a poem's or essay's. Ironically, it was Stein who managed to suggest that the question-and-answer game could conjure poetic complexity. Upon arriving in America for a lecture tour in 1934, she impressed reporters with her verbal lucidity. "Why don't you speak the way you write?" one asked. Her riposte: "Why don't you read the way I write?" The sizable disquisition on cognition, language, and aesthetics that might be unpacked from that breezy reply suggests at least one reason why, these days, the talk writers talk lives on after them.

The question comes in the wake of the proliferation over the past several years of writer interviews in almost every journalistic venue, but especially in literary publications (*Bookforum* included). There's barely a literary quarterly or arts magazine that doesn't publish one or more interviews per issue. As the talkfests pile up, publishers eagerly issue collections of these conversational efforts. (Over the last twenty years, for example, the University Press of Mississippi has published more than 120 volumes in its Literary Conversations series.) The phenomenon becomes particularly notable when one considers the number of publications—intellectual digests, general interest magazines, book reviews—that at one time included fiction or poetry but no longer do. The recent publication of four compilations of interviews, each representing a different era in American literary history—*Mark Twain: The Complete Interviews, Theodore Dreiser: Interviews, Empty Phantoms: Interviews and Encounters with Jack Kerouac,* and *The Paris Review: Interviews, Volume I*—offers an opportunity not only to reflect on whether the author interview constitutes an actual genre of literary performance, but also to experience (in three of these books) immersion in a single writer's oral tradition.

While generally considered to be the first great literary biography, James Boswell's *Life of Johnson* can also be thought of as the template of the modern author interview. Boswell filled a good deal of his book's twelve-hundred-odd pages with lengthy stretches of more or less verbatim conversations he and others had had with the voluble poet and lexicographer. The format is recognizable to contemporary readers—Boswell, in the manner of, say, Dick Cavett, prods his all-too-opinionated subject with deliberately leading questions about matters literary, moral, and philosophical. A typical exchange proceeds thus: "I attempted to argue for the superiour happiness of the savage life, upon the usual fanciful topicks. JOHNSON. 'Sir, there can be nothing more false. The savages have no bodily advantages beyond those of civilized men.... No, Sir; you are not to talk such paradox: Let me have no more on't. It cannot entertain, far less can it instruct.' BOSWELL. 'But, Sir, does not Rousseau talk such nonsense?' JOHNSON. 'True, Sir, but Rousseau knows he is talking nonsense, and laughs at the world for staring at him.' BOSWELL. 'How so, Sir?' JOHNSON. 'Why, Sir, a man who talks nonsense so well, must know that he is talking nonsense.'"

While there is an eighty-year span between the last of the conversations recorded by Boswell and the first of the interviews included in the Twain volume, neither style nor substance changes much. Not unlike Johnson, Twain was every inch the public performer. Indeed, many of the interviews from the book's thirty-nine-year period were given while he was on national or international speaking tours. Twain exhibited a slyly iconoclastic verbal style that meshed neatly with the persona his audiences had come to know through his writing. In full Johnsonian mode, the author deigned to micturate from a great height upon the very process of interrogation: "You don't love the interviewer, I see, Mr. Clemens," a *St. Louis Post-Dispatch* reporter said during Twain's visit to that city in 1882. "No; I don't," he replied. "I have never yet met a man who attempted to interview me whose report of the process did not try very hard to make me out an idiot, and did not amply succeed, in my mind, in making him a thorough one."

The oracular tone and curmudgeonly wit were the author's conversational mainstays over his long career. Reporters from Boston to Bombay, from Cincinnati to Sydney, could count on this patented display of Authorial Presence to fill the pages of their newspapers and weekly magazines. A reading of these reports from distant and familiar quarters, decade after decade, evinces just how rote Twain's responses, as well as the questions, became. The interviews take on something of the ritualized aspect of a minstrel show, with the esteemed author playing comic end man while the reporter serves as Mr. Interlocutor. Invariably, each profile introduces Twain with extravagant honorifics ("the most refined humorist that America, and probably the world, has ever known"), a quick tour of the famous visage ("his long untidy hair, and ferocious mustache; and the grey eyes that are not ferocious, but kind, and gentle, and pathetic"), and some characterization of his voice, which almost always is said to "drawl." The interviewers confronted a known quantity—Twain was easily the most famous author, perhaps the most famous public figure, of his time. "To the present writer," one Australian scribe noted, "the real Mark Twain was in every sense the Mark Twain of imagination."

Given his canny, even prescient grasp of the monetary value of celebrity, Twain understood the value of giving interviews despite the disdain he felt for them. (His financial straits often necessitated lecture tours and the consequent encounters with journalists.) In fact, he often required them to paraphrase his words rather than quote him directly—he preferred, editor Gary Scharnhorst notes, "to sell his words rather than give them away." Still, what Twain had to say—over and over, in these 258 interviews—was somewhat limited; he expatiated broadly on the characteristics of different nations' humor, palmistry, his writing regimen, the joys of cigar smoking ("I never smoke to excess—that is, I smoke in moderation, only one cigar at a time"), the nature of lecturing, and the viability of international copyright laws. He was especially obsessed with the last topic—always at the ready to delve into the economic minutiae of an author's remuneration. He was, by turns, bombastic, pedantic, droll, and charming—his showmanship never flagging. It's a daunting example, one that even the most charismatic contemporary writer might be hard-pressed to match. Twain enthusiastically initiated his commodification unburdened by self-consciousness; he saw no contradiction in hustling his wares while remaining a member in good standing of what Jonathan Franzen, amid his recent brush with notoriety, called the "high-art literary tradition."

If Twain often impersonated a dyspeptic curmudgeon, Theodore Dreiser didn't need to dig too deeply for his performance. He shared a barbed disposition with his friend H. L. Mencken and was rarely reluctant to complain—about small-minded Americans, censorious publishers, Hollywood moguls, plutocrats, the Soviet Union, labor unrest, and the general stupidity (and cupidity) of mankind. He did all this while shrewdly ensuring that his numerous interviews (this volume includes 74 out of what editors Donald Pizer and Frederic E. Rusch estimate to be a total of 165) promoted his publications. For instance, when many major literary houses decided in 1930 to reduce the price of novels to $1.50, Dreiser was not shy about promoting his own limited editions of minor works—"Thus does the Indianan," a helpful reporter commended, "who now dwells in New York beat the publishers."

In what might be thought of as obligatory invocations of the muse before their inquisitions, many authors dismiss or challenge the very legitimacy of the interview process. Dreiser was characteristically direct on this score: Speaking to a reporter from the *New York Herald Tribune* in 1930, he announced, "I will bet you $10 that you cannot get into your paper the things I am going to say." The combativeness is evident from the outset of his career. His first novel, *Sister Carrie* (1900), was withdrawn from publication by one firm and bowdlerized by its eventual publisher, and for decades afterward, the author bore a vigorous grudge. In 1902, he aired the untrue claim that Frank Doubleday had backed out of publishing the novel because the businessman's wife objected to its subject matter. (Doubleday did refuse to produce the book, but there's no evidence he did so because of his wife.) Nearly forty years later, in 1941, the novelist continued to flog the poor lady: "After Mrs. Doubleday had *Sister Carrie* scrapped, kept out of circulation. Why, you'd have thought I was the devil. Nobody would have anything to do with me—none of the people in power." Whenever he recounted the tale, he did so with indignation that could easily be mistaken for relish; Dreiser viewed *Sister Carrie*'s reception as a career-defining moment, and he never tired of making reporters—some of whom, in his later years, hadn't even been born when the book first appeared—understand that he, however currently famous and esteemed, had once been an abject outsider.

Interviewers accommodated Dreiser's debate-team demeanor, sometimes casting their encounters as fraught. In a 1930 interview with the *Jewish Journal*—Dreiser was in San Francisco to visit jailed labor activist Tom Mooney—the author uncorked a series of deliberately bigoted pronouncements: "Jews are marked by a strong feeling for the conservation and use of power. They've always yelled about Justice, but with the thought of making things easier for themselves. Reform Judaism is the only tolerable kind of Judaism." The reporter, Raymond Dannenbaum, smartly led off with these shockers and then set the scene: "He paused for a moment. I had an opportunity to carefully inspect his bronzed face. I noticed that although he spoke vehemently but quietly, and seemed to possess great repose, nevertheless his mind and body were taut.... He returned with a jerk to [the subject of] intermarriage."

When Dreiser was in spirited form, his meetings were hardly tête-à-têtes—in fact, one suspects some reporters felt like Moses questioning the burning bush. Certainly, they all approached the "Literary Mastodon" with an awe and deference that can barely be imagined in our present moment when writers more often are the objects of derision, or stand as the accused in some ethical scandal. Substitute the name of any contemporary figure for Dreiser's in the following sentence and try not to chuckle: "There is something revelatory in listening to Dreiser talk, and in watching him. You see a tall man, lithely put together; you see a sculptural head, massive of structure, and with features formed on a large scale and ruggedly, as if hewn laboriously out of rock." No doubt, even as it is, it's hard not to laugh a bit. The seriousness that attended these interviews—mostly done in the '20s and '30s—reflects their historical moment. Dreiser was queried about all the momentous issues of the day—Freud, the Depression, isolationism—and never took refuge in the feint of merely being an artist. Barreling ahead, he handily threw off what would become provocative headlines—"Noted Novelist Expresses Contempt for Critics in Visit Here"—to grateful newspapermen. When, in September 1942, the seventy-one-year-old author denounced Churchill and the English (the interviewer for the *Toronto Evening Telegram* was at pains to note Dreiser's German parentage), his lecture in that city was canceled, and he was advised to leave Canada. A good deal more than Twain's badinage, this was outright provocation of the sort that Dreiser always played to the hilt.

By the '50s, author interviews had migrated from newspapers to literary quarterlies and, increasingly, radio and television. A collection of *The Paris Review*'s interviews, introduced by the magazine's then editor, Philip Gourevitch, and a hefty volume edited by Paul Maher Jr. of Jack Kerouac's interviews, ably represent a time when a talkative author could be found either on TV (Gore Vidal, Norman Mailer, and Truman Capote were mainstays of various late-night shows) or in low-circulation literary digests—but rarely anywhere in between. Also, interviewers, who had previously been mere ink-stained wretches, were now often well-known authors or journalists. Kerouac was quizzed by Ben Hecht, Mike Wallace, Steve Allen, and Dan Wakefield; at *The*

*Paris Review,* a young poet like Donald Hall was sent to interview another poet, T. S. Eliot; Spanish translator and critic Ronald Christ met with Jorge Luis Borges. Absent from these matchups is the great gulf in intellectual disposition and knowledge that often characterizes those conducted for newspapers. More like peer-to-peer encounters, these interviews tend to come off as real conversations rather than as staged performances in which the lowly supplicant seeks wisdom from on high. There's a strong whiff of shop talk around, say, Hall's curiosity about the elder poet's decision to abandon *vers libre* for quatrains or how Ezra Pound's edits of *The Waste Land* affected the poem's structure. Such lines of inquiry don't afford interviewees much opportunity for grandiloquence; instead, we learn that Eliot's free verse was modeled after Jules Laforgue's, and "this meant merely rhyming lines of irregular length, with the rhymes coming in irregular places." This exchange, from 1959, reflects the fact that, increasingly, the audience for the author interview was made up of academics and aspiring writers—all the tech talk being of keen interest to these specialized readers.

To be sure, Big Questions were still lobbed at certain literary figures, chief among them Jack Kerouac. Repeatedly called upon to answer for an entire generation's cultural predilections, he proved to be an awkward, if endearing, spokesman for the Beat movement. Unlike Allen Ginsberg, Kerouac was too shy to perform in public with abandoned élan. Instead, he managed to sound cryptic and naive at once, avoiding direct responses and sounding embarrassing notes of sincerity. While weathering the first wave of fame in the wake of *On the Road,* Kerouac tried gamely to field searching queries about politics and society. When Ben Hecht asked in 1958 whether Eisenhower was a great man, Kerouac said, "I don't know, we'll figure it out in fifty years." Or when pressed about his Buddhist beliefs, he declared, "I worship Christ. I worship Allah, and I worship Yahweh, who is the Father. I worship 'em all." Years later, Kerouac took to drinking before interviews, in part to cope with the pressure to be some kind of sage—a development all too evident in his 1968 televised face-to-face with conservative commentator William F. Buckley, Jr. *The Firing Line* transcript is a comedy of errors, rife with farcical misunderstandings

(Buckley asked if the Beats were an Adamite movement, and Kerouac replied, "Adamite? You mean Adam and Eve or atom"), rambling (he announced that the Greek version of Spiro Agnew's last name means "son of the reader" and then started in about ancient Greece), and Dadaist non sequiturs (as poet Ed Sanders, another interview participant, tried to explain guerrilla theater, Kerouac piped up, "Do they crucify chickens?"). The tape of the program shows the gravel-voiced, flush-faced King of the Beats gesticulating with his cigar and looking more like a neighborhood blowhard holding court at a tavern than some eminent author dispensing epigrams. Clearly, the genre of the literary conversation had evolved (devolved?) from Boswell and Johnson's day.

In 1958, George Plimpton, the founding editor of *The Paris Review*, interviewed Hemingway, a writer arguably as famous then as Twain was in his time. Hemingway, too, was known as a cagey performer: an author who treated interviews as battles of wits in which someone—himself or the interviewer—had to come out on top. Early in their colloquy, Plimpton took a provocative tack: "Is emotional stability necessary to write well? You told me once that you could only write well when you were in love." Rearing up, Hemingway snorted, "What a question." Yet then, in the spirit of manly competition, he added, "But full marks for trying." If Hemingway's *realpolitik* view was reductionist, it did catch more than a glint of truth: Interrogating writers for publication is indeed an adversarial experience (Twain thought it a kind of "torture").

Authors, as they are wont to do, wish to control their words—something easily done on the page, not so much in conversation—while the interviewer strives to elicit something newsworthy or at least fresh. It is this tension between desire for control and the spontaneity integral to the situation that constitutes the literary interview's chief draw. Interviews with filmmakers, composers, and painters may be of great interest, but since their jobs aren't deploying just the right word in just the right place, there's less at stake. The interview is a particularly high-wire act for writers—sentences they might otherwise rewrite a dozen times turn up in print the way they fell from their tongues. And even though writers seek to impose intentionality on their spoken text and craft their self-presentation as a director might stage a play, nevertheless there's always the possibility of a misstep, maybe even a tumble. Remarks may not be literature, but they are often a prelude to amusement or distress; daily life makes this all too plain to us. Perhaps this is why authors' utterances have elbowed aside authors' texts—conversation can democratize their linguistic dexterity. That extempore genre—the interview—affords us a delightful discovery: When writers talk their talk, even they sometimes don't mean what they say or can't say what they mean.

*Bookforum,* February–March 2007.

# String Theory: The Elusive Art of Harry Smith

"My true vocation is preparation for death." That was the reply offered by polymath, scholar, filmmaker, archivist, and painter Harry Smith when asked what among his many pursuits he believed to be his "truest." "For that day," he continued, "I'll lie on my bed and see my life go before my eyes." If Smith's declaration evokes the gnomic, ironic, dissolute, and fanciful, it also characterizes an artist who prized his own obscurity (and the obscurity of his myriad and often uncompleted endeavors) even within the more rarefied cultural circles of the postwar decades. The underground's underground bard, Smith became famous for his curatorial obsessions (his 1952 *Anthology of American Folk Music* is a cultural touchstone for an entire musical era), his filmmaking (no less than Jonas Mekas claimed that "there are more levels in Harry Smith's work than in any other animator I know"), his mystical Surrealist paintings (many of which he destroyed), and his occultist scholarship (Ed Sanders recounts how Smith inspired his band The Fugs and Allen Ginsberg in their ritualistic efforts to exorcise and levitate the Pentagon). Before he died in 1991, he did enjoy the pleasure of at least one mainstream success, receiving a Lifetime Achievement Grammy for his archival work with folk music. Even so, his was a career lived out in the interstices of culture; since many of his films, artworks, and collections were rarely exhibited and haphazardly maintained, he was an artist and thinker more heard about than heard from. Smith's self-destructive tendencies cannot be discounted either: "I'm not only a filmmaker," he once said of himself, "I'm also an alcoholic."

Nearly a quarter century after his passing, the appearance of the first two volumes of a catalogue raisonné mark another effort to recognize Smith's rightful place as an epic progenitor of ideas that were once obscure but now animate almost every sphere of cultural production—for instance, in the 1950s he anticipated the revivals of ancient spiritual pursuits that have come to inform every alternative belief system from hippie cosmology to holistic medicine. Editors John Klacsmann and Andrew Lampert have taken on the task of sorting through the materials held at the Getty Research Institute, the Smithsonian, and elsewhere to organize them for publication. The new volume devoted to string art—the craft of manipulating a loop to form, say, a "cat's cradle"—has deep origins in Smith's biography. Trained as an anthropologist, he grew up close to Native American communities in the area around Portland, Oregon. His mother taught on the Lummi Reservation, and his studies at the University of Washington (for only five semesters—he was the ultimate autodidact) concentrated on the traditional art and music of this tribe and others. Smith developed a particular interest in Native American string art and began to document the specimens he found in photographs, transcriptions of instructions, and notations about techniques. He hoped to produce a grand anthropological catalogue that would range across indigenous cultures and reveal their underlying universal themes, something not unlike what he achieved with his folk music anthology. But, as was the case with so many of Smith's epic undertakings, the text he wrote is not to be found. According to a research assistant who worked with him in the mid-'60s, it may have been misplaced (quite likely, given Smith's chaotic life and work habits), or perhaps it was simply never written. What survives are notes, film depictions, drawings, and photographs of actual string "compositions" that Smith made. These images, various film stills, and reproductions of handwritten notes and indexes constitute *String Figures*.

Of course, the very notion of a kinetic, three-dimensional, essentially performative art being adequately represented by anything other than the artist forming the shapes in front of you presents a challenge. The string figure exists in an elusive moment, the slightest hand movement altering the configuration. That this "sculpture" cannot be preserved without crucial diminishment may well have played a role in Smith's attraction to the art form, as well as to its necessarily problematic documentation. Directions and drawings for figures such as "Mr Unmake the Younger," "Swinging Below," "Polar Bear," and "Tug of War" offer very specific instructions: "figure produced ... by rotating thumbs in ulnar direction and re-extending." It would be difficult to reproduce these intricate geometries employing Smith's equally intricate directions, which make use of symbolic language for shapes, particular fingers, and hand movements. There are several much clearer manuals to consult. If these meticulously noted texts, on occasion made on envelopes and menus, evidence a ferocious intensity of focus, it is one seemingly at odds with Smith's personal and professional disarray.

Still, this precision shows itself with painterly elegance in the string-figure mountings Smith constructed by affixing white string to black poster board. The minimalist palette accentuates the ornamentality of the shapes and evokes their making: the strings loop, coil, triangulate, crisscross, and double-cross in what almost seems like constant motion. Smith further attempted to solve the problem of representing the figures' three-dimensional state by staging the illusion that they float in what could be the blackness of night or perhaps some more forbidding void. Constellations are as readily conjured as hallucinations—those mutating geometries that might appear behind dilated eyes. Despite the formal beauty of these arabesques, there is an unmistakable cunning apparent in their devising, perhaps, because we cannot quite shed our association of ligature and entrapment with things knotted and tied.

One piece shows, according to Smith's text, "two Eskimo views of the mouth." "On the right," the label continues, "a cross-section (note the glottis), on the left, a front view." Bridging the gap between a literal representation of a mouth and these abstracted anatomies requires the same imaginative capacities a viewer would bring to paintings by Brice Marden, Klee, or Miró—it is possible to see something of what's intended, but seeing that requires seeing so much more than merely what the artist envisioned. The figures aren't confined to static depiction; some portray action-packed narratives: "Cutting up the whale; an Eskimo figure in six stages from Point Barrow. Stage four: The dog that became sleepy and went home." Again, what nuance in the loops of this figure delineates a dog, let alone its sleepiness, only a scholar might say (and Smith's analysis isn't included). But the image suggests enough of the maker's handiwork—the rotation of wrists, the quick extension of a thumb—to stir the air above the page.

What an agile hand might do with a piece of paper instead of a length of string spurred another of Smith's passions—paper airplanes, the subject of another volume of the archivist's work. The extant collection numbers more than 250 specimens that he found on streets, fished out of wastebaskets, or even, as one friend recalls, ran into traffic to retrieve. Planes are as fragile and ephemeral as the string figures, and their intact survival testifies to the high degree of care devoted to what would otherwise have been thrown away. Indeed, many of the planes are annotated with the location and date of their discovery: "Prince nr Wooster 4-5-79"; "Bet 9th & 10th Aves on 49th 4-24-79 In Playground." The variety of colors, paper types, and aerodynamic designs is further enlivened by the multifarious texts visible on magazines, newspapers, phonebooks, loose-leaf pages, menus, political leaflets, commercial handbills, Bible sheaves, manila envelopes, and cardboard scraps. If the planes are found objects, the texts are found poems of particular interest, owing to the reconfiguration of words that the folds create. From what looks like a topless-bar advertisement, the word fragments isolated by creases are "go avail," which are juxtaposed with a young woman's face; the phrase "to remember" appears along another's fuselage, and the wings present, with a little emendation, "christ parade." A complexly folded handbill merges "service" and "business" to yield "serv siness." Another example, devised from a page torn out of a decades-old Broadway theater directory, demonstrates how these bits of ephemera can conjure the past with impossibly delicate specificity. The shapes, too, tease at large ideation by offering an inadvertent retrospective of twentieth-century sculptural forms, in which echoes of Calder, Brancusi, Serra, Noguchi, and many others are easily identified.

Again, the tactile presence of the creator is felt in these constructions—we can envision the bored high school student bending a notebook page, or a contest between office workers, each launching their favorite design from a midtown window. Conceived, folded, and pressed into flightworthiness, each plane reveals in its design and construction a certain sum of labor. And then, of course, that work and its material consequence were offered to the world with no possibility of recognition for the plane-maker. Unless their builders imagined so unlikely a person as Smith, they had every reason to believe they were pitching their planes into the trash.

This spirit of anti-commodification, as well as its attendant art-for-art's-sake aesthetic, no doubt intrigued Smith—the notion of effort heedlessly spent marks his entire career as an intellectual and artist. He gathered with a fervor equal to the idiosyncrasy of the objects; he amassed archives of odd folk relics, photos, and records that, owing to a life lived in a succession of hotel rooms, sometimes disappeared. His archivist's obsession, though, sat comfortably with a genuine insouciance: "I'm leaving it to the future to figure out the exact purpose of having all these rotten eggs, the blankets, the Seminole patchwork I never look at, and records I never listen to.... It is a way of fooling away the time, harmlessly, as much as possible." Taken together, Smith's multiple passions and protean scholarship lack the apparent consistency and evolutionary progression typically associated with artists and academics—but, of course, he was anything but typical. A completist who left so much incomplete, his career zig-zagged, pinwheeled, and often crashed. With these initial volumes, in what promises to be an extensive publication effort, the future has at last begun to figure out the purpose that eluded Harry Smith.

*Bookforum*, February–March 2016.

# Top Secret: Images from the Stasi Archives

Among the many cautionary examples cited by critics of the United States security and surveillance establishment, the German Democratic Republic's Stasi stands out in bold relief. The organization employed over ninety thousand full-time spies and police—but the truly depressing figure is its nearly two hundred thousand informants (some estimates run as high as two million). Since the wall fell in 1989, films, memoirs, and historical accounts have described a society riven with suspicion among colleagues, friends, and family members; a lot of citizens were their brothers' keepers. Berlin-based artist Simon Menner spent two years researching the files of the Federal Commissioner for the Stasi Archives of the former GDR to unearth the photographs he has gathered for this dark but unavoidably comic volume. Menner's collection—*Top Secret: Images from the Stasi Archives*—focuses on images pulled from manuals dealing with espionage tradecraft, as well as actual photos from surveillance operations. A hint of the absurdist humor to come shows in the table of contents' listing of manual titles—"Wigs and Their Application," "Disguising as Western Tourists," "Staged Arrests," and "Practicing the Application of Fake Beards."

The images are constructed in the matter-of-fact manner of any instructional guide, compositional nuance ceding to the requirements of exposition. To teach agents to dress like "Western tourists," two deadpan photos depict a pair of operatives, one sporting red pants and white sneakers, along with a jaunty fishing hat; the other wears aviator sunglasses and cutoff jeans that have been haphazardly sheared as if by a kindergartner with play scissors. Although recognizably "Western," these models are rendered ridiculous not only by their blatant caricature, but by the numerous false fashion notes. Included the section "A Seminar for Disguises," various portraits provide possible modes of dissembling for the same somewhat jowly fellow. But in each case his deliberately bland mien and "casual" pose undo whatever cloaking his garb might offer—he fails to inhabit any one of the costumes, managing instead to master the uncomfortable demeanor of a mail-order-catalogue model.

That these photos of fake mustaches, hand signals, and close-combat techniques all smack of the risibly ersatz doesn't diminish their eerie power: The Stasi, despite its flat-footed training handbooks, proved effective enough. The photos in an "Operations" section titled "Juveniles" document teenagers' "pro-Western sympathies" by showing their bedroom walls festooned with *Playboy* centerfolds, along with Wile E. Coyote and Madonna posters. The secret police were probably right: if you're sixteen and you dig Road Runner cartoons, you're probably an existentialist with scant desire to serve the all-powerful state. A mentality predicated on surveillance and distrust finds emblematic expression in "Spies Photograph Spies," featuring shots taken by Stasi agents observing other Stasi agents while they are observing others. But even that hall-of-mirrors weirdness is topped by a pair of images in which agents photograph themselves; Menner's note that they had "probably attained the highest stage of ... espionage training" is as grimly funny as it is profound.

*Bookforum*, December-January 2014.

# *Unreadable*

# The Lost Generator: Gertrude Stein

We first know her as an icon: the sharply sculpted, masklike face hovering above the piled-upon folds of her body. Her head tilts slightly forward to catch an unnaturally harsh light. Her eyes are askew; one is indifferently wide, the other squints in judgment. Depicting an unsettled Buddha who seems both at rest and about to rise from her overstuffed chair, Picasso's portrait of Gertrude Stein is, perhaps, the most familiar emblem of the Modernist epoch. We can hardly look at this painting and not imagine, standing just outside the frame, Braque, Apollinaire, Matisse, Pound, Hemingway, assorted Futurists, Dadaists, and Cubists—all those who made the art that made the twentieth century. Stein appears enthroned, a high priestess presiding over her charmed circle at 27 Rue de Fleurus. Inevitably, the grand scene the portrait conjures—Paris in the teens and '20s, the Lost Generation—obscures its subject. While we view her as a pivotal, even essential, participant in the artistic turmoil of her times, it is always in relation to her legendary salon, her role as hostess. Yet it was Stein, among all her guests, who truly executed the letter of the Modernist law to "make it new." She did this in some forty books that leave no genre untouched. Whether as librettist, poet, novelist, or essayist, Stein consistently produced work so radical it remains so today. Sadly, this achievement too little informs what we see when we see Stein. Regarded more as icon than artist, more aphorist than author, she is her century's most famous unread writer.

Stein lacks readers not merely because the writing is difficult but because it is, at times, literally unreadable; that is, she cannot be read the way we've been taught, the way we want to read. She sought to reinvent the relationship between reader and page. Arriving in New York to lecture in 1934, she made her intent plain to a group of inquiring newsmen. Surprised by the clarity of her responses, one asked, "Why don't you write the way you talk?" "Why don't you read the way I write?" she replied. Doing that means unlearning the fluid rapidity and instantaneous assimilation we automatically bring to bear. We are sent back to our earliest experiences with written words, when their size, shape, and sound were as consequential as the information they conveyed. By tearing at the seams between sentences, between words, Stein invites readers to join in an almost physical act; she forces the eye to retrace, the mind to rethink. Unraveling one of her punctuation-free run-on sentences can resemble a tug-of-war in which Stein pulls you heedlessly forward while you dig in your heels with imagined commas, colons, and periods. Stein unnerves us; she contorts what we think is the natural flow. The violation of so many conventions upends the implicit contract between writer and reader. In place of that neatly struck bargain, Stein insists her readers read recklessly, with no hands on the wheel and a busy eye on the words ahead:

> I want readers so strangers must do it. Mostly no one knowing me can like it that I love it that every one is of a king of men and women, that always I am looking and comparing and classifying of them, always I am seeing their repeating. Always more and more I love repeating, it may be irritating to hear from them but always more and more I love it of them.

The going can be, by turns, tedious, tiring, or a heady thrill. Much in the way that Schoenberg's non-chromatic twelve-tone compositions disturb listeners, Stein jangles our ears. Too often, her reputation for difficulty has cut short attempts to turn some actual pages. The notion that reading Stein is an unrewarding chore abides, curiously enough, even among her most likely audience: fans of women's and avant-garde literature. The notoriety dates to the early 1910s, when Stein published *Portrait of Mabel Dodge* and *Tender Buttons*. These experiments in nonrepresentational prose inspired satirists and provoked critics to extravagant condemnations. (While Stein struggled to find publishers, *Tender Buttons* was parodied in *Life*.) Believed to be something of a Great Sphinx writing solely in repetitive riddles and double-talk, Stein seemed to epitomize the post-Romantic author's dilemma of recreating an intensely private language as a public voice. The consensus held that she didn't turn the trick, and she became a byword for Modernist and avant-garde excess.

True enough, Stein flouted grammatical convention, reveled in obscure personal reference, and produced books of daunting length, but how did she differ from Joyce and Pound? Modernist monuments like *Finnegans Wake* and the *Cantos*, never candidates for beach reading, have been treated, since their publication, to exhaustive (and exhausting) attention. Stein, on the other hand, has been ridiculed or ignored for the same sins. (Witness the recent flap over editing errors in the new edition of *Ulysses*, while *The Making of Americans* has often been out of print.) Stein's eccentricities appeared to be willful and self-indulgent, the products of a wealthy dilettante's proximity to real genius. Of course, her male counterparts wielded a purposeful obscurity and bent the rules for only the best of reasons—as a woman, Stein couldn't muster quite the same tolerance from critics. But there's a more telling difference. For as much as innovators like Joyce and Pound wore the mantle of the new, they played a game as old as the Talmud. If you have the right education and access to a good library, reading their "difficult" books amounts to solving an elaborate crossword puzzle. The allusions may be complex, but the hierarchical roles of author-as-master locksmith and reader-as-forger of keys remain unchanged. Stein stood resolutely outside this comfy arrangement. She presented the reader with an open-ended game in which interpretations were presumed to be private and always in flux. In the absence of fixed symbols writ large, she devised truly free-form texts that converted readers into writers.

The blurred distinction between reader and writer follows from Stein's belief that writing is simply a way of knowing. In the essay "Sentences," she locates the source of what's written: "A sentence can be in one. A sentence in one sentence has been in one. It has been one." Translation—logos is within; in fact, it defines your being. The writer uncovers what's already penned. To call Stein's circuitous style idiosyncratic is to misjudge its decidedly universal aims. She wanted to capture the rhythms of thinking, an Ur-beat that could be found in "the everlasting feeling of sentences as they diagram themselves." Stein's spiraling sentences mimic the unstoppable quality of thought; she means to draw us deeply in. Her intentionally abbreviated line—"A sentence made slowly"—suggests by its very condensation that the time it takes to write a sentence should equal the time it takes to comprehend it. Consequently, her ideal reader inhabits her sentences' production and reenacts the summing of their parts. This reader surrenders to the jagged pulse of a record being played at variable speeds and is eventually surprised at how right it sounds. If there is a deep grammar, Stein tapped the vein. By stripping the habitual from our sentence-making and reading, she revealed a circularly logical, lucidly incantatory speech, an atavistic tongue flowing just beneath our finely built phrases. Its grammar is the grammar of first speech, the motion and sound are those of human thought.

*

By agreement, Stein's German-Jewish parents had five children, but two deaths in infancy occasioned the births of Leo and Gertrude. A sense of precariousness and unease over owing their lives to the deaths of their siblings would always trouble them both. The family's wanderings did little to encourage feelings of security. By the time Gertrude was seven, the Steins had lived in Pennsylvania, Vienna, Paris, and Baltimore before settling in Oakland. These uprootings sharpened the isolation she experienced as the family's youngest. Although pampered and indulged, she was often left to herself or in the company of Leo. She weathered the chaotic procession of languages—acquiring a child's smattering of French and German—but found in the use of English a private pleasure, as if it were her true home. Her choice to live in Europe among foreign languages would replicate the childhood world in which she was "all alone with english and myself."

Neither parent did much to temper her estrangement. Her mother, who died when Stein was 14, was a marginal presence, "never important to her children excepting to begin them." Her father loomed large as an impatient, argumentative, sometimes tyrannical figure. While mothers appear infrequently in Stein's writing, domineering fathers proliferate. Indeed, Daniel Stein, fictionalized as David Hersland in *The Making of Americans*, is the most vivid and passionately drawn of all her characters. Certainly, he soured her on fathers for good, so much so that she could later link Hitler, Stalin, Roosevelt, and Mussolini through the common denominator of patriarchy: "There is too much fathering going on just now and there is no doubt about it fathers are depressing." Instead, she cleaved to Leo. Bound by the similar circumstances of their conception, they also shared an attitude of superiority toward the rest of the family. She followed him to Harvard, Johns Hopkins, and Europe, hewing to each of his many turns of mind. Snobbishly brilliant and self-obsessed, Leo Stein thrived on the intensity of intellectual pursuit as well as his own neuroses. He was in thrall to one mentor after another—William James, Matisse, Freud—always measuring himself against them, only to be found wanting. What he called his "pariah complex" condemned him to a cycle of hero-worship and frustration. Eventually, in despair over his continued failure and her first successes, he turned his withering condescension on his sister, destroying a bond that had endured for 30 years. Nevertheless, Gertrude was undoubtedly enriched by his aggressive curiosity. Leo furnished her with his style of imperious conviction (which she would leaven with wit) and introduced her to the people who would help supply the convictions.

Stein entered Radcliffe in the mid-1890s and, like Leo, enlisted as one of William James's most avid students. James admitted her to his graduate seminar, where she studied the nature of consciousness and its relation to human behavior. Not just James, but many professors and fellow students were impressed by her intellect and frank charm. A much-told anecdote, in which she walks out of James's final exam after writing across the blue book, "Really I do not feel like an examination paper in philosophy today," lays claim to a precocious degree of self-possession. Stein felt sorely out of place in Cambridge. She was a Westerner with a European glaze among prim New Englanders. Her college essays—first-person confessionals steeped in romanticism—are artifacts of struggle. The grammar is shaky, and kernels of her mature prose—"The eternal feminine is nice to be sure, but it's painfully illogical"—seem less a matter of intent than of verbal inadequacy. The essays portray anxious, strong-willed young women uncertain and frightened of their sexuality. Earnestly melodramatic, replete with hints of incest and sadomasochism, these characterizations were an attempt to control the many selves and voices that had risen up in the years of quiet isolation. Writing, like her interest in psychology, became a means of sorting through the mind's many choruses.

On James's recommendation, she attended Johns Hopkins Medical School to prepare for a career as a psychologist. After four years of study, she grew bored and failed to graduate. Instead, she joined Leo in Europe, eventually settling in Paris on the Rue de Fleurus. There she completed her first novel, *Things As They Are*, a Henry James-like analysis of the emotional entanglements among three well-educated women. Based on Stein's thwarted affair with a Baltimore woman, the novel marked her acceptance of her sexual identity and confirmed her vocation as an author. In 1906, while working on her second book, she met Alice Toklas. Upper-class, Jewish, and a San Franciscan, she was comfortingly familiar to Stein. Toklas became both lover and eternally approving audience, devoting herself to domestic details, which included typing each day the pages Stein would produce in all-night writing sessions. The evenings were reserved for callers, the days for picture-buying and tramping about Montmartre. In her salon and her intimate relations with painters like Matisse, and especially Picasso, a surer, more forthright but decidedly aloof personality emerged—the Gertrude Stein of legend. Although her atelier was common ground for the many pre-war artistic rebels, Stein was too bourgeois to endorse their less-than-proper antics. Yet she drew selectively on the ideas she heard debated nightly. Not a ringmaster but a cryptically wry observer, she preferred a crossroad to a cabal.

After the First World War, Rue de Fleurus became a haunt of the famous or soon-to-be, eventually something of a shrine, and Stein's name spread around the world. Her public persona was the product of deliberate design; she craved fame. Perhaps because of her solitary vantage and abiding sense of aloneness, she greatly desired acceptance; perhaps her literary experiments and the rejection they risked compelled her to declare her own genius. In any event, the decades following the war were dedicated to self-promotion, which culminated in the charming but nakedly egotistical *Autobiography of Alice B. Toklas*. Much like her friend and one-time student Hemingway, Stein labored hard at her myth, bringing forth an outsized creature that ranged beyond her control. As caricatures and jokes turned up in movies, comic strips, and musicals, the Bohemian *doyenne* superseded the author. She delighted in the celebrity, yet even within the ample confines of her fame, she remained an island. Although she had served as midwife to the new century—studying psychology with James, abstract art with Picasso—Stein retained her roots in the nineteenth century. Distant and overwhelmed by propriety, part of her would not respond to the demands of modern fame. When *Four Saints in Three Acts* premiered in New York in 1934, her name was in lights on Broadway; she declined to attend and instead sent a note: "I rarely believe in anything because at the time of believing I am not really there to believe." Stein would hold fast to her apartness, a wise child among foreign tongues.

Thinking, for Stein, was not merely a prelude to composition but both its subject and method. In *Three Lives*, she explored this notion. Especially in the "Melanctha" section, she created characters whose substance derived from an exacting transcription of their consciousness. They came to life in prose that circled at great remove from a bare-bones narrative, touching down only to jog it forward, then flying off. Published in 1909, the novel, her second, decisively announced her uniqueness. There was little precedent for *Three Lives*'s fidelity to the workings of human psychology. Only Henry James, at about the same time, pursued a similar goal. James took pleasure in the mind's propensity for hairsplitting refinements; he traced the balancing act in card-house sentences, sliding clause upon sub-clause. The elegance of his deftly constructed syntax suggests he may have conceived of the mind as an instrument powered by light and air to produce the music of a tuning fork's hum. Stein heard a rougher noise. Throughout *Three Lives*, the rendering of cogitation suggests machinery hard at the task, clanking and catching, relentless. Her use of working-class and Black American dialects acquainted her with the expressive power of staggered rhythm and repetition. From these she fashioned a truer sound, something closer to the core of consciousness.

Having recently arrived in Paris when she started *Three Lives,* Stein found her inspiration in Flaubert and Cézanne. Both were foremost among brother Leo's obsessions at the time. She worked on a translation of Flaubert's *Trois Contes* and absorbed the broad outline of the character Felicité from the story "Un Coeur Simple." Felicité, a dying woman who has suffered quietly through a life of service to others, reminded Stein of the immigrant and Black housekeepers and midwives she had known as a medical student in Baltimore. In their bruised, emotionally cramped lives, she found a reflection of her own sexual and creative frustration. From Cezanne's paintings, she took instruction in a method of depiction. Those paintings emphasized presence, the palpability of a face or vase. She wished to invest her trio of women—Anna, Lena, and Melanctha—with the undeniable reality of Cézanne's washerwomen and cardplayers. She disdained biographical details and narrative plot and assembled her women in the "continuous present." In this newly created tense, "there was a constant recurring and beginning, there was a marked direction of being in the present."

The characters manifest themselves at every point in the telling as a painting offers its subject completely from any particular view. Verbal tics like Melanctha's tireless repetition of the word "certainly" serve as apertures through which she is apprehended whole. Thus, the speaker's rhythms become indistinguishable from the speaker; in fact, they express an essence: "Melanctha Herbert was always losing what she had in wanting all the things she saw. Melanctha was always being left when she was not leaving others. Melanctha Herbert always loved too hard and much too often." Stein used language as an impressionist painter used color, to catch what William James called the "vague and inarticulate" dimension of conscious life. This is not the artful stream of consciousness of Joyce. In the ebb and flow of Melanctha's thought, there is a music as unique and quotidian as a signature; Stein wrote the mind the way she heard it.

If, as Stein proclaimed, *Three Lives* was literature's first step into the new century, *The Making of Americans* (written over several years beginning in 1903 and published in 1925) may find a home in the next. Intractable, interminable, yet strangely mesmerizing, the novel resides in the black hole of literary history. In the 75 years since its completion, *Americans* has been in print only sporadically, most often in abridged editions. Rarely seen, more rarely read, its 925 densely printed pages offer some of the knottiest prose in the English language. Few have the stamina (myself included) to plow from cover to cover. Lacking any formal organization, narrative logic, or even a place to rest, the writing proceeds at full pitch, battering through the notion of the well-made novel. Stein believed *Americans* to be her masterpiece. She regarded it with great affection and kept faith with its most egregious flaws. When she proofed the galleys, few changes were made: "I always found myself forced back into its incorrectness." She knew those flaws: the bottomless sentences, badly joined narrative, and ragged pacing all constituted isolation; she battled the deep suspicion that her unorthodox method was consigned to failure. She both doubted and wished to embrace her "incorrectness"; "I have been very glad to have been wrong. It is sometimes a very hard thing to win myself to having been wrong about something. I do a great deal of suffering." The admissions of uncertainty recur throughout *Americans*. Her "big book," as she called it, was very much about the making of Gertrude Stein. It served as the laboratory of her self-discovery, in which she sought the "great author inside one."

The quest for greatness explains the immense sprawl. *Americans* is overcrowded by Stein's many ambitions. With Olympian naiveté, she said her intent was to "describe really describe every kind of human being that ever was or is or would be." She also wanted to indulge an autobiographical impulse and tell the story of her German-Jewish immigrant family, then draw from their experience—"the old people in a new world, the new people made out of the old"—a transcendent national archetype. Even the novel would take on a representative function as "an essentially American book." Stein plunged ahead on all fronts but failed to keep step. Her rich ideation outraced her ability to shape a coherently multidimensional fiction. The same unvaried single-mindedness that flexed strangely in her prose made for a crude reductionism in the realm of conception. Preferring stark opposition to shading and ambiguity, Stein lacked the intellectual cast to balance the conflicting demands of so many goals. In the end, mythmaking and family history run poor seconds to the psychologist's urge to describe and classify.

*Americans'* fictional family, the Herslands, are recognizable as the Steins, and their daughter Martha as the author, yet there is little of the specificity of detail we expect from an autobiographical novel. Relations between characters are broadly sketched, and narrative development is bound by the continuous present; everyone is in a state of becoming. The extensive use of pronouns—he, she, one, some, they—helps contain the characters' reality within the scope of clinical report. The flatness is deliberate; the characters appear like many different masks behind which Stein makes the case that everyone is different but the same. The Herslands serve as typological specimens for an extended meditation on behavioral patterns and patterns of description: "There are many ways of making kinds of men and women. In each way of making kinds of them there is a different system of finding them resembling. Sometime there will be here every way there can be of seeing kinds of men and women." As in *Three Lives,* the rhythms of speech embody what Stein termed a character's "bottom nature": "Slowly, more and more, one gets to know them as repeating comes out in them. In the middle of their living they are always repeating...." However, the novel is less about "kinds," "ones," and Americans than it is about the mind obsessed with these distinctions. *The Making of Americans* is a driven book, as relentless as many of its dithyrambic, train-length sentences. Stein set herself the task of thinking on paper for a thousand pages until she had "not many things but one thing." What she had was an artifact of consciousness, a mind's true life played out as the "steady pound of repeating."

*Americans* liberated Stein from tentativeness and self-doubt and confirmed her break from any fealty to conventional structure and syntax. She had pushed past telling into a new arrangement with the reader, one in which the reader felt the text become itself. In *Tender Buttons* and her portraits, she pushed even further. Struck by the composition of Picasso's Cubist collages, she noted that "to have brought the objects together already changed them to other things, not to another picture but to something else, to things as Picasso saw them." Stein pursued the same effect. Like the Cubists, she would avoid literal representation in depicting objects and people. She found a compositional equivalent to Cubist recombination by "ridding myself of nouns." *Tender Buttons* describes things without mentioning them, without metaphoric comparison. Instead, Stein adopted the painter's approach of looking at an object from many perspectives, then collapsing the impression into a single expressive image:

> CARELESS WATER
>
> No cup is broken in more places and mended, that is to say a plate is broken and mending does do that it shows that culture is Japanese. It shows the whole element of angels and orders. It does more to choosing and it does more to that ministering counting. It does, it does change in more water.

Although *Tender Buttons* was written in 1911, the boldness of the experiment remains unmuted. We have grown accustomed enough to Cubist and abstract visuals that they can be used in advertisements, but a line like "The change in that is that red weakens an hour" still unsettles us. Yet these prose poems were not meant to shock; they were launched from familiar ground. Stein chose household items—"A CARAFE," "A RED HAT," or "A SELTZER BOTTLE"—along with abstract but homey commonplaces like "IN BETWEEN," "A TIME TO EAT," and "A CENTRE IN A TABLE." To each she responded with a subjectivity so unyielding that the relationship between text and object is indecipherable. "MALACHITE": "The sudden spoon is the same in no size. The sudden spoon is the wound in the decision." "COLD CLIMATE" abstracts abstraction: "A Season in yellow sold extra strings makes lying places." What is a "lying place"? The usage and grammar are still so fresh that we have the impression we are reading a distorted translation from another language, or maybe the ramblings of an aphasiac. The logic of the connections, whether hallucinatory or mundane, is rigorously private. Stein rendered interpretation futile; she preferred her reader to enter the synesthetic domain of the poem and respond as subjectively as the author had.

"Language as a real thing," Stein wrote in "Poetry and Grammar," "is not imitation either of sounds or colors or emotions it is an intellectual recreation." In *Toklas,* she credits her work with "the destruction of the associational emotion in poetry and prose." She was adamant about disconnecting texts from predictable reactions. She believed in the use of language as an end in itself, not as a medium of expression but as a vital expressive element. It's clear that language lacks the plasticity of color or a musical note; it is inescapably tied to a denotative intent. Stein chafed at this limit but recognized it; she simply wanted to lengthen the leash. By placing words in unworn sequences, the dislocated sentences in *Tender Buttons* restored substantiality, a thingness, to desiccated syllables. This was the thinking behind her celebrated line in the poem "Sacred Emily": "A rose is a rose is a rose is a rose." With that expression, Stein remarked, "The rose is red for the first time in English poetry for a hundred years."

Her attraction to painting and its suggestive capacity also led to a series of word portraits in which she attempted to depict with "exactitude" her subject's "inner and outer reality." Usually made for close friends—Matisse, Picasso, Sherwood Anderson—the portraits continued exploring the relation between description and types: "In doing a portrait of any one, the repetition consists in knowing that that one is a kind of a one, that the things he does have been done by others like him that the things he says have been said by others like him...." After having "talked and listened" to her subject, she re-created what struck her as essential. *The Portrait of Mabel Dodge,* written in 1911, introduced Stein's textual Cubism to the literary world. Dodge was so flattered by the piece she had 300 copies printed and bound in Florentine wallpaper (an inspired stroke on her part) and distributed them to the New York literati, who were confused by "So much breathing has not the same place when there is that much beginning. ... So much breathing has the same place and there must not be so much suggestion. There can be there the habit that there is if there is no need of resting. The absence is not alternative." Because it felt arbitrary, it was deemed gibberish. Stein's composition relied less on randomness as a method than on creating the effect of randomness for the reader. No doubt, Stein rummaged freely in shaping her impressions, but her vocabulary was carefully circumscribed by the demands of each piece, and the internal rhythmic and imagistic consistency rarely wavered. She manipulated a sense of semantic chaos so that her reader might find new points of entry into old words or discover a delicious strangeness in an ordinary notion. Her "gibberish" slowed the eye and allowed the words to be pronounced on the tongue and in the ear.

The randomness irked many readers. In 1934, B. F. Skinner publicized experiments that Stein had helped conduct at Harvard investigating the possibility of automatic writing. He charged that *Tender Buttons* was the product of just such a process, and his claim became a convenient reason for dismissing her work. Stein denied, in several contradictory statements, any connection, and her partisans have been at pains to echo her denials. The skill in Stein's wordplay and linguistic technique is too obvious to attribute to chance, but that doesn't preclude some role for the principles behind automatic writing. She wrote each day for a specific amount of time (occasionally sitting in her Ford automobile while Toklas ran errands) and tended to revise very little. The immediacy she sought was diluted by revision and heightened by the need to fill the page. Stein's craftsmanship appears masterful when its improvisatory component is understood: her incremental variations on a single phrase are closer in spirit to what a jazz musician does, say, Charlie Parker, than they are to any other writer.

In her poems and librettos, Stein openly aspired to the persistent music of lyric verse. The repetitions are carefully layered so they accumulate into rolling, melodic tones. Some phrases in *Four Saints in Three Acts* mimic tribal chants: "Saints settled saints settled all in all saints. All saints. Saints in all saints. Saint Settlement." There is a litter of mantra-like bits of nonsense—"windows and windows and ones"—that infiltrate the mind to stay. The long poems—"Lifting Belly," "Patriarchal Poetry," and "Stanzas in Meditation"—thrive on swung measure and song. The availability of line breaks and verse's more open page encouraged Stein to parse out her compound run-on sentences, as if she needed the clutterless white expanse to keep track of their unpackaged parts. The line breaks in "Stanzas in Meditation" create breathing room that the prose lacks and demonstrate just how she built sentences from clauses:

> Full well I know that she is there
> Much as she will she can be there
> But which I know which I know when
> Which is my way to be there then
> Which she will know as I know here
> That it is now that it is there

The metrics are as basic as the meaning is opaque. Typically, abstract words like "which," "when," and "there" have been placed to connote some tangible representation, teasing our expectation that the poem might refer to a reality outside itself. For Stein, the text can be an autonomous thing, its references bound within its actual occurrence, within the continuous present. Meaning isn't a matter of referring but rather of becoming. In contrast, "Lifting Belly," an erotic hymn to Toklas, is rich in specific details about their daily life together:

> Can you can you.
> Can you buy a Ford.
> Did you expect that.
> Lifting belly hungrily.
> Not lonesomely
> But enthusiastically.
> Lifting belly altogether.
> Were you wise.
> Were you wise to do so.

The coy bits of personal trivia—what car Stein owned—don't require exegesis; a better clue to their intimate lives might be found in the poem's odd mix of nursery-rhyme singsong and the language of passion. Regardless of whether her writing skirts second- and third-tier levels of abstraction or turns on a sexual pun, Stein's subject is always herself. By purging language of its stock associations, she claimed she could invest words with a new reality. What she did was shape a language that is wholly her own. At a time when many writers pressed to expand the self to include a world, Stein drew the world in upon herself. She devised a system of relations, a grammar of reference, that posited her at its center.

*

During her lifetime, Stein served as her own best critic. The job was not sought by many. Her writing was too extraordinary to attract a ready crew of village explainers. Having stirred so much curiosity about her life and work, she took to explicating herself. And she enjoyed the task. The strong element of public performance in her essays (even those she never delivered as lectures) indicates she relished the opportunity to instruct. An invitation to speak at Oxford in 1926 provided the occasion for her first critical essay. Appearing before a standing-room only audience, she treated them to the uncompromisingly knotty "Composition as Explanation." What the dons made of roundabout dictates like "Romanticism is then when everything being alike everything is naturally simply different" is anyone's guess. She did make clear that her difficult style was not a clever conceit to be put off when it was time to talk shop. Her method of exploring characters in fiction should be as useful and legitimate for explaining that method in an essay. She insisted that her writing be of one piece. For example, the assembling and disassembling of paragraphs and sentences in *How to Write* discuss her techniques while employing them. Consequently, when she talks about specific works, it becomes unclear where the fiction leaves off and the explanation begins: "The Gradual Making of *The Making of Americans*," a blueprint made in retrospect, could blend imperceptibly into the novel.

The closed circuit of this critical exchange—Stein analyzing Stein—suggests an unabashed solipsism, which she most enthusiastically practiced. But it also gives some measure of her originality and its isolating effect. She could cite no literary forebears for her mature style, and comparisons with contemporaries were limited to those whom she'd influenced. Stein built, occupied, and still dwells in a room truly of her own. Her early publications were self-subsidized; she was 59 and had been writing for over 30 years when an American publisher finally accepted a book of hers; much of her writing was published posthumously, some not at all; today her presence in American bookstores and universities is sporadic, always qualified. It is ironic that a writer whose aesthetic enterprise was so tied to the reader and the experience of reading should find an audience hard to come by.

Nevertheless, she is surely one of the most influential writers of the century. Her list of debtors, direct and indirect, is uncountably long. Sherwood Anderson proudly acknowledged the impact of *Three Lives*; Hemingway, who typed sizable portions of *Americans*, was less candid, but his clipped sentences, repetitions, and notions of suggestive detail are obviously kin to Stein's. ("The worst, he said, were the women with dead babies. You couldn't get the women to give up their dead babies. They'd have babies dead for six days. Wouldn't give them up.") Her stark rhythms and repetitions were absorbed by writers as diverse as Samuel Beckett and Raymond Chandler; the "steady pound of repeating" embodied this century's rebellion against the florid arabesques of the Victorian era. Like Picasso's recovery of the so-called primitive eye through his use of masks, Stein restored to language its connection to the spoken. Her demolition of grammatical constraint stirred almost every American author and practically spawned a homegrown (not European-inspired) tradition of experimental writing. She proved that sentences needn't stop when the rules said so, but could roll on till they exhausted themselves; Faulkner and Kerouac took note. Her painterly approach, the power she sprang from the performance of words as words, launched the Language poets, one of the most vital movements in postwar American writing. In a broader sense, the example of her life, her Yankee stubbornness and subversive vigor, cut the cloth for the American avant-garde style in all the arts. Indeed, she is the mother of us all.

"Think of everything," Stein wrote, "of cowboys, of movies, of detective stories, of anybody who goes anywhere or stays at home and is an American and you will realize that it is something strictly American to conceive a space that is filled with moving, a space of time that is filled always filled with moving." She brought the continuous movement of the mind, with its churned and restive music, to the page. She conjured an immediacy that made reading new. "I am writing for myself and strangers," she announced in *The Making of Americans*. Yet she brings those strangers close to the act of written creation, so close inside her struggle with the sayable that we cannot remain strangers very long. To read Stein is to relinquish our place outside the text and to begin with her to make the words make sense.

*Village Voice Literary Supplement*, November 1988.

# Collected Letters: Ed Ruscha Draws Language the Way It Feels

What is the wordness of a word? Is a word the sum of its letters—the way they look arrayed on a sign or page? Or is a word its sound when spoken, the feel of its syllables on the tongue and in the ear? Or is the essence found primarily in a word's meaning, its service as a vehicle for communication? These are questions that typically occupy poets—whether composing epics to be recited around campfires, songs to be sung by troubadours, or intricate typographic displays for readers to puzzle over, poets have long been attuned to the shape and sound of language. Such focus, though, is hardly confined to writers. Over the past few decades, visual artists have become increasingly engaged with the materiality and meaning of words, and few painters have done so more insightfully than Edward Ruscha.

The publication of *Edward Ruscha: Catalogue Raisonné of the Works on Paper, Volume 1,* a hefty tome that covers the years 1956 through 1976, affords an opportunity to view the Los Angeles artist's developing fascination with what language might look like. The book tracks his movement from an initial interest in signage (the early-'60s drafts for his iconic paintings of the 20th Century Fox logo, the Standard Oil gas-station sign, and the name "Annie" in the comic strip's typeface) to later images that are highly idiosyncratic, downright poetic concoctions ("Thick Blocks of Musical Fudge" is the phrase in one 1976 pastel). With two, three, and sometimes four such reproductions (many with just a single word) on each page, this massive volume is crowded with text in a way most art books are not; in fact, a quick thumb through suggests something more like a child's dictionary. A welter of emphatically rendered words—*gauze, room, range, rut, walk, city, salt, soda, self, squirt, poach, mercy, fever, fix, flood, sin, sure, cement, age, blank, bull, jelly, pudding, ding, dew, pool, radio, vapor, dusty, trust*—tumbles out from the pages, their audible music registering as readily as their visual allure. A catalogue raisonné is generally designed to value scholarship and completist accuracy more than aesthetic impact, and these reproductions—true to the volume's form—are merely adequate. But the book, in its totality from page to page, can be read as much more—as a long synesthetic poem, one that imagines a shape, color, and sound for words and speaks to our profoundest understanding of human expression.

That said, Ruscha's work—his paintings, drawings, and photographs—wears its intellectual richness lightly, a bone-dry wit lurking behind nearly every image. This spirited playfulness is present in an early painting produced for a 1963 show at the Ferus Gallery in Los Angeles. *Large Trademark with Eight Spotlights* reconfigures the 20th Century Fox logo by flattening out the text's usual presentation as a piece of monumental sculpture and elongating the perspective lines that create the three-dimensional effect. The trademark version of the logo is a pyramid-like edifice—the letters formidable and enduring in what is meant to appear like stone. Ruscha de-monumentalizes the text by rendering it in two dimensions, even as he exaggerates the three-dimensional illusion, the pencil-thin perspective lines accentuating the sense of façade. Yet even as the artist slyly undermines the Hollywood icon, he also grants it dramatic stature on the canvas. But the parodic note seems far less important than Ruscha's desire to pry into the space between words as commercial objects and words as objects of design, and to permit the viewer to appreciate, for instance, the difference between the 0 in 20th and the o in Fox.

It's at this diminutive level of attention that many of the works on paper achieve a literary density, form, and content intricately recapitulating each other. Deceptively simple (indeed, almost all of his word-images are), the drawing *Blank* (1963) is matter-of-fact to the point of being stark. If Pop art's influence on Ruscha's early work is evident in *Large Trademark with Eight Spotlights,* here it's the formative role of Op art that's on display. The black-and-white contrast is as sharp and elemental as the sound of the word pronounced aloud; the imperative *bark,* as well as the words *black, lank, lack,* and *bank,* has a ghostly presence among the tightly packed letters; the optical technique (drop-out text, tight leading) encourages us to see these other words as if they were palimpsests, rising and receding in and out of *blank.* The serif communicates officious sameness, implying the word issues from some bureaucratic realm. Yet the elegant design of the text indicates this is a command delivered with finesse, one that, given the word's obliterative meaning, may be intended to deflect suspicion on the part of the viewer and soften the existential import. All of these micro-gymnastics fall within and serve the work's dominant paradox: the assertive, calculated presence of a word that denotes absence.

Ruscha anatomizes a word and its letters to get at its core sensation—its wordness; the goal is predicated on a decidedly physical intuition. In a 1973 interview, abstract artist Howardena Pindell asked him, "Why are you attracted to specific words like 'Annie,' 'carp,' 'lisp,' 'sing?'" "Because I love the language," Ruscha replied. "Words have temperatures to me." He went on to add that words "reach a certain point and become hot words, then they appeal to me.... Sometimes I have a dream that if a word gets too hot and too appealing, it will boil apart, and I won't be able to read or think of it. Usually I catch them before they get too hot." If there's a whiff of the otherworldly in this account of his creative process, that disruptive mood shows itself in the work: Ruscha renovates commonplace words like *toy, flaw, won't,* and *honk* first by disengaging them from familiar communicative contexts; then, by reworking and deploying them in fresh shapes and colors, he directs our attention to those material qualities (rather than the word's potential task in a sentence). What Gertrude Stein aimed to achieve via repetition ("A rose is a rose ...") Ruscha pursues via singularity: When we look at *Honk* (1964), we don't read the word, we *see* it, in the same way we see trees and streams in a John Constable landscape. And if we can almost hear the rushing brook in the English painter's rustic scenes, we can just as well *see* the long *n* sound and its abrupt, clamorous collision with the *k*.

In seeking to free language from mere utility, Ruscha shares kinship not only with other artists who made language their subject (Marcel Broodthaers, Ian Hamilton Finlay, Mira Schendel, Jasper Johns) but with Concrete poets such as Edwin Morgan, Décio Pignatari, Aram Saroyan, and Mary Ellen Solt. One of the founders of that movement, the Brazilian Augusto de Campos, penned a manifesto in the mid-1950s that declared its ambitious goals: "the concrete poet sees the word in itself—a magnetic field of possibilities—like a dynamic object, a live cell, a complete organism, with psychophysico-chemical properties, touch antennae circulation heart: live." Campos's rhetoric may be grandiose, but the underlying sentiment—that language possesses vitality that precedes its role as a transmitter of meaning—is the animating impulse behind much of Ruscha's text-based imagery. His most famous painting, *Oof* (1962), with its incandescently yellow letters pulsing against a night-blue background, portrays a word describing the sound one might make when socked in the gut. It doesn't get more inchoate, more "live," than that.

The 1967 drawing *Self* vibrates in similar, though less visceral, ways. Produced with gunpowder, a material Ruscha happened on as an alternative to graphite or ink and employed regularly for word images in the mid-'60s, the drawing allows the word to unfurl ribbonlike and appear to float just above the surface of the paper. The curlicue script could be lifted from a greeting card, but it also has the flair of someone's signature. In either case, there's a meta-joke: a greeting card you send to your own address, like a florid signature, signals an excessive self-regard that is, well, *self*-referential in the drawing. But when we push past the wry comedy, there is the convoluted shape of the word, the repetition and folding of the loops. The allusion to the Möbius strip and its confusion of interior and exterior is plainly Ruscha's comment on the self, an insight that grows more complex given how the *s* and *f* are made to echo each other. Where does the self begin, and is its beginning found in its end? A visual poem that invokes a topological conundrum, as well as

T. S. Eliot, in pursuit of a metaphysical conceit about identity, is no small labor for a single word.

While the images here tend to be smallish, there is great advantage in viewing all the various iterations of a particular idea. There are three versions of *Self* (all dating from the same year), and each one exhibits minute but telling differences. The texture of the "ribbon," the spacing of the letters, the darkness of the background, and the style of the script subtly evolve from one version to the next. Again, the apparent simplicity of the idea and its execution is deceptive: These drawings have been worked and reworked. The tonal variations in how language resonates across Ruscha's interpretations register most clearly when you study the seven drawings done in preparation for the 1963 painting *Talk about Space*. All dating from that year (in the immediate wake of America's Mercury launches), the images begin with "Space Sketch" and "Space Grid." The sketch presents the basic concept—*space* as a 3-D sci-fi movie title; the grid is done on tracing paper and evidences the artist's meticulousness, as the leading for each letter is calibrated in precise measurements; the subsequent five pieces, all titled "Space Study," reveal Ruscha tinkering with color, the placement or absence of a tiny airborne object, and the incline (rising or falling) of the word. The finished painting set *space* aloft above an empty expanse of what could be sky, its letters slightly canted and receding into the right-hand distance as the word accelerates into the blue yonder. The preparatory drawings demonstrate that there was nothing self-evident about the final concept, and that each trial offered a variation not only of design but of theme. In the second "Space Study," the Cold War mania fueling the space race comes into clear view: *space* now hangs below a daytime hue of orange, and the object (space capsule or bomb?) drops from far above. Is the space in this version less outer and more terrestrial, more our own?

That Ruscha invests these visual poems with such intense care may not be as surprising as how much they reward close scrutiny. The 1971 gunpowder-and-pastel drawing *Adults* neatly conjures so many of that word's associations that it could function as the term's dictionary entry, at least for neurotics and the hyperconscious: The wavering letters evoke the uncertainty of aging; the word's position in the middle of the frame, midway in the air, connotes middle age and its unresolved emotional state; the shadows speak of an evanescent past, as well as the darker implications of the word—sexuality and mortality; and finally, the pluralizing *s*, set the tiniest bit apart from the singular noun, reinforces our awareness of the incremental aloneness that comes with growing older. Yet for all its melancholy, the drawing is a visual delight—the gravity-less atmosphere is expertly rendered, and the rust-colored gloaming treacherously invites the eye. The crafts of poem and picture are seamlessly joined.

As they constitute a kind of dare on the part of the artist, the one-word drawings and paintings earn our fascination, but no less intriguing are the phrases and full sentences Ruscha began producing in the mid-'70s. Cryptic and thus more obviously poetic, these texts extend the Concretist enterprise of freeing the compacted energies to be found in words as well as in syntactic relations: "Chili Draft," "Lame Theme," "Fairly Small Torpedos," "Thinking the Same," "The Chapel Window," "Smells Like Back of Old Hot Radio," "Kidney Beans on Galvanized Steel," "I Live Over in Valley View," "Did Anyone Say 'Dreamboat'?" Most of these lines are set in sans-serif type on monochromatic backgrounds—as if Ruscha had decided that their verbal complexity warranted a proportional diminution of visual invention. They are appealingly clever, and their depths are sounded less in their interaction with how they are rendered than in the candidness of their presentation. *Fairly Small Torpedos* (1974) lays out this puzzling fragment in small (of course) white drop-out type against a deep black background. As musical as it is vivid, the phrase evinces a grim undertow of feeling, yet still bubbles with an off-kilter charm—like a bathroom graffito on a doomed U-boat, a comparison bolstered by the misspelling of *torpedoes*. Ruscha's mischievous sensibility is rarely at rest.

This is only the first of three planned volumes given over to Ruscha's works on paper; there are six devoted to his paintings and two to his prints. Across this long and prolific career, the theme and presence of language have been a constant. One of the earliest pieces in the catalogue, *Study for "Box Smashed Flat"* (1960), a plain pencil tracing of a flattened box of Sun Maid Raisins, features the brand name that puns on the trademark image of a woman harvesting grapes and the "sun made" nature of the grapes themselves. The chiming *ai* in both *raisin* and *maid,* the increasingly smaller typefaces of the name on the front, top, and side of the box, and the repetition of the pun all mark out an essentially linguistic domain. This volume testifies to Ruscha's abiding fealty to a visual poetics that prizes the materiality of words and attempts to explore their anatomies, the wordness that gives them breath.

*Bookforum,* February–March 2015.

# John Yau's Letters for Anna May Wong

In his poem "A Painter's Thoughts," John Yau offers the following speculation:

> I want to paint in a way that the "I" disappears into the sky and trees
> The idea of a slowed down, slowly unfolding image held my attention
>
> Variations on a theme are of no interest. A bowl and cup are not ideas.
> I want my painting to be what it contains: it should speak, not me

The poem, Yau relates in a side note, was a response to what he describes as the "austere still lifes and figure paintings" of William Bailey, an American artist who died in 2020. The poet here takes on this artist's point of view, really any artist's view, to speculate about painting that banishes the painter's presence from the canvas. With its focus on the relationship between the maker and the made, the narrator and the narrated, the poem can also be read as engaging Frank O'Hara's famous "Why I Am Not a Painter." O'Hara describes the compositional progress that follows "thinking of / a color: orange." He goes on: "There should be / so much more, not of orange, of / words, of how terrible orange is / and life. Days go by.... / My poem / is finished and I haven't mentioned / orange yet." To borrow here from Heidegger's phrase, "the thingness of things," both poems address the *thingness* of the art object while positing language as abstract, a symbolic iteration of thought. A piece of art, canvas, paper, clay—what have you—is a thing that is seen, has weight, and can be touched. When that visual art employs language, it becomes something else, something compounded, both a thing and non-thing. It is a text to be read and understood in the rather specific way that language invites understanding, as well as an object whose color, texture, and shape strike us with their immediacy.

*Disguise the Limit,* the exhibition on display at the University of Kentucky Art Museum, affords a comprehensive opportunity to view and attempt to interpret John Yau's visual art collaborations. Overall, we are invited to speculate about the different natures of words written and painted. Rendered on a printed page, a linguistic unit generally appears uniform, legibility being its primary feature. When painted, words acquire a particularity—the precise quality of the brushstroke cannot be repeated with the same precision as any printing process—and that distinctiveness may obscure or alter their meaning. In addition, an intimacy is generated. This is a message that has been shaped by hand. We read with heightened attention.

Such issues are especially salient in the collaborations with artist Archie Rand, specifically the *Alphabet* series, a group of twenty-six canvases completed in two sessions between 1987 and 1994. Rand, an American artist born in Brooklyn, where he resides today, began his career in the late '60s with large-scale color-field or patterned canvases on which he painted the names of African American jazz musicians. His work over succeeding decades has engaged thematically with a wide variety of authors such as Eugenio Montale, Rainer Maria Rilke, Anne Waldman, and John Ashbery. In my conversation with Yau, the poet remarked on the process of their collaboration; it was done speedily and "in some cases Archie put down the image first and I wrote the text. In other cases, I wrote the text first."

The first image "A" appears to set out a theme of deception and disjuncture. "'It is time to start removing our skin,' you whispered, 'its alphabet of disguises.'" Our skin then—something we cannot easily replace—turns out to be a removable disguise, a palpable thing, yet one ordered by the alphabet, by the building blocks of words. A lurid pair of red and pink lips hover just above the verb "whispered," and above the words "alphabet" and "disguise," a floral filigree emerges to creep to the top of the canvas.

The conceptual tone for the series is set: language bears an oblique yet somehow pointed relation to what's depicted. Yau explores numerous linguistic dictions and strategies: wordplay, signage, advertisements, Dadaist non sequiturs, and parody, while Rand deploys an equally diverse range of representations—figurative, abstract, decorative, symbolic, and cartoonish. The text for "C" is "How to Cry Without Really Trying"; for "D" we read "Donkey Man Stew," and thus we learn the alphabet is observed in many cases through the presence of some key word. For instance "E" offers "Ode to Bruce Lee" with four *e*'s but no word that begins with the letter. The text for the letter "G" reads "Say Hello to the Big Blank." Is the "blank" here a sly nod to the lack of a word beginning with "g"? As might be expected in an alphabet of disguises, the indeterminacy is intentional.

In "T" Rand sketches out the Empire State Building as seen from below; the conventional depiction is flanked on either side by words in list form: "Tree, Free, Feed" and "Dropping, Droppings, Dropping." Following from "tree," Yau sounds out the assonance with "free" and "feed"; the repetition of "dropping" might be suggestive of the long way down from the building's spire, with the middle iteration lending an "s" to register a slightly scatological note. The text here isn't quite a poem; the drawing not quite a work of art. Together, though, we can experience the lists as a kind of falling—the long "eee" sound suggesting the whistle of air while plummeting, and the repeated iterations of "dropping" the beginning of a notational ladder indicating gradations of descent. Yau and Rand deliver an elemental part of the wordness of words, their felt physicality.

Of particular interest are those collaborations referencing the Chinese American actor Anna May Wong. In *What It Means to Write About Art*, an anthology of interviews with art critics, Yau recounts seeing Josef von Sternberg's pre-code film *Shanghai Express* at the age of 16: "I'd never seen such a beautiful Chinese woman on the screen.... I became completely fascinated with her." Born in Los Angeles in 1905, Wong began appearing as an extra in films while she was in high school. At the time, she could not win leading roles. Anti-miscegenation laws not only prohibited interracial marriage but also interracial kissing on screen. Wong was relegated to supporting and stereotypical roles, in particular being cast as the "Dragon Lady," a deceitful, mysterious temptress. She did, however, attain starring roles in several British films. In the 1928 silent film titled *Piccadilly,* a kissing scene with a white love interest was filmed but cut before release. Years later, in another British film, one titled *Java Head,* she appeared in a scene kissing her white husband. This was one of her favorites.

Although it's not part of this *Alphabet* series, a collaboration with Richard Hull is worth noting. It depicts an anonymous torso whose head is overtaken by a swirl of shapes. The overall iconography of the image is that of a wanted poster: the face presented in frontal view, the name of the criminal in large type above or below the portrait. Yau's text reads: "Wanted the Lost Films of Anna May Wong." What is being suggested here? Are the lost films those literally lost due to decay or misplacement? Or are the "lost" films those that Wong was not permitted to make because of her ethnicity? In any case the obscuring of the "wanted" figure's face not only subverts the conventional meaning and utility of the wanted poster but amplifies the theme of loss—the actor's face and identity are indeed *wanted* by the poet but they have been concealed by time and, more crucially, by the film industry's racism.

In Yau's 1988 poem "No One Ever Tried to Kiss Anna May Wong," he seems to be recounting a moment from *Shanghai Express.* In the film, which also starred Marlene Dietrich, a group of train passengers is captured by a warlord during the Chinese Civil War. Wong is cast as a prostitute. I say "seems" because the train in the movie travels from Beijing to Shanghai, but the poem begins:

> She's trying to find a way to turn her cup / upside down, while sequestered on a train / from Dublin to Vienna

Yau may be referring to the biographical fact that Wong played the lead in an opera in Vienna. Critics at the performance praised her fluent German. But in this fantastical train ride Wong wears "a crescent scarf / and a chilly snake high smile." This allusion to the Dragon Lady stereotype is quickly undermined by the next line, "others claim she's all skin and eyes." The poet deems this assessment—one Hollywood filmmakers would likely have made—to be "oily chatter." For Yau, Wong represents a Chinese American artist who has been caricatured and diminished, reduced to what's obvious. Worse yet, as the poem proceeds, her various cinema fates are catalogued, with an emphasis on the role of the white filmmakers, the ones who decide: "she's been told to be scratched, kicked, / slapped, bitten, stabbed, poisoned, and shot." The dark comic effect of this alliteratively composed list is enhanced by the passive construction; it's the white filmmakers—those concocting these indignities—who *tell* her what she must endure. The poem concludes with an image both lyrical and enigmatic as we return to the train compartment the speaker has entered: "On the seat beside me I find a circle / smaller than the one left by a wet apple."

Yau expands such fictive personae and experiences in the five *Alphabet Series* paintings devoted to Wong. In "B" we read the rather straightforward caption "Anna May Wong at the Cedar Bar." The Cedar Tavern, of course, was the famous Greenwich Village hangout for many Abstract Expressionists, as well as Beat and New York School writers like Kerouac and O'Hara. Placing the actor in such heady company connects her to the avant-garde movements of the 1950s, a time when Wong's long career was just beginning to be recognized; she received a star on the Hollywood Walk of Fame in 1960, a year before her death at age 56. She was the first Asian American actor to be included. Yau prefers to situate her in less mainstream company; Rand's ghostly figure, too, suggests another kind of recontextualization, as it resembles the Delphic Sibyl in Michelangelo's Sistine Chapel fresco. Wong appears, it could be said, as a prophet among painters.

These imaginings can take a comic turn: "F" performs a cultural remix that combines film lore and politics. The text "Forbidden Love by Anna May Wong + Harry S. Truman" posits a movie titled *Forbidden Love* starring the actor and President Truman, a most unlikely leading man. What is forbidden, we know, is any interracial romance. Yau has chosen a president whose connections to China are multiple: in the 1952 campaign he was alleged to have "lost China" owing to the 1949 Communist revolution; Truman then refused to recognize the new Chinese government; and finally, he prosecuted the Korean War, a conflict in which the threat of China's involvement always loomed. Rand's unrealistic rendering of the Great Wall (it's doubled here on either side of a river, perhaps the Yalu River, which constitutes the border between Korea and China) alludes to both the racial barrier in films as well as the antagonistic stance of the U.S. toward China. As a nation, China itself was and remains a forbidden love.

"Anna May Wong in Dracula's Laundromat and Bakery" (the relation to the letter M here is, frankly, an elusive one) works a similar ploy, partnering Wong with a slightly more possible co-star, one we can assume to be Bela Lugosi, who played Count Dracula in the 1931 film. That the fearsome vampire is now running a laundromat and bakery is an inspired jest; the laundromat is included, no doubt, as an allusion to the stereotypical association of Chinese Americans with laundry services. Like Wong, the Hungarian actor was confined to parts emphasizing his foreignness. Although it should be noted that some European-born actors succeeded in playing roles outside their ethnic category. In the case of the adaptation of Pearl S. Buck's bestselling novel *The Good Earth*, German-born Luise Rainer was chosen over Wong for the leading role of the Chinese farm wife O-Lan. Wong eagerly sought the role (one for which Rainer won an Oscar) but was turned down. With Paul Muni as the male lead, the production code ban against miscegenation meant Muni, Rainer, and the other white actors performed in yellowface. Wong was offered a minor role but refused, saying: "If you let me play O-Lan, I'll be very glad. But you're asking me—with Chinese blood—to do the only unsympathetic role in the picture, featuring an all-American cast portraying Chinese characters."

In another *Alphabet Series* painting—"J"—we find Wong listed with Asian and Asian American figures: Hong Kong born Bruce Lee, Japanese American James Shigeta (who was cast—or miscast—as a Chinese character in the film adaptation of Rodgers and Hammerstein's *Flower Drum Song*), and the Filipino boxer Speedy Dado who fought in the 1920s and '30s. An idiosyncratic roll call, the list's very randomness is strangely compelling. The hand at the top of the canvas has the aspect of priestly benediction, conferring on this group a kind of blessing. Is the hand that of the poet who, by uttering these names in paint on canvas, invests them with power? Certainly, that's the case in the final Wong canvas: "Q." Wong is announced as the Queen of Diamonds. Yau thus crowns the actor with belated dignity, no longer, as he wrote, "scratched, kicked, / slapped, bitten," but elevated to deserved status.

A name acquires its "thingness," its material presence in the world, via its declaration in print, paint, or ink. To paraphrase Yau's lines quoted at the outset, a painting might be what it contains: it should speak. The collaborations in *Disguise the Limit* exemplify Yau's wish to bring language more fully into the material domain. In the case of his invocations of Anna May Wong, he seeks to disrupt the stock biography by suggesting alternative lives, ones less constricted by anti-Asian prejudice. Through Rand's images and Yau's words, the persona of Anna May Wong, now enriched with inventive possibilities, speaks to us.

Paper delivered at the Louisville Conference on Literature and Culture, February 2024.

## Renee Gladman's *One Long Black Sentence*

When you cross the *t* in your signature with a decorative flourish, you likely don't brood on having crossed the boundary separating writing from drawing. That slender gap between visual and linguistic meaning is one explored by poet, essayist, and novelist Renee Gladman. In *Prose Architectures*, a volume published three years ago, she offered a series of ink drawings that resembled handwriting, architectural blueprints, anatomical illustrations, maps, and scribbling while not quite resting within any one of those categories. Her drawings move energetically between figurative and abstract elements, between the legible and the inscrutable. *One Long Black Sentence* extends and deepens her investigation of that liminal zone by virtue of its overall design. The jet-black cover embossed with lustrous white fabric, black pages, almost exclusively white ink, and the evocative title all denote the more-unified whole associated with an artist's book. While Gladman continues to suggest—and dismantle—recognizable forms, the relationship between the drawings can be understood as continuous, organically developing, and aimed at sense-making—much like the grammatical unit she names in the book's title. In many images, elliptical looping lines dance through stacked rectangular shapes, suggesting an intimate connection between the biological and the built that recalls Paul Klee's *Twittering Machine*. Such tensions not only animate each drawing but operate between them. Turn a page and the intricately fused boxes that conjure a cityscape mutate into a burst of lines that might be synapses or muscle fiber. Another paired sequence shows (possibly) a globe? a planet? or the earth's curve, accompanied by her indecipherable notation, perhaps mimicking some rocketeer's telemetry; in the next image, a pincer-like ladder rises beneath another seeming planet. Elements of speculative fiction are in play, only grasped, though, by the viewer's inchoate sense of how such stories *move*.

Gladman's white line—which reads more as a lack of color than as any specific hue—generates emotional presence via its varying degrees of intensity. It shifts in and out of wordless expression that whispers (a delicate arc that dangles an airy triangle), murmurs (a string of minute squares snakes toward a green disc), and declaims (a brutalist construction so tightly packed with scribble that it is nearly all white). These dynamic, anti-literate forms require a fresh way of reading as they articulate the voice, if not the entire body.

"This sentence comes in the form of an open tangle," writes Fred Moten in an accompanying essay, "Anindex." The paradox Moten notes—a tangle that is nonetheless open—is threaded through Gladman's project. Not only is her sentence one that doesn't employ language, but its blackness is found not in its inscription but in its background. Indeed, many pages are devoid of any marking. Is the long black sentence the motionless container, the space around the restless, declaratively white line? The question arises from drawings that assert both presence and absence, stillness and action. Gladman's sentence is unspeakable even as it defines the essence of speech.

*Bookforum*, September-November 2020.

# Post Modern: Ray Johnson's Contrarian Sensibility Inspired Mail Art

From our current vantage, it's not hard to acknowledge that one of the presiding spirits of early 21st-century art is Ray Johnson's. Collagist, painter, poet, and the originator of mail art, Johnson took up the appropriative strategies of Marcel Duchamp and Jasper Johns, infused them with John Cage's ideas about Zen Buddhism and chance composition, and energized the mix with his brand of deadpan Conceptualism. The art he made beginning in the early 1950s until his death in 1995 ingeniously merged artist, artmaking, and art object in ways that were once disquieting but are now considered routine. The strong strain of performativity and self-reflexiveness—qualities that mark the work of artists such as Matt Freedman and Ryan Trecartin—was the animating force behind Johnson's collages and texts and, more pointedly, what he chose to do with them. Rather than show in galleries, he mailed his work (often multiple Xeroxes) to hundreds of people, and encouraged them to embellish it and send it out again. The republication of his artist's book *The Paper Snake* and the selection from his voluminous letters in *Not Nothing* are an opportunity to sample one of the most subversively witty intelligences to paste, draw, and type in the last half century.

A twenty-two-year-old Johnson arrived in New York in 1949 after studying at Black Mountain College, where he met, among others, Cage, Merce Cunningham, and Willem de Kooning; in the city, he soon contacted like-minded artists such as Johns, Cy Twombly, and

Robert Rauschenberg. Within a few years, he knew everyone on the scene. No less ambitious than any of his contemporaries, Johnson nonetheless chose to work small—he began making collages on the 8-×-11-inch cardboard sheets that came inside laundered shirts. He juxtaposed glamour shots of movie stars, advertisements, photos of writers, newspaper text, and images from physical-culture magazines in suggestive, mischievous ways that made clear there was a joke, but one so recondite that maybe only Johnson laughed.

Despite his art-world pedigree, or perhaps because of it, Johnson poked at the myth of the autonomous, heroic artist. One of his more famous pieces shows the Lucky Strike logo pasted onto an iconic photo of James Joyce; the ad hovers next to the author's head, and he seems to be contemplating the bright red circle and its slogan, "It's toasted," with placid disdain. Another untitled piece from the series "The Luckys" sets two of the bull's-eye logos on either side of the words "F. Scott Fitzgerald Crack-Up." The recognizable name and images are put into dynamic play—one icon is set to playfully duel the other for visual dominance, even as a more covert tension animates the field of potential meaning: Is Johnson commenting on these writers' careers, the haphazard distribution of fame, or the variable nature of aesthetic judgements?

Johnson's fascination with authors is no surprise given his own prodigious writerly proclivities. *Not Nothing* offers a small portion of his mail art—a conceptual project that remains his signal accomplishment. The process—one public yet intimate—by which Johnson put his collages and letters into circulation embodied his core aesthetic of motion and mutability. He dubbed his collages "moticos," an anagram of "osmotic" (a word chosen at random from a dictionary), and he thought of them as recombinations designed for further recombination—by him (he constantly altered his own work) and his correspondents. A sampling from a mail-art list titled "102 Moticos" from the early '50s gives some sense of the concept's unsettling ambiguity: "matching for them," "two pound one," "Australian contemplating a ladder," "the fan can name," "bearer away," "the Zebra feet girl," and "used Switzerland." None of these, or any of the other items, in any way define a motico and indeed they can each (and in aggregate) be regarded as anti-definitions. The move is characteristically Johnson's—he also staged Zen-inspired events called "Nothings" in response to the '60s vogue for Happenings.

This oppositional impulse guided Johnson's approach to his letters, which are in fact metatexts, letters that parody and undermine not only the genre's forms but the very notion of person-to-person communication. The New York Correspondance School (Johnson's misspelling) was the official-sounding name he gave to his postal round-robin; the moniker mocks the idea of artistic "schools" while alluding to actual correspondence schools, institutions that once offered high school degrees or certificates in, say, appliance repair. (The ritualized impersonality of sending homework back and forth between students and instructors no doubt intrigued Johnson.) His correspondents were artists and writers (Joseph Cornell, Christo, Marianne Moore, Andy Warhol, Lynda Benglis, James Rosenquist) who were teachers of sorts, providing him with inspiration (he asked to trace Moore's tricorn hat; she declined) and encouragement.

A glance reveals that this is no ordinary collection of missives: Every page is distinct, as variations on collage, drawing, handwriting, and typography are all energetically exercised. Styles and forms also run the gamut; there are lists, poems, diary entries, koan-like tales, and annotations. Some are addressed to particular people, others aren't addressed to anyone; some employ plain paper, others use loose-leaf, or stationery from hotels, businesses, and government offices. Johnson's calibrated deployment of these elements demotes meaning in favor of the mode of presentation. The entirety of the mail-art experience—the use of the postal system, the process of opening an envelope, puzzling over the contents, the choice about whether to respond or discard—trumps the quaint idea that Johnson had something he actually wanted to say to someone.

What might art historian Gregory Battcock have made of the 1967 note Johnson sent him, which reads: "An exhausted mushroom hunter from Leghorn, Italy was captured in Helsinki. The mush-room hunter was found in a zoo, catching its breath after the flight from Leghorn, more than 1,300 miles away. An identifying band was found on its leg. An exhausted musroom." This absurdist tale, with its deliberate misspellings and confused pronouns, surely delighted Battcock as a send-up of the newsy missive, but its underlying premise—that personal communication is ultimately uncommunicative—offers a more profound insight about human relations.

The same gibe registers graphically in "Poem in 64 Word Form – for Larry Poons – by Dick Higgins," a numbered list that repeats a hyphenated version of the word *tidbit* ("tid-bit") eighty-six times; the neologism, though, has been overtyped in about half the instances, rendering much of the text illegible. But not really—while straining to discern the typed-over letters, you still know "tid-bit" lurks within the palimpsest. Johnson's game cuts to fundamental questions about how we use language and how language uses us. His affection for enumerated lists and even letters entirely composed of numbers (the only constant feature in these documents is the standard epistolary inclusion of dates and the address of the sender) may testify to faith in digital accuracy over verbal nuance. Or it may be nothing more than Johnson's love for the contours of numbers. The author's intentions are as indeterminate as the texts.

In 1965, poet Dick Higgins collected some of the many items he had received from Johnson in *The Paper Snake*, a volume meant to solve the problem, as articulated by Higgins, of how to present mail art, works "so rooted in their moment and their context" but nonetheless "seemed to acquire new and larger meaning as time went along." The essentially poetic nature of Johnson's expressive range comes clearly into focus in this compilation of pieces addressed to a fellow poet. The Steinian wordplay and disruptive grammar appear to be the most natural means of rendering his contrarian sensibility, one that delights in all manner of incongruity:

> Dear Dick,
> I enclose some fur. I enclose my signature.
> I enclose a novel of suspense.
> I enclose a three-legged animal. I enclose a Lucky Strike.
> I enclose a Y (a fragment of RAY).
> I do not enclose a man with his left hand in his jacket pocket

with a black shoe on his left shoulder.
I do not enclose Jesus Christ.
I do not enclose Luck Str
I enclose hands stirring and hands mixing.
I enclosed a highly magnified view of potato rot.

The comic collision between a business letter's formal diction ("I enclose") and the ridiculous ("shoe on his left shoulder"), the improbable ("three-legged animal"), the pseudoprofound ("Jesus Christ"), and the just plain weird ("potato rot") owes as much a debt to Dada as Monty Python might owe to these lines. This is the spirit of the moticos—moving in many directions at once, everywhere and nowhere.

In January 1995, Johnson drove to Sag Harbor, Long Island, and apparently committed suicide by leaping off a bridge. He was last seen lazily backstroking toward open water. His lifelong obsession with numbers appears to have determined the date (the 13th), his motel number (247: 2 + 4 + 7 = 13), as well as the decision itself: he was sixty-seven years old (6 + 7). At his home, friends discovered all the artwork turned to the wall or covered, all except one large photo of Johnson himself. It was the self-portrait he had repeatedly distributed, typed over, and collaged—one in which his round face and close-cropped hair lend him a lunar aspect. His intense gaze and parted lips denote apprehension—the moment just before. A handwritten letter from 1977 ("Dear Dick Higgins, I'm sitting here waiting for something to happen") serves as a gloss both for the image and for Johnson's career. The anticipation of opening an envelope before reading a letter, the shape of the words before their comprehension, the nothing before the something—these are the experiential locales that his art maps with aptly fluid boundaries. His work is self-regarding and hermetic, to be sure, but Johnson's interiority is carefully positioned just—but not quite—out of reach. To appreciate the joke, you have to not try. It's like the mail: it comes when it does. And then you get it.

*Bookforum*, Summer 2014.

# Correspondence School: The Changing Face of Letter-Writing Manuals

A few mumbled words may get you a cocktail, but only smooth talk will net you that great job or date. The learning curve that governs speech once held for writing, too. In the not-so-long-ago phoneless world, letters enabled us to marry, get a loan, or save a friend from drink and dissolution. If you wanted things done, you wrote; if you wanted them done well, you wrote with bells on. Letter-writing manuals once taught us how. Tailored for use by the newly literate classes, guides to letter writing date back to the 18th century. They anthologized scores of letters—from marriage proposals to condolences—demonstrating the felicities of composition by example. These exemplary letters, which served as templates for the most intricately personal transactions, testify to the trust once placed in rhetorical expression, and to the vigor such expression conveyed.

Published in 1832, *The Fashionable American Letter Writer: Or, the Art of Polite Correspondence* was designed for waistcoat pockets, a volume to be kept close and consulted often. Its user possessed enough education to understand the references to Cicero in the preface, but was by no means a scholar. Likely candidates would number among the burgeoning ranks of professionals, especially those anxious to signal their recent social elevation. Indeed, the issue of class is addressed unembarrassedly, and informs almost every piece of advice: "Proverbial expressions and trite sayings," we are told right off, "are the flowers of the rhetoric of a low-bred man." Readers are also warned about the pitfalls of tautology, using Latin quotes, alliteration, and the right way to fold a letter—it must be "strongly pressed with the proper instrument." By standardizing the window dressing of correspondence, letter manuals ensured writers a modicum of self-regard; to produce an acceptable piece of mail meant you could sashay among the ladies and gents. But rules also democratized letter writing by encouraging conformity (watch that Latin!) and emphasizing the practical rather than belletristic ends to which letters might be put.

*The Fashionable American* promises "a variety of plain and elegant letters" on subjects like courtship, business, and marriage; in short, love and money hold sway. An exchange of notes from "a Tradesman to a Customer Demanding Payment of Money" shows how bullish insistence can be channeled in such roundabout ways that modern readers will have to peer deep to see that someone is being dunned. "I have a very large sum to make up in the course of a week," the Tradesman writes, "and shall esteem it a very particular favour, if you can let me have the amount of my bill delivered within that time." When the Customer pleads lack of cash, the Tradesman bores onward: "I have sent the bill by my clerk for your acceptance, not doubting that it will be duly honoured, and that you will excuse this liberty from, Sir, your most obedient and humble servant." Today, this ritualized deference appears farcical, if not manipulative, but such an approach would not have rung false to a 19th-century audience. Deftly strung phrases made a euphemistic music that eased tensions and buffered disagreements; unadorned, straightforward cadences registered with a truculent clang.

Courtship has always tested the letter writer's ingenuity, and this guide doesn't disappoint, offering a nuanced menu of romantic approaches. Beginning with the simple "From a Gentleman to a Lady, disclosing his passion," the manual moves on to "From a Gentleman of some fortune who had seen a Lady in public, to her Mother." Not mere pleas for affection, these are extended disquisitions on hearts broken by the cruel, cruel world. You can get a very precise sociological take on 19th-century women's situation from the letter to be written by "a young Lady to a Gentleman that courted her, whom she could not esteem, but was forced by her Parents to receive his visits, and think on none else for her Husband." How crucial a role the letters manual played in private life is indicated by the specificity of these samples; correspondents turned to these books not for general guidance but for a very particularized language that would turn the trick in their lives at that moment.

When a "rich young Gentleman" wants to propose to a "beautiful young Lady without a fortune," he must first smoothly engage certain social givens: "It is a general reflection ... of the present age, that marriage is only considered as one of those methods by which avarice may be satisfied, and poverty increased; that neither the character nor accomplishments of the woman are much regarded, her merit being estimated by the thousands of her fortune." Perhaps an opening like that won't turn her motor over but in the wake of his senatorial oration, this suitor can pitch his serious woo: "I have been always determined to consult my own inclinations, where there is the least appearance of happiness; and having an easy independency, am not anxious about increasing it, which leads me to the discovery of a passion which I have long endeavored to conceal." Windy words like this may have cloaked awkward realities, but that delicacy still permitted frank dealings over sticky issues. Imagine a contemporary correspondent venturing to cross a similarly mined field without benefit of overdressed sentences—"Yes, I know you're poor, but I'm going to tell my family to stick it, and marry you because I want to." Somehow, you know this modern bachelor will stay single.

The samples in this letters manual were not intended to be copied word for word—the general popularity of the guides would lead to quick detection—but rather to immerse writers in a temperament. Before dipping their pens in the inkwell, they would drink in a rhetorical show of lithe pirouettes and earnest declamations, the elaborately dramatized mechanisms of persuasion. They became masters of the passive-aggressive tack—the ability to get what you wanted by never really asking. Of course, from our current vantage, it's difficult to read this deflection as anything but devious.

At least as serviceable a death knell for the letter as the first transatlantic telephone call is "*Take a Letter ...*": *Putting Persuasive Power*

*Into the Day's Dictation*, a 1929 guide by Jack Garrett. Inside are the ur-texts of "junk mail," a moniker that permanently smeared the reputation of epistolary communication. The advent of the Dictaphone undermined the worked-over written quality of the letter, replacing it with the newly prized conversational feel. Envelopes no longer would house voices, but hold chatter instead. With a dismissive tweaking of the past, Garrett announces the brave new letter: "A generation ago, when Grandfather parked his Spencerian pen in a potato, business letters were few and far between.... Using letters to *build business* was something that never occurred to him." Garrett's formula—"Get attention, arouse interest, create desire, inspire action"—is familiar as the grating mix of sexual come-on and military command that we've come to know as modern advertising. Exploiting the letter's natural intimacy—you hold it in your hands, it is addressed to you—along with its equally personal language ("dear" and "sincerely"), the sales letter poisoned the well. Like a Trojan horse, it enters your home under the pretext of bringing you news from an old friend or at least an invite to dinner, only to betray you. Decades of unfolding letters beginning Urgent! and closing with Act Now! have not only worn out the letter's rhetoric, but the physical occasion of reading it. Still, a memory of real correspondence survives. It accounts for our opening those Publishers Clearing House envelopes, which we do, in part, to reenact a familiar rite, and because we harbor a dim hope of finding something human inside.

The waning of these reflexes shows in Lillian Eichler Watson's 1948 *Standard Book of Letter Writing*. She presents the letter as a "visit" on paper, and seeks to help you "MAKE YOUR LETTERS SOUND THE WAY YOU DO." A glance at the table of contents clues you in to the letter's decline in importance. No longer do we read missives from uncles advising nephews on "the pernicious habit of drinking to excess," or fathers cautioning daughters about "coquettish behavior." After a century of exhaustive overuse, the rhetoric of letter writing just isn't up to it. In the '40s, the mail brought mostly party invitations, condolences, thank-you notes, and business letters. Some less perfunctory categories—"Vacation letters to the folks back home," "letters to a son in a foreign country"—are covered, but it's clear the emotional ambit of the letter has shrunk and the writer's voice is cramped by a telegraphic style. A letter of condolence that begins, "There's not much we can say at a time like this," and then closes two lines later with an invite to call if "there's anything we can do," looks like a semaphore signal when set next to the older manual's several hundred-word epistle from father to a son titled "on the Immortality of the Soul." That there would be much to say "at a time like this" was precisely the point for the 1832 correspondent.

Some slender thread of written life carries on in a recent renovation of the letter-writing manual, *Personal LetterWorks,* by Judi Barton and Nate Rosenblatt, a book and computer disk loaded with letters for the '90s. Not surprisingly, many are complaints—"Your Waiter Made Sexist Comments to Me," "Your Salesperson Has an Offensive Odor," "My Guests Felt Snubbed by You," or "I Won't Support Your Addiction." A section devoted to sensitive issues bangs out terse notes for talk-show topics like "Stop Stalking Me" and "Stop Seeing My Husband." Long gone is any preamble, any mincing of words: "If you don't end this adulterous relationship, *you* will be the one who suffers the consequences. (1) I will tell your husband. (2) I will go to your office and tell your boss and co-workers. (3) I will post a notice on your church bulletin board describing your behavior. (4) I will take additional action without prior warning."

In the age of terrorist demands, the letter as threat or ransom note has arrived. If we will no longer dance to rhetoric's tune, we will certainly sit up and take notice when knife-sharp sentences like these come in the mail. The art of polite correspondence hardly needs a manual now; our letters read the way we speak—blunt, pissed-off, and loud. Ritualistic communication—and letters are nothing if not carefully staged rites of self-representation—has collapsed under the wave of the gestural. Anything even a tad ornate will be tagged as greeting-card prose, or worse, as bullshit for not expressing our true feelings. We are now free to sling our plainly put sentiments at will, although bothering to write them down risks making us look like dandies. To look at a book on how to do it would make us frauds.

*Village Voice Literary Supplement,* October 1994.

# Tour of Duty: A Baedeker's Dozen

Some years ago, during my first visit to Paris, I mercilessly ran my companion ragged chasing down the onetime homes and longtime graves of everyone from Stendhal to Gertrude Stein. Flush with assorted maps and guides, we trudged around Père Lachaise in the cold and trespassed through private buildings. When we were unceremoniously booted from the courtyard adjacent to Stein's atelier, my embarrassed friend snatched my paperwork and demanded we do something real, instead of stalking three-starred highlights from a map as big as a rug. By "something real," she meant sitting in a café and just watching people, or maybe strolling down anonymous, unsung streets. What she didn't mean was hunting for the exact spot where Hitler stood above Napoleon's tomb in that famous wartime photo.

Eventually, she took ill, surely to spare herself my mania; a few months later, we broke up. But I wasn't distressed enough to ever abandon faith in the *Baedeker's* way of knowledge. In the face of the fashionable travel ethic that prizes spontaneity, casual discovery, and the nuances of everyday life, I remain a doggedly literal and dutiful tourist who treasures the books that tell me where to go and the maps that show me how to get there.

If a journey of a thousand miles begins with a single step, my trek also starts with page one, chapter one: How to Use This Guide. Even when roaming close to home, I need to know the lay of the land around me—I own over a half-dozen guides to New York City. I could no more live here just off St. Mark's Place without my Lower

East Side handbooks than explore the Mayan ruins of Uxmal bereft of accompanying text. (From different sources, I've learned Ira Gershwin lived in my building, and Frank O'Hara wrote "Second Avenue" across the street.) A travel guide deepens its chosen geography, restores lost years, and inscribes blank turf with names and deeds; it illuminates that unseen place which shares coordinates with, for instance, the New York Public Library steps where, if you stood there a mere lifetime ago you would have been blowing bubbles at the bottom of a vast Egyptian-style reservoir. In Rome, I once had to be restrained from chancing a dark alley littered with dope peddlers to find the once bloody ground where Brutus stabbed Caesar. Inane guidebook facts, perhaps, but also keys to luxurious cities of ghosts.

Of course, travel guides perform a far more basic job—getting folks from here to there. Make a right at the used car lot, you tell a lost motorist, the one with the fifty-foot tire out front, go about one mile past the baseball field, then take the first left after you hit the railroad tracks, look for the neon Dunkin' Donuts sign and head straight for it. If you bother to point out that some kid tried to kill himself by jumping off the tire, Tom Seaver pitched Little League on the ballfield, and after your prom, you passed out in the donut shop, you've got the makings of a guide. Or even a novel because directions and descriptions lie at the heart of storytelling. Travel itself is essentially narrative in both its arc and propulsion, a matter of putting one step in front of the next sentence. So it shouldn't surprise us that how to get there and what to see have long been the questions first answered by scribblers.

What is Homer's *Odyssey* other than a *Frommer's* for the ancient Mediterranean world? The blind bard provides information about what to pack—spear, shield, and tunic, navigational aids for skirting Scylla and Charybdis, advice on how to dine with a Cyclops, tipping suggestions for the ferryman at the River Styx, and entertainment highlights like Circe, who, we're told, is belting out some of the catchiest strophes this side of the Pillars of Hercules. And there's the *Divine Comedy*, the template for the modern guidebook. Although Dante hired Virgil as his afterlife escort, we can benefit from guidance almost as personal by reading the Florentine's handy, geographically organized, tourist-friendly account. Whether it's a rafting trip down the Mississippi or a chartered cruise in pursuit of a whale, the big-time classics amply remind us it's not the feat, it's the motion.

In the mid-19th century, the German publisher Karl Baedeker helped inaugurate the age of industrial travel by publishing a series of highly detailed guidebooks illustrated with "numerous Maps, Plans, Panoramas, and Views." One might also be warned about gratuities in a city like Naples, where "the insolence of the mercenary fraternity has attained an almost incredible pitch." Restaurants, churches, museums, and natural vistas were poked and prodded by a judicious, efficient prose—"The large vestibule on the *Ground Floor,* adorned with mosaics by Salviati in the style of the 14th century, contains antiques and weapons, including an Aragonese breech-loading field piece of the 15th century"—that presumed an indefatigably curious audience unaccustomed to wasting time. For such newly wealthy travelers, these dense but pocket-sized volumes became the definitive battle plan as they laid siege to foreign shores from Cairo to Copenhagen. A *Baedeker's* not only told you where to go, and what to look at, but it kept a dauntingly precise record of where you'd been—a checklist of sorts, of those sites that had been done, as in "We did Versailles." The little red book was pivotal: it drained leisure travel of its peripatetic cast and injected the purposeful intent of religious pilgrimage and modernity's driven pace to create that thing abhorred most by every tourist: tourism.

But that's what happens when you give the middle classes a handbook, they take an arm. We've overrun the globe, elbowing one another in the Medici Chapel, jostling for a camera shot of a ritual cremation in Bali. You can blame the Wright Brothers for most of this, and travel guides for the rest. How many people would risk jet propelling themselves into downtown Bangkok or the fjords of Norway if they hadn't been properly prepped by Uncle Karl's myriad successors, *Michelin, Fodor's, Frommer's,* the *Blue Guide,* and *Birnbaum's?* If they hadn't been assured, in a worldly, connoisseur's tone, about friendly locals, drinkable water, and the general worthiness of paying a visit? Like Helen's face, guidebooks have launched many ships. The imperial calm with which their authors meet any travel anxiety—the exchange rate in Istanbul, a pissoir in Prague, driving a wisp of a car in Italy—challenges us to get off the sofa, buck-up, and grapple with cultural difference. An almost martial undercurrent seeps through—these books bang the drum for foreign adventure, and then parade us, single file, past the bad bouillabaisse and across the Bridge of Sighs, with an insistently eager sightseeing beat.

Numbering myself among the great unwashed and unleisured, I find this taskmaster approach just fine; I don't have the time to be nonchalant about travel, and I too deeply crave the obvious attractions, often because of their very typicality. At places like the Piazza Navona or the top of the Empire State Building, the travel-guide traveler percolates with a sense of achieved apex; they are welcome in the throng. At this late date in our mobile century, any real novelty, I'm certain, lies well beyond the reach of even the most eccentric traveler. However much we resist admitting it, a good deal of what we think we discover—the shabby trattoria in a working-class quarter of Rome, the secluded, pink coral cove in Tortola—is, in fact, old news to legions of Germans in sandals and socks. When we travel, hooked like fish to our guidebook itinerary (the hip, unconventional one; you know it's offbeat because the title tells you so), we chiefly experience the phenomenon of tourism, certainly far more than what we quaintly wish to be authentic life in some foreign clime. We cheer signs of such realness, like laundry hung in the Barceloneta, but that too is written up in the guidebooks.

This isn't necessarily bad. There is something both communal and profoundly knowing about joining the tourist bazaar of all nations as you simply fall into place, hand over your ticket, savor a taste, and move on. You have surrendered to guidebook law and, depending on your guide, you will be led forth justly. This is how we get around in the global village, never cozier than being someplace strange while lost in a hometown sentence. On the subject of Venice being overwhelmed by both prose and tourists well over a hundred years ago, Henry James noted the dawn of the Baedeker era, "There is as little mystery about the Grand Canal as about our local thoroughfare, and the name of St. Mark is as familiar as the postman's ring." Yet, "It is not forbidden," he continued, "to speak of familiar things." Of course, he did speak, and speak, about every famed and overrun attraction in his beloved but much publicized city. True, the travel book has become the subway map for whole continents, but there remains an intricate delight in counting and watching the stations pass.

Still, as my wife says, "It's hard to read and look at the same time." And it is. You might end up tumbling headfirst into the sacrificial cenote at Chichén Itzá or giving yourself whiplash davening from book to ceiling in the Sistine Chapel. Worse, you can end up digesting facts while seeing nothing. I once climbed all morning to the top of Half Dome in Yosemite, where I spent almost all of the brief time I had there fooling with a trail guide and map, trying to figure out the names of every distant peak. Great fun for any cartophile, but what I remember is the ceaseless sky and believing for a few seconds that I was inhaling sunlight. Standing in front of Masaccio's frescoes while reading about Renaissance patronage may be a common enough sight, but it is no less idiotic; I know, I've done it. Guidebooks are pocket-sized for a reason—sometimes they should stay in your pocket.

Just how much you want to mediate experience with words comes down to cases, and the words in question. For instance, Kate Simon's *Italy: The Places in Between* may well be an intoxicating masterpiece of lush prose and deftly served detail, but Simon sees so much and writes so well, her sensibility threatens to crowd out my far more mundane responses. Better to have some workmanlike *Michelin* in hand on whose bare prose I can manage to hang some shred of personal insight, than to be superseded by Simon's gorgeous eye. This is a book to read for recalling a long-past visit; only then can I permit myself the delusion that my own slack perceptions mirrored hers. In the heat of the touristic moment, what is needed is plain, precise facts. When a guide declares a church in Cortona to be open from 3 to 5 o'clock and it turns out to be *chiusa*, it can hardly be faulted for the whimsical Italian way with time. But if it says that the tapestry above the door was a key inspiration for Provencal troubadours yet neglects to mention there are three doors, each with a tapestry over the portal, your thwarted literary-historical revelation can certainly be laid at the publisher's door. Most cruel, though, is the "moderately priced" restaurant in Venice where the bill ends up looking like a ransom note. Going by the book has its traps and tricks; surely, a guide to the guides needs to be written.

In the preface of one of my 19th-century *Baedeker's*, it says, "The Handbook will also, it is hoped, be the means of saving the traveler many a trial of temper." The phrase is particularly felicitous. What else might be the object of some great journey other than new worlds that might shake the cobwebs loose and try one's even temper? This was certainly true of a different age, before American Express cards, connecting flights, chain hotels, and the establishment of English as the tourist world's lingua franca. And before the proliferation of travel guides. Of course, we still fret over lost bags and inadequate plumbing, but we are hardly Lewis and Clark. Travel guides are designed to reassure, familiarize, and spare us the disasters that follow from stepping into dark, unlit rooms. They cannot make the worlds we visit new again, but they can make them fresh sites for an ancient ritual—finding our way by reading the magic words.

*Village Voice Literary Supplement*, February 1994.

# The Criminal Within: A Genre of How-To Manuals Indulges Our Darkest Fantasies

At the information desk of a downtown Manhattan Barnes & Noble, I ask about a title—*Be Your Own Undertaker: How to Dispose of a Dead Body*. The young man behind the desk doesn't miss a beat. "Has it begun to smell?" he asks, with a perfunctory grin that acknowledges yet undercuts the small joke between us. He knows there's no corpse in need of disposal; my inquiring openly about such a book in a Barnes & Noble is proof enough. And I know he knows this; indeed, any slight self-consciousness on my part stems from my awareness that buying this book is akin to purchasing one of those tourist T-shirts depicting a revolver above the tired tagline "Welcome to New York." But this book is a hipper jest, something truly arch. That doesn't mean it lacks gruesome details on how to rid yourself of an inconvenient body: Before you sink the stiff in the river, author A. R. Bowman advises, don't forget to "take a long, sharp object, like a tire iron or a very, very large screwdriver, and drive it through the corpse numerous times" to allow for the release of buoyant gases during decomposition. And if you've got to remove incriminating ballistic evidence from a head wound, you can "cut the skin off the forehead, break up the skull bone behind it, and reach in with long tweezers, chopsticks, or something similar." Bowman's earnest, intimate tone—"if you find yourself gripped by a constant urge to visit or look over the site ... resist it" is both eerie and hilarious, but the true capper to the joke is my purchase: I, a mild-mannered work-a-daddy, seek out, among the gardening books and cappuccinos of a corporate superstore whose cheery employees are only too happy to help, a book whose predicated reader is a recent murderer.

*Be Your Own Undertaker* is published by Paladin Press, of Boulder, Colorado. A descendant of the underground presses of the 1960s, Paladin, along with another quirky publisher, Loompanics Unlimited, located in Washington State, displays an antigovernment, antisocial tilt with its numerous titles devoted to drug production, bomb building, and anarchism (even though the company got its start reprinting Army manuals). Paladin and Loompanics have updated the marginal mimeograph-and-stapler approach of the ad hoc '60s press and now pump out hundreds of titles apiece. Both publishers report sales of more than 300,000 books each year, with roughly 90 percent ending up in American hands, and this overwhelmingly native popularity, together with the lower-middle-class mindset ostensibly being catered to, implies that these books are no longer blueprints for the revolution but rather the literary equivalent of pink flamingo lawn ornaments.

For the most part, retail sales for both companies are catalogue-based, but the Virgin Megastore in Times Square carries more than two dozen Loompanics and Paladin books grouped together, genre-style, on their own shelf. The books shrewdly ride the current mainstream trend toward how-to and self-improvement manuals, with the difference being that their readers find instruction in knife fighting, survivalism, methamphetamine manufacture, sniping, lock picking, wiretapping, shoplifting, and smuggling. The Paladin catalogue lists fourteen different titles on gun silencers alone; Loompanics lists over a dozen guides to psychedelic drugs. Together, the offerings constitute a riotously intensive and extensive encyclopedia of underground arcana.

Loompanics claims to offer "The Best Book Catalog in the World," and, unlike mainstream specimens, whose actual books must be read in order to inspire or to entertain, their catalogue is itself an object of literary delight. My guess is that most readers don't order either of these from the publishers to find just the right book on street fighting, but rather for the camp thrill. They have a laugh over the choice juxtaposition of *Close Shaves: The Complete Book of Razor Fighting* and *Breath of the Dragon: Homebuilt Flamethrowers*, or they savor a presumed cause-and-effect relationship between *Threesome: How to Fulfill Your Favorite Fantasy* and its adjacent title, *How to Dump Your Wife*. With hundreds of carnivalesque pages, these catalogues score high on what television programmers term the "Hey Mabel" effect—"Hey Mabel, you can use Liquid-Plumr and Tylenol to build a bomb!" Although the offerings appear to give voice to a chorus of libertarians, it is difficult to believe that the whole thing isn't a put-on, an elaborate media prank offering a satiric tour of our homegrown lunacies.

If the editors are winking at their readers (does "Loompanics" combine "lampoon" + "comics" + "panic" + "loom"?), it is impossible to say so for sure. The same ethos governs many of the nation's over-the-top sideshows—the *National Enquirer*, *Jerry Springer*, *Melrose Place*—and, like them, Loompanics and Paladin books appear to be self-parodies. All of these books state that they are "sold for informational purposes only," but this legal hand washing acknowledges potential danger with what seems to be another big wink. The guidelines for prospective Loompanics authors may call for "stuff that rattles the cage of consensus reality," but the cage-rattling fellow with a dead body on the kitchen floor isn't going to dash out and buy a book about getting rid of it; that book will be bought only by someone whose very distance—social, psychological, and economic—from such a likelihood makes it both legally safe and emotionally tolerable for him to own it.

To say that how-to manuals on knife fighting and blowguns are but clever party favors for the smirking cognoscenti is not to dismiss the practicality of the information conveyed. If your bar-brawling skills are in need of polishing, look no further than Kurt Craven's *101 Sucker Punches*. He analyzes "seriously effective moves used by the FBI, bouncers, and security guards for Elvis Presley" to school you in such strategies of the sweet science as the "Kiss-My-Ass Kick" and the "Grab-Hair/Smash-Face-Against-Table Attack." While arguing over a parking space, you can give the Modified Hair Lift a try: "Take a pinch of hair between fingertips and thumb at each of his temples and lift sharply a few inches.... [O]nce the victim grimaces and comes to his toes, spin his head in either direction by pushing with one hand and pulling with the other. Pain and momentum will turn his head and shoulders into the proper position for the application of a Choke Hold." Such is the fate of the hapless sucker who trucks with a Paladin reader. Unless, of course, your sucker has read Peyton Quinn's *A Bouncer's Guide to Barroom Brawling: Dealing with the Sucker Puncher, Streetfighter, and Ambusher*. Then you may be pitting your chapter against his verse.

As if readying to serve as a satisfied "straight" customer in a Paladin advertisement, James Edward Perry, a one-time convict and street preacher, seemingly set out to prove the value and utility of the book *Hit Man: A Technical Manual for Independent Contractors* in 1993. According to Maryland prosecutors, Perry employed twenty-two of the book's pointers when he performed contract murders on a mother, her son, and the boy's nurse; the book was found in his home after the arrest. An attentive reader, he had followed the instructions of author Rex Feral, a purported professional killer, to run a file down the gun barrel in order to foil ballistics tests and to shoot out the eyes of his victims to ensure death. Rex Feral, it turns out, was a divorced mother of two (as of this writing, Paladin refuses to divulge her real name) who had originally submitted the manuscript as a novel. In a letter to the publisher at the time of her submission, she wrote that her ideas came "from books, television, movies, newspapers, my karate instructor." In the book, she dispenses business ethics that could be cribbed from the Rotary Club: "Expenses generally run between $500 and $5000.... The money will cover travel, lodging, food, accessories such as disguises, and equipment. Any amount left over belongs to you. But don't cut any corners trying to make an extra buck. Give the man the most professional job his money can buy."

That Rex Feral did not, as the author confessed in the letter to Paladin, "even own a gun" probably wouldn't have dampened Perry's appreciation of her fourteen-point shopping list for making a disposable silencer. No doubt he checked off such tasty kill-tech items as "drill rod, 7/32 inch" and "80 grit sandpaper." And it is precisely these kinds of details—with their shop-talk snap and crackle—that the ironist finds exquisite; they occupy the camp juncture where methodical and serious intent meets flippancy and disbelief. The survivors of Perry's victims are suing Paladin for aiding and abetting the murders, and the Supreme Court has refused to hear the publisher's appeal to dismiss the case on First Amendment grounds. Howard Siegel, the survivors' attorney, doesn't buy the free-speech argument, and last summer described Paladin in *The Washington Post* as "a correspondence school for crime" and *Hit Man* as "a recipe for murder." By the time this case goes to trial—with a pro-Paladin brief submitted by other, more mainstream companies, including *The New York Times, The Baltimore Sun,* and ABC—this paperback, with its comic-book cover (a shiny-suited gunman, replete with fedora, holds a gun outside a half-opened door), may supersede its camp niche and end up being sold in gift shops everywhere, right next to Dilbert calendars and magnetic poetry kits. Until then, such publicity only sharpens its kitsch cachet and lends to the aura of danger a thin undercoating of actual blood. Oklahoma bomber Timothy McVeigh was another proud Paladin reader; he owned a copy of *Homemade C-4: A Recipe for Survival.* No doubt the whiff of carnage informs other Paladin and Loompanics titles, thus twisting their ironic reception into a double reverse: it's a joke, but the book is very real, which makes it even more of a joke, because you wouldn't use it, though you could, if it weren't a joke.

This duplicity draws an audience whose attraction depends on *apparent* authenticity. We can claim to keep a skeptical, if not dismissive, eye; we can say that we enjoy these books solely as "cultural artifacts"; yet central to this pleasure is the belief that someone, somewhere, takes them seriously. This is the "real reader" of these "real books," and against the foreground of presumed un-self-consciousness (at least on the part of the publishers) and credulous reception by a not-so-great unwashed, the ironic reader can fancy himself interested in criminal how-to books only insofar as they are tokens of trailer park Americana. Held aloft by sociological distance, he can imagine himself skimming the surface of a turgid pool of pathological defectives who buy *101 Sucker Punches* because they truly want the answer to Craven's opening query: "What is a Sucker Punch? And why should we use it?" But just as it hardly matters whether the editorial intent is straightforward or not, it is equally irrelevant whether such readers exist; it is enough that they *should* exist.

If the appearance of authenticity gets someone to buy one of these books, what gets him to keep it? Could it be that very same faith in authenticity? If honest-to-God criminals and miscreants might use these books, the purchaser might reason, then maybe there's some information within worth having around. This is the same reason I held on to my *Boy Scout Handbook*: it was full of detailed instructions on how to track deer, tie a knot, rig a sail, or hoist an injured buddy. These how-to books are the *Boy Scout Handbook*'s dark cousins; they can help you out if you ever need to rig a bomb or hoist a buddy's corpse.

Just as pipe-smoking dads of the '50s maintained a shelf of woodworking, car-repair, and fly-fishing manuals, the *Popular Mechanics* male still prides himself on his fix-up chops. But nowadays, you can't remedy the glitch in your software with a ratchet wrench, or restore the cruise control in your car with a mallet. Grittier than the rarefied guides that accompany your new printer, Loompanics and Paladin books serve as objects of nostalgia for a more hands-on epoch. Ryan K. Kephart's *Rolling Thunder: Turning Junk into Automobile Weaponry* has that irresistible bang and clang of hard-core know-how. With it, you can trick up your Honda to bristle with options like a timed detonator, a gasoline mine, or a directional projectile launcher. Kephart's schematic diagrams and peremptory, numbered instructions—"1. Obtain a 20-ounce cola bottle (minimum) and hollow out the neck end"—percolate with the reassuring rhythms of American manhood's Ur-language. The countdown rhetoric propels the reader toward accomplishment—in twelve easy steps, your car could be ready to electrocute a menacing hitchhiker: "[F]lick the switch, wait for a reaction to the impulse ... then get out and run. Leave the switch on while running and don't look back."

The can-do ethos of such dark-side handbooks not only links them to rugged individualism but bolsters their appeal as *objets trouvés*, relics of a bygone era when problems were solvable on the kitchen table or at the workbench. In *Silent Death*, a treatise on "poisons and the art of killing with stealth," the author, Uncle Fester, waxes melancholic about the decline of technical smarts: "It is a sad commentary on the brutish times we live in that the use of deadly substances as a means of homicide is virtually unheard of. Instead of the quiet dignity of an effective poison, those with homicidal intent seem to impulsively reach for a gun, knife or club." The deliberate put-on factor may sound high, but any doubt as to the practicality of the information he provides is quickly dispelled by a meticulous, citation-heavy account of poison manufacture. "For those unable or unwilling to tackle the more technically demanding tasks of nerve gas manufacture or botulin culture," one chapter begins, "Mother Nature's bounty has provided a considerably more low-tech alternative: Ricin." Ricin, we learn, "is an exceedingly toxic protein found in castor oil bean," good for both "assassination" and "mass-attack situations." One big advantage is the "delay in the onset of symptoms," which means that "a target most likely will not realize it is under attack." As exhilarating as it is disquieting, this kind of thing can't be read without a thought to who else has read it, and in this way the book acquires a certain potential energy in your hands. Are these the same sentences, you wonder, that a terrorist or scheming husband has underlined?

For an audience weaned on action movies, the obvious appeal of this terrain is obvious. More than a few screenwriters, no doubt, keep these titles handy for those scenes when someone has to explain, for instance, why the head won't sink. But not all the vicarious thrills involve knives and detonations. Identity changing, Loompanics reports, is the hot trend now. There's brisk trade being done in titles about disappearing and ID switching, and no wonder, since books such as *How to Disappear Completely and Never Be Found*, by Doug Richmond, *Fugitive: How to Run, Hide and Survive*, by Kenn Abaygo, and *The Heavy Duty New Identity*, by John Q. Newman surface at the convergence of two American narrative traditions: self-help and the getaway. The potent allures of disappearing have been evident ever since Huck lit out for the territory. The day you burn your driver's license might be the day you skip merrily free of an avalanche of debt, or a maddening spouse, or unsavory revelations about those photos you've been downloading from the Internet. "To a man of a certain age," writes Richmond, "there's a bit of magic in the very thought of cutting all ties." This cowboy romance, long comprising equal parts fear of being fenced in and desire for frontier expanses, has slid markedly toward paranoia. The crazies who rant about bar-code IDs being branded on our arms merely register the extreme end of a broader American suspicion of credentials and dossiers. There's something un-American about identity papers, after all; in movies, the voice asking for them is often a foreign one.

Much of the language describing the physical side of identity change and disappearance could just as easily be recounting religious conversion. Like a country preacher baptizing a sinner, Newman warns, "You must leave far, far behind your old lifestyle and city.... You must break these old habits 100%." If you're thirty pounds overweight, lose it; short hair, grow it longer; dress dumpy, start dressing better; speak with an accent, suppress it; "swing your arms about yourself" when you walk, stop it. Now no one will "think twice about the 'new' you being connected to the 'old' you." Best of all, no one who knows that you cleaned out the family bank account, sold your brother-in-law's car, and knocked up his wife will know the new you either. An abiding faith in self-invention as self-redemption undergirds these makeover plans. As an immigrant people we are a nation of runaways, and this heritage bequeaths a promise of not merely the pursuit of happiness but the pursuit of a "permanent new identity [under which] you will be able to live the rest of your life, or at least until the statute of limitations has run its course."

Leafing through scram manuals in a lawn chair behind the split-level is as far afield as most purchasers will ever get. Yet imaginations will surely tingle at the tale, retold by Richmond, of a hassled dad who couldn't earn enough as a schoolteacher and was forced to pump gas on the weekends: "Can you imagine the humiliation of a forty-year-old man pumping gas, or the anger that grew inside him every time a neighbor or colleague pulled in for a fill-up?" To avoid crushing alimony and child support, he split. He "found a job more interesting than he ever imagined he could get. And he's with a wonderful woman now who earns her own keep, to boot." Stowing an escape manual around the house is like having a boat in the backyard: every so often, you take a look at it and dream.

If Loompanics and Paladin how-to books satisfy our inner Boy Scout's craving for practical know-how, they also tap into that desire's underlying creed: Be Prepared. We have to be ready, and readiness means knowing how to do things, whether that's flinging Minuteman missiles across the ocean or wiring your passenger seat to electrocute a carjacker. You don't have to be a survivalist to feel the fear; even ordinary Americans are proactive paranoids: we build bomb shelters, stash pistols in the nightstand, rig our homes with alarms, and videotape our babysitters. In *Getaway: Driving Techniques for Escape and Evasion*, Ronald George Eriksen draws on the code system of awareness used by the 82nd Airborne: "In Condition Green, you are completely relaxed and unalert. If you are violently attacked while in this condition, you will most likely be destroyed. In today's violent times, one should never be in this condition." Eriksen recommends that you "vary the times and routes to and from work.... Always park so you have a fast exit from your parking space... [c]heck rear-view mirrors frequently." Condition Orange, when "your mind is focused on the danger," is the place to be.

In the radiant light of Condition Orange, these publications glow with the promise of preemptive solutions. This is the knowledge "they" don't want you to have; hence the samizdat appearance of the physical books. In *Gravity's Rainbow*, Thomas Pynchon describes "creative paranoia" as "developing at least as thorough a We-system as a They-system." Books filled with the rough science of criminal mayhem are passports to an alluring, homegrown We-system, one that allows the reader to recast himself as a rebel against government and conventional morality even as he seeks a salve for his anxiety.

"If you're a typical American," Jack Luger writes in *Snitch: A Handbook for Informers*, "someone has probably already informed or snitched on you." His guide to ratting for sheer spite or cold cash (a bald man on the cover whispers into a pay phone as it spews coins) conjures cartoon-paranoiac scenarios in which you report your plumber to the Internal Revenue Service because he signs over your payment check to someone else, indicating that he may be avoiding taxes. "At home," Luger instructs, "observe your neighbors carefully, and note how they live. You may notice that one neighbor has a car that's apparently beyond his means, or that his wife wears a mink coat that makes you wonder how he can afford it on his salary." What may tempt you to accept this view of society as a nest of predatory spiders is the way it charges day-to-day living with the luminous heat of the hunter and the hunted: the new administrative assistant is a company spy; you can curry favor with the cops by squealing about the marijuana plants next door; somebody's asking how you vacationed in Hawaii. *Snitch* grants you a peepshow look at an underworld of dirty deals and betrayals just beneath the surface of your glad-handing, please-and-thank-you life. It's a world you fret over yet somehow long to wade into, prepped with savvy, and mastery. According to Luger, "The fundamental principle of security is information control."

A candidate for the flagship of the Loompanics and Paladin lines could be Victor Santoro's *Gaslighting: How to Drive Your Enemies Crazy*. Santoro, the author of several other titles on revenge, gets right to the matter: "The purpose of gaslighting isn't pure physical destruction, but destruction of your target's intangible assets: his confidence, self-esteem, and reputation. With just a little bit of luck, you can eventually reduce your target to a shapeless mass of shivering, quivering jelly."

The trickery Santoro outlines may range from fiendish—telling a male friend who has been sleeping with your wife that you are HIV-positive—to farcical—slipping an anti-abortion bumper sticker on a co-worker's car when his supervisor is a pro-choice advocate—but most of it falls within the familiar precincts of backstabbing. For instance, "Exposing a minority target's incompetence on the job," Santoro notes, "will have several healthy effects: It will justify the feeling that your target is holding his job only because of 'quota hiring.' He'll be frozen out socially, and fellow employees won't offer him the help they might provide to others having a difficult time at work.... Incompetence, if properly documented, can stand up as grounds for termination." Glaring bigotry aside, *Gaslighting* is quite funny in places. Consider the effort involved in thinking through what could be done with an enemy's unattended camera: "use it to take a close-up picture of an accomplice's genitals"—but the reader is ultimately creeped out by the instructions. People do write poison-pen letters, tape colleagues, make harassing phone calls, and get co-workers fired, and the book's utilitarian aspect therefore hits so close to home that there is something distasteful about buying it. I didn't bat an eye picking up my corpse disposal book at the neighborhood bookstore, but *Gaslighting* I preferred to receive through the mail.

Although often posed as "How can I hurt them?" the underlying question asked by Paladin and Loompanics titles is "How will they hurt me?" And perhaps this explains why these books seem to *require* an ironic response; anything else would be an admission that you are really afraid of someone disappearing on you, of being sucker-punched, of being poisoned, of being sent unprepared to a federal prison camp. Could it be that their popularity, rather than proving the vitality of an anti-government, survivalist movement, attests instead to a growing We-system of bedwetters, whose night terrors may be faced only between book covers?

In his 1964 essay "The Paranoid Style in American Politics," Richard Hofstadter notes that our various national anxiety attacks are marked by "this appearance of the most careful, conscientious, and seemingly coherent ... evidence for the most fantastic conclusions." The Loompanics-style how-to guides muster up just such a facade for suspicions both public and private. Their meticulous preparations against everything from nosy neighbors to nuclear war justify, indeed amplify, the very fears they seek to allay, so that, at best, holding on to Uncle Fester's rules of "good poisoning" becomes an act of bravado, announcing (to guests, to yourself) that you worry so little about a nerve-gas attack on the subway that you keep its recipe on your bookshelf.

*Be Your Own Undertaker* opens with this commonplace assessment: "In today's world, any person may, at any time, suddenly be subjected to a violent and probably senseless attack with no provocation. Given this sad fact, it is clear that self-defense must be taken seriously and may someday mean the difference between surviving such an attack and becoming a faceless, lifeless statistic." Regardless of whether there is "careful, conscientious, seemingly coherent evidence" for this view, we hear it all the time. Many people reject this worldview as too corrosive, a kind of self-poisoning, but others are drawn to its stark, Hobbesian candor. Are these the people who buy a Loompanics or Paladin book and then keep it around because it satisfies some need for a legible, navigable world? "Think before you act," advises Abaygo in *Fugitive*, "but trust your instincts. Learn the ways of nature. She will provide for he who takes what she offers—and strike down the man who hesitates." Trust your instincts—the ones that tell you to run, to hide, to lash out. You would never really do these things, of course—I mean, who would? But if, after it has outlived its usefulness as a coffee-table conversation piece, you hold on to that book about performing a contract murder, or getting rid of a corpse, or changing your identity, or ruining a colleague, or creating automobile weaponry, can you ever really be sure why?

*Harper's Magazine*, March 1999.

# In a Word: Jackson Mac Low Restlessly Reinvents the Line

At the poetry readings I attended around New York City in the '80s and '90s, a familiar figure often occupied the front row: an elfin gentleman with dramatic eyebrows and a great wave of hair to match. At my very first events, he drew notice because he sat with pen in hand, writing throughout the reading, as if he were taking dictation. I recall wondering if he was a journalist or another poet cribbing lines from his fellows. I soon learned that he was the legendary composer, performer, and poet Jackson Mac Low (1922–2004) and that in all likelihood he was culling words and phrases to deploy in the many recombination schemes he used to create his texts. With roots in the Fluxus movement and an early association with John Cage in the '50s, Mac Low emerged as one of the most rigorously adventurous American poets in the decades that followed. Not the least part of his unconventional profile was his energetic work across genres and art forms: writing poems and prose in diverse modes, composing and performing music, collaborating with theater and dance companies, and creating a body of visual art that might be said to incorporate something of each of these multifarious pursuits.

A sampling of that work—mostly done with pen or crayon on paper—is currently on view at the Drawing Center in a show titled "Lines–Letters–Words." The title is literally accurate in that it describes the pieces on display, which, indeed, depict lines, letters, and words. But the sequence of the terms makes the title especially apt, as it gets at the heart of Mac Low's enterprise as a poet and artist: understanding the construction of communication; that is, how mere lines are bent to configure something called letters and these letters are assembled to create that improbable result, a word. The sequence is equally relevant when run in reverse: for Mac Low, disaggregating meaning from sound, sound from words and letters, and ultimately from the random marks on a page achieved the same end: revealing the relation between meaning and its constituent parts.

The very bold strokes of the earliest pieces in the show—1947 through 1953—bear strong resemblance to the gestural work of Abstract Expressionists like Jackson Pollock and Franz Kline. Soon after, though, the inked strokes emerged, like figures in the carpet, as the beginnings of letters, and even elementary words can be discerned. In three untitled drawings from 1953, we can readily make out an *h*, an *if*, and *Hi*. From the sinuous chaos of lines, there is actual communication: a resonant preposition announcing possibility and a warm greeting. These pieces are hung in close proximity and offer a rarified gag, not unlike the cartoon that depicts evolution from ape to modern Homo sapiens. (In fact, another two pieces from this period present *Ape* and *Pie*, as if setting the alpha and omega of human progress.) All of these words are sizable, scrawled, set askew to the viewer, so the intensity of their depiction takes precedence over ready legibility. They are intended to be more felt than read.

This tactile, pronounced-aloud quality of the visualized word is carried forward in the drawings of the '60s, featuring handwritten poems or sentences or utterances (take your pick). Theatricality attends this script in its variability from thin to thick, print to cursive, small to large. These qualities, as well as the strategic arrangement of the letters and words, bring to mind the audible modulations of a musician or an actor. The drawing *What is a nail* crams the thickly rendered text "What is a nail. A nail is a unison" onto a standard letter-size piece of paper. The seeming question (there's no question mark, so perhaps it's a statement) and its apparent response are heard as if they've been shouted into a tiny box, each syllable's sound colliding with its successor. The effect sets the poem's delicately crafted enigma in contention with the bluntness of its clamorous voicing. Mac Low—whose texts were often meant to be performed and, truly, were best comprehended in that manner—has staged the words on these "pages" as carefully as a director blocks a complex scene.

A piece titled *Boxing* presents dozens of lines of cramped writing jammed in every which way and overwritten by a large phrase in loopy script that might be read as "nobody goes into the ring to knock out the other guy," but could also be "to knock out the other guy the ring nobody goes into." It's hard to say; the sheer amount of text and the complexity of the resulting spatial interactions offer more readings than any single viewing could accommodate. Some of the text is sideways and upside down, and I would have required a ladder or license to, as it's said, flip the script and fully assess the juxtapositions. Again, the paper size here isn't much more than a notebook leaf, a fact that encourages our sense that what we see is the product of some feverish spell of transcription. The prose itself is likely drawn—as Mac Low often did—from extant, carefully randomized sources. There's much in this piece on the subject of the sweet science, its abolition, its relation to combat, its presence on television, the phenomenon of the knockout—and then sundry incongruous lines ("Pouring Chanel Number Five over a dead mackerel" or "A youngster who did not like to adhere to routine"). It's like reading the transcripts of several simultaneous conversations. That I had to squint here, cock my head there to even take in some of the text made me think that maybe Mac Low was again connecting the visual and aural experiences by inviting behavior similar to what I'd do if I were trying to listen to one voice amid a welter of overtalk—leaning in or cupping my ear.

Mac Low's abiding interest in Buddhism and chance led him to a lifelong interest in process-driven composition as a way of eliminating the ego from the creative process. A series of drawings called "Gathas" employs such "nonintentional procedures," as the poet Sylvia Mae Gorelick describes them in the show's catalogue. The word *gatha* means "verse" or "hymn," and these pieces done on graph paper—each letter in its box—present "transliterated mantras." Thus, the resonant thrum of one titled *AUMMM Gatha* is recognizable even as the rigidity of the diagrammatic image both defamiliarizes and amplifies our understanding of this meditative vocable. Another piece that derives from Buddhist thought, *Om in a Landscape*, deploys the mantra in hundreds of minutely inscribed iterations, as if the syllables were insects swarming inside a consciousness. Again, the repetition may conjure the contemplative essence of the chant, but the chaotic array of *Om* upon *Om* suggests an insistence more unnerving than serene.

Drawings from the '70s and the most recent works return to Mac Low's earlier fascination as they leave off from whole words and sentences to investigate the foundational element of any written language—the line. While some of these works might initially appear to be reiterations of the Expressionist mode, they lack the gestural dynamism of that style. Instead, Mac Low brings scrupulous focus to bear on the line's shape, possibility, and presence. Not unlike the work of Sol LeWitt, these images manifest concentrated, rather than impulsive, energy. In a series titled "Skew Lines," Mac Low groups straight lines of various colors in pointedly oppositional arrangements. The lines—singly and in clusters—vibrate with the power of force fields, and I couldn't help noting a resemblance to the flow arrows representing attack and counterattack on a military map. The thought isn't entirely unconnected to the undeniable purposefulness of written communication: lines on a page, when formed into letters and then, say, into an essay, poem, or political slogan, do muster a kind of martial power. Words both invade the mind and offer its only defense.

In another group of drawings (several are titled as birthday poems for Mac Low's collaborator and partner Anne Tardos), the inchoate, wayward, permutational quality of the line is, as befitting the occasion, celebrated. The black pen's scribble in *Happy Birthday, Annie* is as wild as it is determined to obliterate the whiteness of the paper. The ghostly product of an equally untamed red pen can be seen threading through the dark tangle. Are these lines in a prelinguistic state searching for a form? Or perhaps lines freed from their bondage in sentences? Mac Low was always pressing such inquiries, looking for origins and consequences. All of these drawings testify to an ever-restless mind and pen, a pen that didn't merely employ language but performed its physicality. I was never able to spy out what Mac Low was putting to the page during those readings—it may have been overheard talk, a line from the poet on stage, a phrase from someone's T-shirt, or a dash becoming a line about to become a letter. What I couldn't have seen—what Mac Low saw—was its sound hovering just above the paper.

*Paris Review Daily*, March 1, 2017.

# The Bookness of Not-Books

I once owned a hardback edition of Somerset Maugham's *The Moon and Sixpence* that had served time at the top of a bedside pile; its cover and spine had acquired several islands of melted wax from the candle it helped support. Running my fingers from the smooth dollops to the grainy fabric—an illegible but sensual braille—always afforded a small pleasure, even if the reading itself offered much less. That long-ago volume came to mind recently while holding a copy of an artist's book by Deborah Dancy titled *Winter Morning* in the rare-book room of the Baltimore Museum of Art. Dancy's slim book is made from wax-impregnated paper into which snippets of found text have been pressed. Light as wafer, the book almost floated in my hands, and turning its stiff, deeply yellowed pages felt like exploring a precious archaeological artifact.

I was fortunate to handle this rare and fragile *objet* at the invitation of Rena Hoisington, a curator at the Baltimore Museum of Art, where she mounted the current show "Off the Shelf: Modern and Contemporary Artists' Books." The extensive range of artists and writers includes, among many others, Grace Hartigan, Pablo Picasso, Frank O'Hara, Ed Ruscha, Wassily Kandinsky, Susan Howe, Vladimir Mayakovsky, Barbara Kruger, Robert Creeley, Kiki Smith, and, of course, the master of the artist's book, the Swiss Conceptualist Dieter Roth. Equally wide is the breadth of approach: from Ruscha, there is an edition of *Twentysix Gasoline Stations*, the photos printed on an accordion-folded sheet in the order they appeared on Route 66, going west to east; from Barbara Kruger and Stephen King, a large-format volume with a stainless-steel cover and an embedded digital clock; from three authors—Pier Paolo Pasolini, Luisa Famos, Andri Peer—and the artist Not Vital, a series of poems written in Rhaeto-Romansh (the national language of Switzerland) and printed on pages custom made from cedar bark that sport attached objects, such as a saw blade. The rich variety of constructions and materials, as well as the methods of representing text—thickly rendered in paint, printed in chaotic typefaces, scrawled across images—beckons the viewer to reach out and touch.

If there is a single operating instruction for any book, it has to be "Turn pages." But the art part of an artist's book makes exercising that common function a privileged experience. Like most paintings, prints, or sculptures, these books are inherently delicate and typically produced in limited editions. Curators can't just set them out on table with tiny chains like they often do for exhibition catalogues; museumgoers are restricted to one or two (presumably well-chosen) pages under glass, with no opportunity to touch, for instance, the woody grain of that paper made from cedar bark or graze the metallic coolness of Kruger's cover. One of the books on display is a beat-up suitcase that Dieter Roth filled with six enlarged and laminated lithographs based on postcard images of London's Piccadilly Circus that were silkscreened over with his abstract designs. Straightforwardly titled *6 Piccadillies*, the piece possesses qualities of a series of prints, but also sculpture (one is overlaid with iron filings), a book (you open the case to find "pages"), postcards (meant to be written on, stuck on walls), and, well, luggage (the bag is ID-tagged for travel). These elements compete within our response, suggesting as they do both ready utility and restrained regard, even as we are guided by the artist's comic intent, a joke about the function of art that reaches back to Marcel Duchamp's *Fountain*.

A similar jest emerges from an encounter with another book in the show, a collaboration between Francesco Clemente and the Italian author Alberto Savinio titled *The Departure of the Argonaut*. Clemente's lithographs cover the entire page, often obscuring Savinio's translated account of his experiences in and around the Mediterranean during

World War I. The text references the Greek myth of Jason and the Argonauts, and the imagery, at least the spread on view—depicts a seemingly heroic human figure who bestrides the pages, the gutter neatly bisecting the body. Even if not encased in a vitrine, the book would be a difficult one to peruse: it's enormous, measuring more than three feet in width when open and more than two in height. Surely not intended for the beach or bedside, the book calls to other employments: the corporeal image and overall capaciousness may invite you to slip into its pages and wrap them around you like a cloak. But reading—in any typical sense of the activity—isn't easily accomplished; this book subverts its very nature.

Our reaction to these artists' books moves along the continuum between seeing and reading. Included are Barry Moser's wood engravings for Lewis Carroll's *Alice's Adventures in Wonderland* and Mark Twain's *Adventures of Huckleberry Finn*, both of which could be said to fall into the more common category of illustrated books. These images serve to enhance the text, to make our reading experience more literal, more detailed, and perhaps more comprehensible. (Of course, many argue that such visual aids, like film adaptations, in fact encumber the imagination.) This sort of book—at least in its mass-market edition—is meant to be handled and read, its images checked against our visualizations. When the art part of the book—the possessive in the "artist's book" is telling—becomes increasingly salient, the experience of the text can become subordinate to the experience of the visual and even end up almost incidental. (In *The End of the World as Filmed by the Angel of Notre Dame*, Blaise Cendrars's words, when exploded in a variety of typefaces and colors, are hardly distinguishable from Fernand Léger's colliding shapes, which appear throughout the collaborative volume.) These are books and pages intended to be seen but not necessarily read.

That the volume produced by Picasso and Surrealist poet Pierre Reverdy—*Le chant des morts, poèmes* (*The Song of the Dead, Poems*)—lands somewhere in the middle of this continuum probably has much to do with their collaborative process. The poems were handwritten by the author, and elegantly so. The accompanying caption relates how

Picasso, after seeing a sample of the text, remarked that the cursive was "almost a drawing in itself." His brushed additions of bright red nodules, looping shapes, and circles occupy the empty areas of the pages, rarely trespassing on Reverdy's script. The poems are legible, and the artist's approach to the text could almost be said to mimic that of an undergraduate annotating their textbook: Picasso underlines and parenthesizes with bold strokes that respond to the emotional tenor of particular lines. He said he avoided figurative imagery so that he wouldn't interfere with the "curved quality" of the poetry; in doing so, he deferred to the bookness of the collaboration.

Alas, those eminently readable pages go unturned in their case. But in the library with Rena, I was able (carefully, my potentially messy pen replaced with a pencil) to page through a luxurious volume that combined Robert Motherwell's art and Rafael Alberti's poem "Motherwell's Black." The book is complexly built with foldout pages and irresistibly touchable deckle-edged parchment and thickly inked with swaths of color; its material essence is palpable and therefore meaningful. Turning each page involves removing a protective sheet of paper and slowly unfolding the sheet to full size. The ritualistic quality of our "reading" suggested occasions in a distant past when books were rare and one-of-a-kind, when reading was done at a podium in cloistered circumstances (think depictions of Saint Jerome) or in churches with high ceremony. We moved through the book, enthralled yet deliberate as its allure evolved from page to page. Later, back in the gallery looking at the beautiful array of barely opened volumes under glass, I felt even more forlorn, wondering about the unseen pages, the unfelt textures. But knowing myself to be the sort of person who has stained nearly every tie I've owned, I was also glad these beauties were out of harm's way. Spilling wax on a two-dollar used book created a homey curio. I doubt some errant contribution to a Picasso would cause as much delight.

*Paris Review Daily*, June 22, 2017.

# Nonsense and Sensibility: The Absurd Humor of Glen Baxter

Opinion about the English sense of humor can prove a handy means of cleaving any social gathering into two mutually uncomprehending factions—those that think it exists and those that don't. Despite the debate's rather low stakes (this isn't surveillance versus security), it is a revealing one, personality-wise, and if you've ever labored to convince someone that *Monty Python*'s fish-slapping dance *is* funny, you know the gap in sensibilities isn't trivial. Glen Baxter's drawings, which have been collected in over twenty books since the late '70s, amply evidence his native clime's tradition of nonsense and just plain silliness—from Lewis Carroll and Edward Lear to P.G. Wodehouse and Benny Hill—and in doing so cause bafflement as easily as belly laughs. The very first cartoon in a new volume—*Almost Completely Baxter*—of the cartoonist's work exemplifies the effect: Viewed from behind, three young men inspect the darkened entrance of a cave; if the kitchen utensils they wear on their heads are immediately apparent, the fluffy dog tails that sprout through the backsides of their pants are not. (Realized by the same quick dashes that articulate the folds on their suits, the tails are nearly camouflaged, so we see them via a double-take.) The text in most cartoons would at least hint at an explanation of the almost otherworldly scene, but here we have only a deadpan declaration: "It was precisely six-fifteen."

Baxter's comic realm—the space between image and text, between perplexity and the mundane—is a locale where uncertainty emerges as weird and weirdness recedes into uncertainty. The funny arrives as a slow-motion detonation that seems to dissipate as quickly as it boomed. This disquieting physics is surely the reason that Baxter has found a ready audience among the literati. In 1974, he gave a reading at St. Mark's Church in the East Village "before an audience of poets, painters, and filmmakers," he recounts in this volume's introduction. "I stood at the lectern, dressed in a tweed suit, and began to speak. People burst into spontaneous laughter. I had arrived." (The cheeky essay, though attributed to one Marlin Canasteen, a former "Security Advisor at the Bolick Mandolin Conservatory Society," is clearly Baxter's own.) Since that New York debut, his drawings, with their erudite nods to Dada and Surrealism, as well as allusions to mid-20th-century popular culture, have been regarded as a kind of visual poetry. Frequent comparisons to René Magritte and Edward Gorey aptly note the philosophical and satirical elements at play in Baxter's humor; but his drollery is warmer, more gemütlich, owing to his affection for old movies (particularly Westerns and adventure flicks) and his apparent nostalgia for the hairstyles, clothes, and home décor of 1940s Britain. His world could be lifted whole from an Ealing Studios soundstage—pith helmets, sweater vests, fireplace mantels, and properly stodgy actors, too, all rendered in busy, typically colorless line work that deepens the vintage feel by evoking cartoons from that era. (Even Baxter's nickname, Colonel Baxter, conjures an association with Colonel Blimp, the bloviating English military man in David Low's satiric comics from the '30s and '40s.)

These staid and tweedy scenarios, however, are always upended by Baxter's anarchic invention: In one of his rare color drawings, a distinguished gentleman, bald, with box tie and cigar, sits with his tea setting by a picture window through which snow can be seen falling. As he reaches into his jacket pocket to retrieve, most likely, a pair of spectacles or a handkerchief, a chap in short pants, perhaps his nephew or protégé, plays the violin. The expression on each man's face bespeaks nothing more than the comfy equanimity of a winter evening in a well-appointed home. The narration, though, has another tale in mind: "Slowly," it reads, "but with unerring precision, Dr.

Tuttle reached for his Luger." The cozy image—the vacant yet kindly look on the older man's face, his placid, deportment in an ornate chair, the sprinkle of snow and almost audible violin notes—takes on an entirely new meaning when you read the text, which presents the sudden specter of not only a gun but a German World War II weapon. This, along with the imposition of "unerring precision" on the languid composition, is as shocking as it is ridiculous—like a blood-curdling scream uttered by a grown-up on a teacup ride. When governed by his sly caption, Baxter's scene, familiar from any number of English films set in country homes, grows comically sinister: The doctor's calm suddenly resembles a psychopath's deliberation, while the younger man's innocent focus on his instrument acquires the pathos of his imminent victimhood.

But not quite. The stock quality of the tableau and the carefully deployed language (is there a more harmless-sounding moniker than "Tuttle"? A grimmer lineage for a handgun?) announce their contrivance. The joke relies on our awareness of the artifice and a familiarity with its cultural references. (*Monty Python*'s Proust-summarizing contest isn't a hoot unless you at least know that there's a lot of Proust to summarize.) This is humor that is both knowing and nonsensical, sparking laughter that depends on a savvy apprehension of details (the teapot, the short pants, Tuttle's resemblance to Churchill) even as its mainspring is improbable, gruesome, and downright goofy.

Marcel Duchamp's learnedly obscene subversions come to mind, and it's no surprise that a young Baxter—attuned to the French artist's droll seriousness—once wrote him in hope of obtaining a catalogue of his work. Baxter gleaned from Duchamp a sense of language's malleability, the function of repurposing, and the power of the enigmatic. Indeed, in explicit homage to Duchamp's kinetic works and readymades, Baxter invents and recombines objects: a cane with a lightbulb, giant teeth, a club-size pen attached to orthodontic headgear, and an assortment of implausible-looking machines imported, it seems, from *Flash Gordon* comics. Odd viewing contraptions proliferate. In one panel, a policeman has detained a motorcyclist and points an object—what could be a tiny telescope or flashlight inexplicably mounted on a display platform—toward the chest pocket he's unbuttoning: "'I'm afraid I'm going to have to show you my nipple, young lad,' announced the constable gravely." With its peephole, lamp, and spied-out nudity, Duchamp's infamous *Étant donnés* is the unavoidable reference, one Baxter employs, it could be suggested, to shrewdly mock the prudish reaction that greeted the work when it was first displayed at the Philadelphia Museum of Art in 1969.

This mischievous tack often tweaks the pieties of the art and literary worlds: underneath the depiction of a man roped to a tree in a gloomy forest, we read, "Edgar had attended many a poetry evening." A cowboy with a gun drawn breaks up a fight: "'We'll have no alliteration in this here bunkhouse,' snorted McCulloch." Two children in bathrobes carrying an old-fashioned lamp stumble on a family secret: "Daddy seemed to be running a lucrative little sideline churning out Mondrians." And tagging Monty Python's Proust routine, a pair of Western mountain men observe smoke signals in the distance: "'It's the second chapter of *À la recherche du temps perdu*' explained Big Jake." While Baxter's staged collisions of high, low, and middle usually work, they are sometimes less than pointed. At book length, they begin to feel perfunctory: His wit is best enjoyed not in extended sittings but rather, as is the case with much waggish art, in small doses.

An ideal example of an image whose dire-to-daft transit makes for evergreen laughter presents a barren landscape marked by a few boulders, great tumbling clouds, and birds wheeling among them. At first, we might mistake the two objects at the bottom of the panel for more rocks, but they are the heads of men who have been gagged and buried up to their necks. The strong filial association with Samuel Beckett's Nell and Nagg, who peek out from trash cans in *Endgame*, casts an existential spell on the scene, but the grim reality of such a torturous death isn't negated by the literary ideation—it is a genuinely unnerving moment rather than one of Baxter's campy outtakes from *Brief Encounter* with parlor lamps and pocket squares. Or at least until you catch the caption: "The summer term was always a bitter disappointment." Lickety-split, the viewer departs the desert, the circling carrion birds, the inevitable demise from heat and suffocation, to land in the faculty lounge, where tiny annoyances are regularly inflated into episodes of epic suffering. And there, between dying in the dust and cursing the copy machines, Glen Baxter finds his mark.

*Bookforum*, April–May 2016.

# Bruce Nauman: The True Artist

As one of the contemporary art world's pre-eminent jesters, Bruce Nauman is hardly a barrel of laughs; known as much for his deadpan wit as for his dire take on mortality, his art engages bleak themes (the failure of language; the body's betrayals; the repetitive, claustrophobic nature of daily life) even as it sparks a knowing, gallows grimace. How else to react to, say, *Sex and Death/Double '69,'* one of his trademark neon sculptures, which arrays four figures of indeterminate gender in an arrangement (two hang down between two standing) felicitous for simultaneous oral and genital copulation by both pairs? The iconography may owe a debt to high school bathrooms, but the tension between the pulsing colors and the matter-of-fact postures of these doleful sybarites evokes the title's universal and enduring linkage, as well as the more particular moment of its creation at the beginning of the AIDS crisis in 1985. The scary sense that the core of our human enterprise may be nothing more than a garish amusement park diversion feels inescapable—and as such, we are invited to grin and bear it.

*Bruce Nauman: The True Artist* offers the fullest survey yet of this protean artist's work. Still, even with its numerous reproductions of Nauman's sculpture, photographs, and drawings, the volume necessarily falls short of adequately representing his videos, performances, and installations (included stills and photos must suffice), and that is no small issue for an artist whose efforts in those media are regarded by many critics as decisively influential. Indeed, it's impossible to talk about the careers of any number of contemporary video artists without referring to

Nauman. Peter Plagens's accompanying text takes smart measure of that current relevance, while also providing a detailed account of Nauman's aesthetic evolution in California during the 1960s. A longtime art critic for *Newsweek* who kept a studio in the same Los Angeles neighborhood as Nauman, Plagens bolsters his strong art history chops with a memoirist's site-specific insights. He recalls his early ambivalence—"Nauman's art bothered me. It was both psychologically and culturally threatening, and the very fact that it bothered me bothered me"—and notes that his first reviews of the artist were negative. This first-person, journalistic tack is a welcome approach to an artist who often attracts jargon-fond academics.

That's not to say Nauman doesn't warrant high-energy contemplation; his vigorous connections to, say, Ludwig Wittgenstein and Samuel Beckett animate his representations of language's doubleness and the intrinsically slapstick nature of repetition. The philosopher's influence marks a 1967 sculpture titled *From Hand to Mouth* that literalizes the locution by presenting a disembodied, snakelike hand, arm, shoulder, neck, chin, and mouth. The macabre object undermines the commonplace quality of the expression by charging its conventional meaning with corporeal fact: To live hand-to-mouth is to be hungry, perhaps feeble. Plagens notes how "like Beckett, Nauman was compelled to exteriorize these troubling thoughts" and finds that the incessant permutations of the famous "sucking stone" passage from Molloy "in cadence and content parallel Nauman's way of artistic thinking."

The kinship is borne out as if scripted by the Irish author in *Clown Torture*, a 1987 video installation featuring four monitors and two video projections set in a darkened space on which audiences watch perpetual loops of a clown screaming "No," opening a booby-trapped door, balancing a fishbowl on the end of a broom, and retelling the same joke. Loud, abrasive, and disturbing, the "torture" the clown endures isn't funny. But it is. Or at least we are, as we stand there in the dark, subjecting ourselves to what Plagens calls the "pointless seriousness—or serious pointlessness" that makes Nauman's art a test of our tolerance for his grim vision.

*New York Times Book Review*, December 5, 2014.

# Made Men of Letters: Our Thing about the Cosa Nostra

Walking through Greenwich Village a few years ago, I passed Vincent "Chin" Gigante, the reputed boss ("reputed" being the decorous fig leaf of technical innocence) of the Genovese crime family in New York City. A shrunken old man in bathrobe and slippers, with unbrushed hair and a clueless stare, he stood in a shop doorway, shielded by a trio of beef slabs in knit shirts who scuffed the sidewalk and smoked. I gave them all a wide berth, tamping down the urge to gape openly at this wizened former boxer who once weighed 300 pounds and now shuffled around these streets like a punch-drunk has-been. His bulked-up associates looked like planets that had no choice but to orbit a collapsed star. Prosecutors had long maintained that Gigante's addled state was a ruse to keep him out of court—a successful one until he was ruled competent to stand trial last year and convicted this July of racketeering and conspiracy to murder. As I passed "Chin" that afternoon, I felt a slight yet unmistakable rush. It was the excitement, I'm sure, of seeing someone famous. But it was also that rarer frisson, the one you get from seeing a killer.

And how we love that shiver. Especially when the murderers dress in black, wield a mean Fifth Amendment, and have a taste for great scungilli. Especially when they are Mafia. One need only check the literary record to measure our devotion: a flood of novels, confessionals, histories, and true-crime books (the Library of Congress lists several hundred Mob-related titles), and still every season sees an Explosive

New Tell-All Mafia Thriller. Indeed, if the Mafia owned a copyright on itself, the Men of Respect wouldn't need to make a killing, except on the bookrack. And, of course, at the box office.

Mob stories fall out as either myth or countermyth. Fiction necessarily belongs in the first category, and report, biography, and confessionals, in the second. If novelists deliver operatic killers, dressed for the stage, true-crime books promise the real lowdown, passed on by Mobsters, their kids, ex-cops, or anyone currently in the Witness Protection Program. The very salable notion that a web of mystery—specifically, *omertà,* the Sicilian code of silence—is being swept away is what drives nonfiction Mafiana. In *Mafia Princess,* Chicago boss Sam Giancana was plumbed in print by his daughter; Nicholas Pileggi has gleaned two bestsellers, *Wiseguy* and *Casino,* from former Mafia associates Henry Hill and Frank Rosenthal; onetime FBI agent Joseph Pistone penned *Donnie Brasco,* a behind-the-polyester-curtain account of his time undercover; and in *Joe Dogs: The Life & Crimes of a Mobster,* Joseph Iannuzzi tells the salutary tale of how he ratted out his Mob buddies to get revenge for being beaten half to death. Indeed, '90s Mob guys are so market savvy that you can almost imagine them breaking someone's legs, then going home to work it into their pitch.

And then there is *The Godfather*. Mario Puzo's book (and Francis Ford Coppola's movie) is the benchmark for all literary Mafias, but it is Mob nonfiction that measures itself most aggressively against *The Godfather*'s mythmaking. The writers of these books know that their audience is looking for the myth to be stripped away, and the result is a peculiar form of literary self-consciousness: Former FBI agent William F. Roemer Jr. titled his recent book *Accardo: The Genuine Godfather*. The first sentence of *Killer: Autobiography of a Mafia Hitman,* by "Joey," is "Fuck *The Godfather*."

The Mafia has sung for its supper since its inception in America, the lure of celebrity handily overwhelming centuries of tradition. After setting the standard for gangster-as-media-showboat, holding press conferences and even turning up on the cover of *Time* magazine, Capone pitched his autobiography to wary New York editors (this was, after all, 1930) and later considered converting his notoriety into cash by becoming an evangelist. Even a solid, tucked-under-the-brim guy like Charles "Lucky" Luciano, an architect of the modern Mafia and the first *capo di tutti capi*, caught the bug. During his last years in exile in Naples, he collaborated on a screenplay about his life that was about to go into production when he was strongly advised to forget it by certain critics back in New York. In 1980, Mafia capo Joseph Bonanno did, in fact, write his autobiography—*A Man of Honor*—in which he detailed the entire structure of New York's Five Families, providing authentic inside dope that fueled prosecutors for years. Upon the book's publication, Gambino family *consiglière* Joe Gallo offered his close reading on an FBI tape: "It makes you wonder. Is this son of a bitch senile, or is he just a fucking nut? ... This is a new kind of plea bargain, or what? Go to the slammer or write your memoirs and make your friends look lousy?"

But perhaps the biggest secret spilled in these books is that criminal life is, apparently, a bore. FBI agent Pistone recounts the epic tedium that reigned in the back room of a Brooklyn storefront where "half ass" wiseguys played gin and bullshitted for hours on end: "The Mob was their job. You got up, went to the club or wherever you hung out, and spent your day with those guys." Even for the bosses the high life ain't so high. In *Wiseguy*, Henry Hill recalls Mob boss Paul Vario putting a surveillance camera outside the window of his Brooklyn apartment: "He used to sit on the bed in his underwear for hours trying to spot G-men. 'There's one,' he'd say. 'The guy behind the tree. Didja see him?'" The reader is often left with the impression that Mafiosi are pretty much just stressed-out collection agency hacks with terrible tempers.

This is not quite the outlaw fantasy you call upon while sitting at your desk sorting through yesterday's Post-it notes. What you want is something like Elmore Leonard's *Get Shorty* or George Dawes Green's *The Juror*, both recent Mafia novels starring preternaturally cool enforcers who could burn a hole through a pad of Post-its with a glance.

In *The Juror*, Green gives us "the Teacher," a Mob killer/philosopher/aesthete who is as likely to be found sitting in a half-lotus position as torturing someone with an electric cattle prod. He tells one bloodied victim, "If your spirit ran *with* the Tao, I swear to you that no bliss could elude you." The Teacher wields a lordly omnipotence, assuring a female juror in a Mafia trial, "Anywhere. End of the earth, we'll find you." This is the gangster as Dark Angel, who, like Milton's Satan, is fascinatingly evil. The all-too-real "Joe Dogs" hardly fascinates, but he does know how to win friends and influence people:

> "[I)f you don't do what I tell you, I'll kill your father. I won't kill you, but I'll maim you. And you will have to live with the fact that you got your father killed. We will even let your mother live, but let her know the reason her husband got killed."

Sure, he may be blowing smoke, but he can afford to do it sans style, in much the same way that he orders confederates to teach someone a lesson: "I told the spades to break one leg, smash the knuckles on his right hand, and blacken both eyes." No grandiose threat or Taoist hoodoo here; this beating is strictly business.

Although explicit commands may get results, they read too clunkily for the skillful novelist. Elmore Leonard's Chili Palmer, in *Get Shorty,* is a winsome, gentle shylock who rarely raises an angry hand. Instead, his technique is the deftly tuned psyche-out: "You never tell the guy what could happen to him. Let him use his imagination, he'll think of something worse." In answer to the question "Who the fuck are you?" he's ready with the cryptic yet threatening "I'm the one telling you how it is," which sounds a lot like God's tough-guy reply—"I am that I am"—to Moses. Garbed in natural fabrics, Chili and the Teacher are well-rounded, articulate achievers and thus suitable as objects of projection for middle-class power fantasies, unlike the *fuhgedaboudit* knuckle draggers most nonfiction books deliver. Mafia fiction offers the eloquent threat, one you might air out while pushing for a raise; Mafia fact serves up body parts in garbage bags.

Still, whether delighting in the romance of the Cosa Nostra or a grittier workaday syndicate, fans recognize the Mob for the meta-story it is—one that provides a frame for dozens of other cozily familiar yarns, many of them about belonging. Think of mobsters testifying in a courtroom or before Congress, always accompanied by labyrinthine charts tracing the hierarchy of Mafia families, the *capos,* and their *caporegimes.* The balance of power in this shadow government readily compels attention because we can't help but wonder, as we might about Bohemian Grove or Yale's Skull and Bones, not only how you get in but how you get the cool nickname.

That's why the initiation ritual is such a staple of Mafia storytelling. Its details were first revealed by turncoat Joe Valachi in his 1968 confessional narrative, written by Peter Maas and published as *The Valachi Papers*. Sat down in 1930 by then boss Salvatore Maranzano (a punctilious, erudite man who read Julius Caesar in Latin and had once studied for the priesthood), Valachi was shown a gun and a knife and told in Italian, "This represents that you live by the gun and the knife … and you die by the gun and the knife." Next, Maranzano set fire to a picture of a saint and put it in Valachi's cupped hands and had him repeat, "This is the way I will burn if I betray the secret of this Cosa Nostra." Finally, his trigger finger was pricked with a pin to create a blood bond with his new family. In *Underboss: Sammy the Bull Gravano's Story of Life in the Mafia*, Maas elicited much the same tale from another eventual turncoat, whose ceremony took place nearly fifty years later. A portentous mix of ethnic hokum and kid stuff, these hieratic rites spark the imagination in part because these "made men" can be so handy with an ice pick. But the rituals owe their effectiveness to more than blood; the shadows and accented whispers invest mere greed and viciousness with the illusion of meaning as surely as the ever-popular "kiss of death" bestowed upon traitorous friends recalls the betrayal of Christ.

A tribe with rituals must have a sacred language, and Mafia authors, even those with tin ears, can't help but chime out the gruff jangle of *dese* and *dose*. At its most inventive, Mobspeak is a poetry of the oblique. The very name Cosa Nostra translates simply as "this thing of ours." (Present here is a level of devious abstraction) "Whacking" better connotes the paddling of a coddler than it does six shots to the back of the head. "Clipping" a rival means more than a little off the top. To corrupt a judge or jury member, someone "makes the reach," a mechanical yet metaphorically apt way of noting the gulf between being "in the life" and out of it. "Made guys," or "button men," know how to identify a fellow member to another made guy as a "friend of ours" and a nonmember as merely "a friend of mine."

Such neutral, prosecutor-proof vocabulary often produces a Dr. Seuss-like phraseology. Seventh-grade dropout Capone, we learn in Laurence Bergreen's biography, could craft beauties: about a self-important mobster he had eliminated, he quipped, "his head got away from his hat." Hit man Gravano is no slouch either. Of his duties for Gotti, he says, "John barked and I bit." Mafia fiction can hardly outdo this telegraphic eloquence. Puzo, in *The Last Don,* gets carried away with his gangland patois, coining overtly symbolic terms like "Communion" for murdered bodies that disappear and "Confirmation" for those left to be found. Real Mobspeak is somewhat more direct: "You tell this punk," Gotti once announced on an FBI tape, "I, me, John Gotti ... will sever your motherfucking head off! You cocksucker!"

An undeniable humor attends the oxymoron of law-abiding mayhem—the idea that baseball bat pummeling, dope peddling, and loansharking should all be carried out with businesslike vigor, with an eye toward public relations and the bottom line; that, as Capone sagely opined at a press conference, "there is enough business for all of us without killing each other like animals in the streets." Valachi recalled the expulsion of many Mob guys in the late '50s for being "unfit": "twenty-seven contracts ... ended in complete misses, slight wounds, and bodies being left around in the street." Henry Hill points out a macabre attempt at etiquette in *Wiseguy,* noting how, when one mobster's son was whacked for misbehaving, the executioners "left the kid's face clean so there could be an open casket at the funeral." The broken-toothed gears of mobster ethics allow innocence and malignancy to coexist peacefully in the same conscience, and because Mafia evil appears safely sealed within its own world, unconnected to ours, we can laugh at the gangster's moral bifurcation in a way that we cannot when presented with stories about, say, Himmler being a wonderful father. True evil, we seem to feel, demands a familiar victim—specifically, one of us. But as long as the wiseguys are killing other wiseguys, that's entertainment.

Rule busting is a national birthright, and we reserve a particular affection for rebels with a cause—especially if that cause is cash. As Hill puts it, "Anyone who stood waiting his turn on the American pay line was beneath contempt. To wiseguys, 'working guys' were already dead." However, since most of us are on that line, we do expect the nobler virtues to be paid some lip service. Perhaps this is why, in movies and novels, the antisocial attitude gets muted, if not turned inside out, when Mafia bosses are portrayed as pillars of the community. Forever doling out such Dale Carnegie platitudes as "friendship is everything" or "a man who is not a father to his children can never be a real man," Puzo's Don Corleone could easily be a GOP candidate for the U.S. Senate. After all, he's for unrestrained capitalism, family values, and the death penalty. Capone, a rags-to-riches bootstrapper who beat two men to death with a bat, once bragged, "I have always been a Republican, and my young men are 100 percent Republicans." Mafiosi are tough on crime too—at least other people's. After FBI agents stole back a car that Mob killer "Lefty Guns" Ruggiero had stolen from them, Pistone recalls Lefty's angry *cri de coeur*: "Fucking Puerto Ricans! They musta seen the Christmas presents in the back seat, that's why they took it." He sounds like the stock suburbanite on the evening news shaking his head woefully and saying, "This used to be such a nice place to live." After all, the theft took place near Manhattan's Little Italy, a locale generally thought to be watched over by an unseen, all-seeing eye.

Most mobsters aren't getting over on the straight world to the extent that the loss of some Christmas presents doesn't sting. Except for the top *capos*, your average Mafia soldier puts in long hours for highly speculative returns, without medical benefits, pension, or sick leave. If he's a "good earner," he's expected to pass a substantial "piece" on up the family tree. Hence, the Mob tale embraces another irresistible saga—that of the haves and have-nots. "All these big puffers with their cigars and pinkie rings," Pistone quotes one crypto Marxist hood complaining, "they're taking down all the money. It's gotta change." Capeci and Mustain detail up-and-coming Gotti's resentment at Paul Castellano, the brother-in-law of the legendary Don Carlo Gambino, for having inherited his position. Castellano was born to Mafia royalty, while Gotti grew up dirt poor, one of thirteen children, in the South Bronx. His rise from a tenement to the cover of *Time* is a Horatio Alger tale, except for the less-than-inspirational fact that his ascent was achieved via six bullets to Castellano's head.

The tabloids and television news alike celebrated Gotti's entrepreneurial panache. One newspaper deemed him a "frontier risk-taker"; another suggested that he be named superintendent of schools. And the public agreed: he was asked for his autograph in restaurants and eventually received thousands of fan letters in jail. In gangland, class struggle isn't a frustrating, incremental process that takes decades; rather, it's swift, decisive, and dressed in blood. For a grudge-holding, perennially snubbed citizenry, the Mafia story enacts an effective path to social change. In *Wiseguy*, Pileggi describes the best candidates for criminal success:

> They were not the smartest kids in the neighborhood. They were not born the richest. They weren't even the toughest. In fact, they lacked almost all the necessary talents that might have helped them satisfy the appetites of their dreams, except one—their talent for violence.

It is the Mafia boss's unreflective exercise of primitive will that makes him a figure of epic stature, and stories about men with that singular character flaw—Capone, Luciano, Giancana, Costello, Gambino, and Gotti—link us to tales once told by firelight of underworld wraiths and vengeance. Since Homer, the "hit" has been one of the hardest-working gimmicks in showbiz, one that serves comedy as ably as drama because it is seen as a push-button affair, free of psychological complexities. Woody Allen's *Bullets Over Broadway* hardly dims when a Mafia hit man ices his boss's girlfriend because she's a bad actress. Billy Wilder's *Some Like It Hot* features not one but *two* group executions with no discernible ebb in the chuckles.

In both drama and true crime, the ceremonial staging of the hit cloaks the ugliness of the deed. What we recall about the killings in Coppola's *Godfather* is their cinematic grace—a baptism crosscut with machine-gun fire—while Capeci and Mustain's account of the Castellano rubout fascinates because its military precision is coupled with farcical detail: the hit men wore "identical tan trench coats and Cossack-like fur hats." Like witnesses to the crime, we remember only the strange garb, not the killers' faces, and not the two men—fathers, husbands—dead in the street. But beneath the theatricality lies a deeper pull: our distinct suspicion that these petty, money-grubbing turf wars are, in fact, exemplars of a timeless battle, one properly devoid of morality's window dressing and pared down to Darwinian essentials. Mafia stories provide a rigged moral measuring stick by reassuring us that life truly is nasty, brutish, and short, and thus affording us forgiveness for our own shortcomings. After all, what's a little tax chiseling or extra-marital sex compared with cold-blooded murder?

Most closely resembling a monarch, the Mafia boss conjures images that are decidedly pre-democratic. Whenever Gambino appeared in a cafe in Little Italy, a crowd would immediately form outside. One by one, supplicants would pass through bodyguards to approach the Boss of Bosses with their request. Restaged as the memorable opening scene in Coppola's film, the narrative antecedent for this audience of petitioners lies in both regal history and Arthurian legend. Albert Anastasia, New York's "Lord High Executioner" in the 1930s and '40s, ruled with such increasing capriciousness that he was eventually dethroned. He happened to be watching television one night when he saw news of a young Brooklyn man who had spotted the notorious bank robber Willie Sutton after seeing his wanted poster. "I hate squealers!" Anastasia screamed, and he instructed one of his men to "hit" the guy. The pointless, attention-grabbing murder was condemned by Anastasia's fellow bosses, who subsequently had "Lord High" gunned down in a barbershop. We've heard this story before, of course, only the angry sovereign was Henry II and his victim was Thomas à Becket.

In this age of political and judicial paralysis, the appeal of a despot hardly surprises. In September 1995, after Gigante's ninety-four-year-old mother was mugged in Greenwich Village, the remorseful suspect apologized in court through his lawyer, saying he was "sorry the situation occurred and he acknowledges that it was wrong." The newspapers, one of which dubbed him the "Nitwit mugger," presented the case humorously and with the assumption that while the legal system could barely elicit admissions of guilt, let alone apologies, an old man in pajamas could surely make those trains run on time. No doubt most readers nodded knowingly at this piece of news, not only confirming the mystique of the Mafia boss but also signaling some small yearning for a draconian king. Who wouldn't want to live in a town where the muggers say they're sorry?

The Mafia's ability to intimidate effortlessly is perhaps its most potent and theatrical lure. In *Get Shorty*, Chili Palmer gives a movie star a lesson in giving "the look," telling him, "Put it in your eyes, 'You're mine, asshole,' without saying it." The actor gets it wrong and Chili remonstrates,

> "You're squinting, like you're trying to look mean or you need glasses. Look at me. I'm thinking, You're mine, I fuckin' own you. What I'm not doing is feeling anything about it one way or the other. You understand? You're not a person to me."

Of course, if you just want to spook your opponent, you can turn on the old *malocchio*, the evil eye. When Gravano testified against Gotti, a young man who had once been very close to the turncoat was sent into the courtroom to glare at him. Prosecutors took this threat seriously enough to force the young man back to the second row and have federal agents block his view. All this heavy eye contact may recall high school drama club productions, but the self-conscious spectacle of gangsters mimicking De Niro mimicking them testifies to the dizzying power of Mob entertainment. After all, the evil-eye bit in the Gotti trial appeared to be inspired by a scene in *The Godfather*. And Gotti's trial, much to the Dapper Don's delight, was attended by Mickey Rourke and Anthony Quinn, both of whom claimed to be researching upcoming roles.

It's always been hard to say where the movies leave off and the real hoodlums begin. As early as 1928, bona fide bootleggers served as "technical consultants" to the makers of the film *The Racket*, one of the first to be modeled on Capone. (Having given away too many trade secrets, though, the bootleggers tried to block the film's release by threatening to kill its stars.) Before he was thirty-two, Capone had inspired two more movies—*Little Caesar* and *Scarface*—and was the undisputed template for gangster iconography. (Ever the social conservative, though, he worried that "these gang movies are making a lot of kids want to be tough guys.") But it was Puzo's book and Coppola's movie that together became the *Hamlet* of Mob dramas. *The Godfather* gave us what felt like the definitive look at the Mafia and served as a bang-up recruiting vehicle, too. Capeci and Mustain describe Gravano as one of the young Brooklyn men the movie had sent "gloriously floating out of theaters" when it opened in 1972. Less keenly aware of the gap between fact and fiction than you would imagine of a man who had participated in nineteen very real killings, Gravano later waxed wistful to a federal prosecutor: "Now, years go by, and the only thing I can love about my life is the movie. There's no honor, there's no respect. Everything is a double cross."

Gravano's nostalgia for bygone days lies at the heart of Mafiana. The narrative arc for the Mob is always in decline, always falling away from some golden age when there was honor among thieves and young people had *respect*. Titles like *The Last Mafioso* and *The Last Don* proclaim that the jig is up and that the Mob is a passing thing, not unlike an America where you didn't have to lock your doors. Pistone says that Mafia old-timers lament the transition of "'Our Thing' to 'My Thing,' in the hands of a lazy, selfish younger generation." Hill, in *Wiseguy*, recalls the young guys in the '70s who ran so wild that the "violence began to damage the business." And Gotti, doing a cross between Lear and B. B. King, was taped by the FBI moping about the difficulties he had with his unruly *capos*: "[They] break my fuckin' heart. Who the fuck wants to be here? We got nothin' but troubles. I got cases coming up. I don't feel good."

Even the FBI mourns the Mafia's supposed demise, because the Chinese, Russian, and Vietnamese crime groups are terra incognita when compared with the Italians. All in all, things ain't what they used to be, and who doesn't feel that way? The loss of a good thing—"We were given paradise on earth, but we fucked it all up," says one goodfella in Pileggi's *Casino*. This is another long-standing trope; it's forever curtains for the Mafia, and all the while Mafia movies and books soldier on.

If the Mafia is, in fact, on the ropes, it is there in large part because mobsters can't help telling one another the tough-guy tale they fell in love with as kids. Listen to Tommy Agro threaten Iannuzzi on an FBI tape:

> "I got people that will eat the fucking eyes out of your fucking head! You dumb bastard! And they're as loyal as a motherfucker. With balls the size of cows.... Why do you think people fear me? Because I was a hard-on, you fuckin' moron? You think I got where I was because I was a jerkoff in the street? You're easy, you motherfucker. The most wrongest thing you ever did was fuck me."

Clearly, the man is a lover of the mother tongue, one who gets an author's kick out of giving the audience a chill. But you hardly have to catch wiseguys chatting about dismemberment; a simple job description will do. The federal racketeering statute (the Racketeer Influenced and Corrupt Organizations Act, or RICO) makes the very existence of a Mafia family illegal, so when a gangster merely says the words "boss" and "Cosa Nostra," as Gotti did on tape, it's next stop, maximum security. Picky editors, the feds. An *omerta* stalwart, even if it meant going to prison for life (as he has), Gotti nevertheless suffered from a prolixity of Johnsonian dimensions. He loved to talk Mob, and in just six hours of taped conversation, he gave away the whole show—the Mafia hierarchy, his income-tax situation, and a handful of murders. In contrast, Gravano was taped for thousands of hours and didn't say enough to warrant a parking ticket. Both men loved "the life," but Gotti, the tabloid hero, couldn't stop massaging himself with its gritty particulars. He committed the ultimate sin for an inside Mafia storyteller: he said "Once upon a time" ... without government immunity.

With Gotti and an aged Gigante now in prison, perhaps we have seen Puzo's last don. It doesn't matter, though. The fable of blood and honor is so familiar, if not downright homey, that we might easily think of its endless retelling as the narrative equivalent of bead counting. Before turning the first page, before the opening credits roll, you can already hear the *fiiitt* of the silencer, already see the don bring the espresso cup to his lips, and you can remind the hit man in *The Godfather*, as his victim slumps over the steering wheel, "Leave the gun. Take the cannoli." Our fascination with Mob tales provides the surest clue to what makes evil tick: Taking place in an idiosyncratic moral realm where honor percolates fitfully alongside the survival of the fittest, these recitations of greed and guns satisfy a need to see ourselves in an elementary, id-like state. We come to understand the act of murder—not done for love, not out of hate, but for "business"—as an inescapable, necessary part of what humans do. And, finally, our trifling moral dilemmas can be neatly resolved in the home team's favor in the face of the Mob's serene, relentless enactment of the will to power. For all its decorative trappings, it is a simple story about our deepest wish: unrestrained self-gratification. The Mafia dream is the American dream, the one where you get to have your cannoli and eat it too.

*Harper's Magazine,* October 1997.

# Lost Highways: Finding Our Way Home with the *National Geographic 1998 Road Atlas*

A continent you hold in your hand. Fold up and jam under a car seat. A portable anthology of landscapes you can tour on the cheap; ravines, suburbs, foothills, downtowns, basins, and borders you flip through. The view is aerial—Olympian in scope, encyclopedic in detail. The wide world un-widened, abridged for handy perusal. For getting around the United States, Canada, and Mexico without getting out of your chair, the *National Geographic Road Atlas* is the epic sojourn of choice. Pack light.

Where are we? Where are we going? Posed from a philosophical point of view, these are heady, existential queries lacking any definite answer. But asked of a map when flooded with wanderlust or claustrophobic panic, we can readily pick another spot—Terre Haute or Montana's Little Belt Mountain Range—and trace out a straight or dilatory route with a finger's imperial skim. A map may provide little clue to your soul's peregrinations, but it does pin down your corporeal self with ruthless precision—the *Atlas*'s close-up of Manhattan fits me right into the grid, between two red crosses for hospitals, across from a pale green square that indicates a park, a remnant swatch of a colonial-period meadow. Fixed in geography as well as history, I am right there. I can move to other pages for larger views, first, to situate myself on the whole island, then to see Manhattan snuggled into the coast, and finally to measure out my foothold on the continent. It's a form of home construction; a way of putting the *firma* in my *terra*.

With its cover and each page trimmed in the familiar bright yellow of *National Geographic* magazine, the *Road Atlas* partakes of its cousin publication's climb-every-mountain drama. Of course, there are no images of Navajo hitchhikers or Nova Scotian fisherman hauling their nets—the *Atlas* only acknowledges the inhabitants of its terrain insofar as our geometry is visible—the broad, hard-angled bands of interstates or Mondrian-like blocks produced by city borders. Evidence of a resident population can also be found in the myriad names of our towns, rivers, and counties; in fact, they warrant such a density of print in some locales that the map is as much a text as any article in the magazine. Self-descriptive or enigmatic, the place names ring out with incantatory music—Flatwoods, Frametown, Left Hand, Looneyville, Rosedale, Belva, Bazoo, Mount Nebo, Muddlety, Pond Gap, Chimney Pitch, Strange Creek, Swandale, and Gilboa Zela. (Is it happenstance or combustible history putting Boomer right next to Smithers?) All found within one small patch of West Virginia, this cluster of hamlets alone forms a Whitmanesque catalog of American speech.

Scattered along spidery mountain roads, such names conjure up tales as well as the solidity of their stony turf. Proust lulled himself to sleep reading the town names on railroad schedules—he found the unwritten novels suggested by each name restful to contemplate. The particularity of a place name, amplified by its specificity on the map, naturally gives rise to images and narrative. A speck of a town, Chilly, in southern Idaho, lies between the Lost River Range and the Sawtooth National Forest. Route 93 is the lifeline that connects it to the slightly larger burgs of Challis and Arco. Who lives here? Hardtack descendants of pioneers, recent refugees from big cities, or just plain folks who happily drive big jeeps sixty miles to work at the government weapons laboratory or, on Sundays, to visit the nearby Craters of the Moon National Monument. Are they hardy souls? Transcendentalist spirits? Survivalist jerks? Do they go stir crazy during long winters? These questions ripple outward from Chilly's black dot; its geography predicates a spacious, tangible world. We can loot the appropriate image banks for the visuals—flatbed trucks hauling timber, low-slung cinderblock stores, gun racks and tow-headed kids in pickups, an A-frame Mormon church—while working our way deeper into the feel of the place. Nightfall in Chilly. An explosion of stars. Is there even one streetlight?

Geography may not be destiny, but it surely constitutes a good part of our mental atmosphere. While steering you from state to state may be the *Road Atlas*'s chief job, it also serves as a guide to far-flung psyches. As you follow that long, curved stuttering of islets to end up at Key West, you gain a good idea of what living at the end of the line means. Except for one sliver of road, suspended on dozens of bridges, there's no way out but the ocean. In central Pennsylvania, the raised striations of the Appalachian Mountains run east to west with few breaks. Since most roads run through the valleys, the locals often drive up to thirty miles to get to a neighboring town right on the other side of the ridge. Walking there would mean a half-day of hard hiking. Of course, you don't have to look to the hills to speculate about how geography individuates a sense of time and distance. For many Manhattanites, the slender width of the East River (thick as a pencil mark on the state map) proves an insurmountable obstacle to Brooklyn. What a New Yorker means by "far" is quite different than what a citizen of British Columbia or Nebraska might think.

The *Road Atlas* parses us down to our basic coordinates—urbanites hunkered down amid crowded print (we become clearer in the blow-up views of city streets), prairie dwellers strung out along the vast rectangular grid of interstate highways, fans of sun and sand sewn into the ragged cuffs of Florida, New Jersey, and South Carolina, or altitude addicts, wedged against the rumpled green folds of mountain terrain. Locally distinct vocabularies are recorded, if not generated, by road maps. Every East Coaster travels "95," the highway that links Florida to Maine, just as Montanans drop references to the "Hi-Line," a rail and road line that once marked the northern edge of the settled plains, and in California everyone knows the difference between driving "1" or "5" is the difference between jaw-dropping splendor and mind-numbing boredom.

If the road map has our number, down to the last kilometer, it also charts our past. It is a record of all those goings hither and comings and, being motion-mad Americans, this means our most powerful memories are to be found threaded through its latitudes and longitudes. The name of a hometown, the poppy seed size lake near an uncle's summer house that once seemed impossibly vast, the wiry road you took to get there that always made you carsick, the double-chambered, heart-shaped island in Maine where you nearly drowned in a motel pool. Find the Utah town of Mexican Hat that you passed through twice, once in your twenties camping with a friend, years later with a woman you wanted to marry but would never see again after that trip; trace over your route, remember how both times you stopped to take roadside photos near Natural Bridges; how the first time driving the zig-zag of switchbacks (smoothed out to gentle waves at this scale) made it difficult for you to see the forest of ochre cliffs, and how the second time, you again took the wheel so she wouldn't miss the view.

Whatever we do, we do it someplace. A compendium of geographic facts, the *Road Atlas* is a cartographic source of melancholy. The map provides the dispiriting reminder that everywhere we've been or might go, someone has been there before; yet there's some useful consolation in its endlessly circulatory web of roads—there are two ways of getting somewhere—fast or scenic—and there is always a way back home.

*Village Voice Literary Supplement*, July 1998.

# Off the Map: The Way of Some Worlds

The overstuffed boxes and shelves in my apartment attest to an enthusiasm for saving maps. I have hundreds of all kinds: 19th-century maps, restaurant place-mat maps, tourist guides, charts of the heavens, maps of the stars' homes, hiking routes, atlases, aerial photographs, geological surveys, transit maps, amusement park plans, and so on. When I travel, I can't leave a town, park, or country without having some map to commemorate being there. On airplanes, I study the maps of flight paths printed in the back of the in-flight magazine, that is, if I'm not gawking out the window trying to match the landscape below to the map I've brought along. I will never throw out my detailed road maps of, say, Provence or the Yucatán, where I once drove years ago. I even have maps of the island of Saint Helena, the ocean floor, and the moon, none of which will ever be of use. Maps are codes, they are pocket-size pieces of the planet. I employ them to get to places I'll never go, as well as to discover exactly where I am now. I daydream over them. But I don't dream about the joys of travel or exotic sights; instead, I try to discover the liminal place where the map leaves off and the terrain begins. Where paper edges into rock, where ink bleeds into asphalt. Here are four maps of mine in which that sweet spot has sometimes felt within reach.

### *Sinclair Gas Station Road Map: Pennsylvania*

I keep a bundle of old gas station road maps that belonged to my father. He worked as a truck driver, piloting eighteen-wheeler tankers, and he used them to get around. They date from the early '70s and carry dark smudges such as you might expect on items that were stored in the cab of a truck delivering materials for the chemical industry. These much-folded and refolded maps were quite literally tools for my father: They enabled him to steer his tractor and its trailer—a sixty-foot steel tube brimming with, say, hydrochloric acid—across states, through cities, down back roads, and over interstates within the time allotted by his employer. Like most ten-year-olds, I loved all manner of vehicles, and big trucks, especially. One time, my father drove his rig by our house and allowed me to climb into the cab and go for a very short ride—I was thrilled. Looking over the roofs of passing cars, I was airborne. To me, his maps were key to this imperial mobility; to master them would mean mastering that immense truck. After the dinner dishes had been cleared, I often watched him sit at the kitchen table with a map spread out in front of him. He jotted route numbers, place names, and scribbled arrows in a notebook; these notations, which filled page after page, seemed to me like mathematical formulas, indecipherable yet suggestive of some secret capacity to go far, to go far fast, and to do so from a great height.

In the intervening decades, I haven't gotten very far—I grew up in Philadelphia and now live in Brooklyn. Still, my father's road maps, retrieved from his house when he died, are talismans of one moment of possibility, my own and, not to sound overly grand about it, America's. Or at least that of America's car culture. Gas stations don't give out maps anymore, at least not free ones, and the cheery, bow-tied pump attendants pictured on the map covers are long gone, too. Gulf, Esso, Phillips 66, Mobil, Sinclair, Shell, and Sunoco are some of the oil companies represented in my cache. The company names and their logos handily reference the geography and geology of the petroleum industry: the location of oil rigs offshore from Louisiana gave Gulf its name; Shell's seashell and Sinclair's dinosaur reminded patrons of the tens of millions of years it took to brew up the gas they blithely pumped into their GTOs or Chevy Impalas. The time before gas shortages, compact cars, fuel efficiency standards, and emissions controls was a kind of golden age for American drivers. Esso bid us, "Happy Motoring." Phillips 66 struck a didactic note, "It's performance that counts." And a solicitous Sinclair let it be known, "We care about you and about your car."

The earliest road map—a twenty-foot-long parchment that depicted the Roman world—dates from the 3rd century. No doubt, even at twenty feet, the Peutinger Table, as it came to be known, would be easier to stow than it is to correctly refold any gas-station map. A version of this Roman plan was revived in the Middle Ages and served as a guide for pilgrims bound for Jerusalem and, like automobile maps with their gas advertisements and hotel icons, noted the locations of hostels and stables where you could refresh the horses. By studying this guide, pilgrims learned that their epic journey was possible; they had only to hew to its thinly sketched lines to reach an unimaginably distant goal. The map was an almost magical thing.

The cover of Sinclair's Pennsylvania map features a gleaming white service station and a bright yellow car with tail fins in the garage. The building is shaded by a huge tree and, in the near distance, a mountain can be seen. It's as rustic a vision as might be found in any painting by Thomas Cole. No sign of grease or exhaust. Most of the cover is taken up with the powder-blue expanse of a near-cloudless sky: a wide-open space that belies the empire of tiny-print towns and interwoven roads depicted within. After my father left on a trip, for instance, to Reading or Youngstown, I'd trace out possible routes, usually ones far more circuitous than he'd ever take. Truckers take the shortest course and stick to the turnpikes and highways, but I imagined paths winding heedlessly among the Allegheny Mountains or threading through towns named after any manner of flora—Daisytown, Primrose, Pine Bank—or through strangely dubbed burgs like Blue Knob, Drab, Normalville, Gump, and Puzzletown. Sitting high up in the diesel cab, I would give the airhorn a blast as I rolled through their main streets. The closer I bore down on the unfolded sheet, the more I saw myself lifted above the conjured landscape. Eventually, I found myself peering down as my father's truck moved steadily down some road. He was driving on, his workaday pilgrim's progress marked on my map, one inch (equaling ten miles) at a time.

***Heart of the Grand Canyon: National Geographic Topographic Map***

The spot where I thought I might die isn't on this map. It lies several miles to the east of its right-hand border, right along the Colorado River on the Escalante Trail. I bought "Heart of the Grand Canyon" over twenty years ago during my first trip to the park; it depicts the most touristed and most obviously dramatic section of the canyon. The famous postcard landmarks are clustered here: Bright Angel Trail, Phantom Ranch, Isis Temple, and Shiva Temple. Unfolded, the sheet easily covers a good-sized desk. The coated stock sharpens its colors—various shades of reddish-brown, green, and blue—to give an accurate report of the landscape's actual hues. The thousands of hairbreadth-thin lines that indicate changes in topography appear almost vibratory, like those in cartoons that are meant to suggest sudden motion. If the precipitous depths of the actual landscape are both entrancing and foreboding, they are something else when drawn by a cartographer; the steep pillars and great battleships of stone appear to tremble ever so slightly, as if caught in a freeze-frame of their geological evolution.

Like every tourist in the gift shop, I wanted to take a little piece of the park away with me, and this map promised more sublime reverberations than a Hopi bowl or Grand Canyon sweatshirt. After that visit, I often lingered over the map's intricate gorges and buttes, which were drawn to give the alluring effect of tridimensionality. If I relaxed my eyes (in the way one does to see the "hidden picture"), I could almost feel the dizziness, the near-religious sense of awe I'd felt there. I used the map to unfix time and space. I tried to reanimate the rapture—there's no other word for it—that overtook me when, after hiking about halfway down the canyon, I stopped at Plateau Point, lay flat on the ground, and inched my torso out over the drop, the roaring Colorado a still, soundless ribbon beneath. "I take space to be the primary fact of America," poet Charles Olson had once written. And there it was—wide and gaping, and beckoning me in a not-un-sinister way. A few hundred feet below, I could make out a falcon riding the updrafts, tracing the inseam of the void. For months afterward, toppling headlong into my map, I chased that high. But the thrill grew thinner over time. Mere paper—coated stock, to boot, wasn't enough; what I wanted to retrieve was beyond mere imagining. I had to go back.

On the next trip, two days into a cross-canyon trek, I slipped on a talus slope about seventy feet above the river. I tumbled backward down the steep incline, and every time I tried to get up, the weight of my pack threatened to tip me over. Once again, the river was below me, much closer this time, and hardly quiet. Indeed, if inhabiting the canyon map had been serene, this moment was not: the rush of the river below joined and amplified the braying alert that was sounding in my head. The rocks seemed alive, but not as they had seemed on the map; now they radiated my humming dread. On this day, I thought, under this enormous sky, I could fall—and not get up. Again, I was touching the hem of the cosmos, but not the grand part that comes with its own organ-music accompaniment; instead, I heard the dull thump of a tumbling body. Dying in a locale this beautiful struck me as a kind of vandalism, an unfortunate staining of three-hundred-million-year-old rocks with my small mortality.

It would be convenient to say that, amid these dire thoughts, I recalled my "Heart of the Grand Canyon" map and realized that it, that any map, was a grievous reduction, not only of space—of the feel of *unbordered* space—but also of the possible emotions real rock and sky might spark. I had never experienced fear staring across the vertiginous peaks when they rested on my desk, but that fear—of falling, of losing oneself in an impossibly vast landscape—is as much a part of experiencing the canyon as is awe. I didn't think any of this, but I could have if only I hadn't been clinging to a rock while struggling to find a foothold. With the help of a rope lowered by my hiking companion, I managed to crawl back to the trail, dragging myself over a nub of cactus in the process. (I would be plucking tiny needles out of my arm weeks later.) Safely perched on a shelf of rock above the slope, I gazed down. There were no topographical indicators at hand to delineate my ascent. Instead, there was only the measure of distance between two scenarios—a very bad day that almost came to pass and another that was, even as I breathed in some of the great sea of air around me, already getting better.

***Panorama of the City of New York, Queens Museum of Art***

I was nine when I saw it the first time—at the New York World's Fair in 1964, a scale model of the entire city, with every building and street carefully set in position. The faux landscape covered nearly ten thousand square feet and would have easily swallowed my sizable collection of Matchbox cars and trucks. Still, I longed to climb over the railing and drop to my hands and knees and play. It was the biggest toy I'd ever seen, and now, many years later, I feel the same way when I visit it in New York. Refurbished since the World's Fair, the panorama is reasonably up-to-date (a red, white, and blue ribbon graces the Twin Towers). Robert Moses, who commissioned the model, insisted that there be less than a 1 percent margin of error between the model and the actual landscape. With binoculars—visitors are confined to glass walkways that skirt the perimeter—I can spy out, for instance, the buildings where I've lived among the nearly nine hundred thousand other structures. There's also the Tompkins Square Park playground where my son sat in his first swing or the downtown rooftop where I watched the Statue of Liberty Centennial fireworks. It's an Olympian view of New York and, for me, since I've lived here for more than twenty-five years, it's a God's-eye view of my own life.

In *Jason and the Argonauts,* one of my favorite movies from childhood, Zeus and Hera peer into a pool in which the world of mortals appears. Below them, they see all and intervene in events by moving ships, monsters, and other gods like chess pieces, dropping, for instance, a wave-making Poseidon in Jason's path. Casting an eye over the sprawling miniature city at the Queens Museum, I'm almost similarly empowered. My world appears readily comprehensible in a way it never has before. When I've stood amid the West Village's nest of oddly intersected streets, I've never really been able to orient myself, but from this vantage I plot with ease the shortest route from Westbeth to Sheridan Square. The fuzzy mental geography we carry around in our heads, a geography owing largely to our getting around by subway, car, and foot, is clarified from the bird's-eye perspective: LaGuardia Airport doesn't sit at the other end of the Midtown Tunnel; Prospect Park isn't deep in the middle of Brooklyn; and Eighth Avenue is hardly the far west side of Manhattan. And, while New York's not Venice, we are indeed surrounded by an awful lot of water (which we often ride beneath). New Yorkers are much more conscious of living on islands of a different sort—your home is on the atoll of West End Avenue, you commute to the isle of Chelsea, and shop along the archipelago of upper Broadway. We island hop from one destination to another, never especially conscious of what's in between or out of sight. What's concealed from us as we tread our narrow paths is laid out to the very last brick in the panorama.

If the model helps dilate my sense of space, it does the opposite to time. As I scan my various residences, places of employment, homes of friends and lovers, sites of memorable occasions, and do so all at once, time—my lifetime—is collapsed. This version of Legotown sorts a confusion of years into a single geographical narrative made up of *wheres* rather than *whens*. In the sweep of an eye, the relation between one place and another is made plain; on the grid of avenues and cross streets, I can isolate any number of events that occurred over decades and here are "viewed" in an instant. The panorama provides not just a sense of mastery over territory but over one's own memories. If New York City is too labyrinthine and large, too peopled by others to be truly known and personalized, then the view from this catwalk allows me the illusion that it can indeed be grasped, that it can also—in its epic totality—be a real home. At this micro-scale, the city sheds its forbidding particularity; it's not composed of thousands of streets, millions of rooms, tens of millions of windows, each with its own view. Instead, it appears singular and whole—infinity downsized to a front yard's worth of acreage. Scanning the painted streets and toy buildings, I see precisely how I've inhabited this town. My goings hence and comings hither are visible, measurable. It may be a jury-rigged omniscience that's offered here, but until I can drop by Olympus, it'll have to do.

### *Holy Sepulchre Cemetery Map*

I have a single, small sheet that appears to have been separated from the rest of a pamphlet devoted to the Holy Sepulchre Cemetery in North

Philadelphia. This portion was found among the boxes of paper I carted out of my parents' house. It's a map of the cemetery where my father's mother, Rose, and his brother Nick are buried. My father has written "Nick Mobilio, Section 42, Range 9. Lot 13" along the border, and he has also drawn a tiny rectangle with the notes "Mom's" and, inexplicably, "Burns's Grave." (Inexplicable because I don't know anyone named Burns.) My grandmother's grave is located not far from the intersection of St. John's and Assumption Roads. Other road names mark similarly religious events and personages: Annunciation, St. Gabriel, Visitation, Immaculate Conception, and Epiphany. Curving into broad arcs and circles, these roads trace a fanciful course, like the path an amusement park monorail might take to provide views of Monkey Island and Pirate's Cove. The expressway and avenues that border the cemetery form an angular frame for the graveyard's curlicues. There's a clear demarcation between the hard-edge domain of the living and the undulating terrain of the dead.

I've only been to Holy Sepulchre once, when I was a teenager, and I recall it being bewilderingly huge. I sat in the backseat of the car with the flowers; up front, my parents tried to navigate the maze—a repetitive landscape of grassy knolls and headstones. Very likely, my mother held this particular map as she directed Dad to "Take a right on Transfiguration." It was a Palm Sunday sometime after Uncle Nick's demise. Nick had lost a leg in World War II and never married. Instead, he dispensed loud and lewd remarks at family dinners. Concerning some especially pricey toy that I wanted, he imparted this unsavory bit of wisdom: "You want the money? Put one hand on your ass and wave the other in the air. You'll get something in one of them." Even as an eight-year-old fond of all things irreverent, I found this very disturbing. He sat there cackling, his left pant leg rolled up and safety-pinned, his forehead as shiny as his wide satin tie. Did they bury his crutches with him? I thought about such things when we finally found his grave that day, Section 42, Lot 13.

The cemetery where my parents are buried isn't nearly as large as Holy Sepulchre, but I never owned its map; since it was close to home when I was growing up, we visited Immaculate Conception

Cemetery often. As a kid, I could find my way to the family plot by way of certain statues and names on the headstones: downhill from the blue and white marble angel, past the Toricelli family, to the right of the Kapinskis' Sacred Heart of Jesus bas-relief. But when I arrived on the day of my father's funeral, I soon got turned around. Was it the Toricelli's or Tenaglia's? And everywhere I looked there was another damned angel. I was supposed to meet a priest and a few relatives, but I was early—there was no cluster of vehicles to guide me. I had brought Dad's ashes in the trunk of my car and was wandering among the headstones holding the urn in a cardboard box. (Don't think me cheap; my father would have loved such bargain-priced élan.)

When I was a child, the stone that marked my mother's parents' graves and now hers had loomed for me as something ominous, even monumental. But as it finally came into view, I saw how ordinary it was compared to the others. A modest marker among bright angels between whose wingspans it could easily fit. I sat the box in the grass and watched as cars began stopping on the road just up the hill. The handful of other mourners found their way easily enough, it seemed. My father was the last of seven brothers and sisters—Uncle Nick being the oldest, my father the youngest. Each now had a locus on some map, their own coordinates: a plot number neatly penciled in somewhere, it could be hoped, close to a road named Resurrection, if not Ascension.

My map of Holy Sepulchre provides me the key to getting around a destination I'll never visit again. That's what makes it a favorite—its perfect uselessness. Because surely, we get to where we're going, with or without a map. My father found his way to his square foot of topography, his book of route numbers and road names lost along the way. Someday, of course, my maps will be scattered, or maybe they will be saved by another map collector. With or without them, though, I won't be traveling blind.

*Tin House*, Spring 2005.

# On Camera

# Blue Is the Color of Blockade: Boris Mikhailov

As its title—*Refracted Times*—indicates, Ukrainian photographer Boris Mikhailov's current exhibition at Marian Goodman Gallery offers a historical narrative, one recording three chronological points during his country's troubled passage from Soviet domination to independence. A series of C-prints titled *Salt Lake,* taken in 1986, shows vacationers at a factory-adjacent beach in southern Ukraine; *By the Ground,* a sequence shot in 1991—the year the Soviet Union collapsed—presents signs of urban dissolution; and, finally, *At Dusk,* a group of blue-tinted photos from 1993, extends that meditation on social disarray. The uniformly gritty content doesn't make for an optimistic before-and-after tale; while those bathers may be clustered around a drainage pipe in the shadow of smokestacks, they are at least on holiday.

Mikhailov began his career as an engineer but turned to photography in the late 1960s. Associated with the Sots Art movement (the Russian version of Pop Art), he employed various darkroom interventions: hand-coloring, superimpositions, and the use of found images. Evidence of this period can be found in one of the show's videos, *Yesterday's Sandwich* (late 1960s–'70s), a fluid collage of photos altered to create Surrealist juxtapositions. As this wasn't the sort of thing sanctioned by official culture, Mikhailov operated at its margins, sometimes reported by his street photography subjects to the police, who then ordered him to open his camera and expose the film. By the early 1990s, though, with the Soviet downfall imminent, his first exhibitions abroad took place.

Within the context of Western European art, Mikhailov's experimental work was hardly shocking, echoing as it did decades-old compositions by Man Ray, Claude Cahun, and Hans Bellmer. Still, the Soviet censors, ever alert to formal innovation's subversive properties, understandably took note. Yet the documentary-style photographs on display at Marian Goodman would have been far more prejudicial to the regime. The bathers featured in *Salt Lake* sit on a rocky dirt embankment sloping abruptly into water that looks unappetizingly murky, given the harsh contrast of the black-and-white film. Seemingly unconcerned with an open concrete duct likely leading from the nearby factory, the swimmers (well, more accurately, waders) stand about under a cloudy sky and converse. The pictures, taken the same year as the Chernobyl meltdown, don't evoke a socialist paradise so much as another ongoing environmental disaster. Mikhailov subtly presents this Soviet-era paradox—amid awfulness, Ukrainians find what pleasure there is to be had.

For the images gathered under the title *By the Ground* (the phrase, Mikhailov reports, was inspired by Maxim Gorky's play *The Lower Depths*), the photographer employed a horizon camera to produce panoramic views of street scenes. Shooting from hip height, he would capture awkward, unstudied moments: babushkas wearing heavy coats stoop over shopping bags, children play around a rubble-strewn basement entrance. The use of sepia toning lends the pedestrians a palpable weariness, as if their passage over cracked pavements and crumbling facades could only be described as trudging. But that overdetermined reading is countered by more perplexing acts: a young woman (seen from behind, as are many of Mikhailov's people) peers over a ramshackle fence; what she seeks is unknown, but her tensed leg perched on a rock reveals an acute need to see *something*. Her youth, her effort, even her anonymity suggest a vitality and possibility that are otherwise drained by the series' portrayal of so drab a domain.

The more than two dozen prints comprising *At Dusk* somehow chill the room in which they are hung. Produced just two years after *By the Ground,* in this series Ukraine's declining fortunes remain fully in evidence, but Mikhailov has accentuated his depictions of decay and human distress by hand-coloring the photos in cobalt blue. This choice is an attempt to conjure the night sky of his youth in Kharkhiv during the Second World War. "Blue," he explains in the gallery text, "is the color of the blockade, hunger, and war." In addition to the tinting, some of the photos have been stained and scored, giving them the appearance of relics from a catastrophe. Again, the frame is panoramic, shot from waist level; again, figures are seen from behind, often only the lower half of their bodies. Mikhailov places viewers in the midst of a city's street life; its mundane chores, random debris, and incipient chaos swirl around us.

At what might be a public dump, a shabbily dressed woman lugs two buckets as she moves past several garbage bins; above her, large birds caught mid-flight look ominous, even predatory. Around an outdoor concrete table, several men stand, hands in the pockets of their bulky coats. On a street corner, a man stumbles to the ground while passersby rush along. The subjects that occupy this bleak and wintry locale are isolated, lonely; and when a face is visible, it's often grim, staring out from within a closely wrapped headscarf or fur-lined hat. When people do interact, the scene is fraught: a couple, blurred and indistinct, clutch one another in an open plaza. Mikhailov has applied smudges all around them so they look as though they were huddling against a storm of dark scars. In a rare composition, another embracing couple directs their gaze at the camera: the young man allows us a neutral regard while his female companion broaches a smile. Whatever optimism might spring from their apparent contentment is blunted by their surroundings (they share the frame with a man walking past, the blankness of his dark silhouette a kind of refusal—if not a rebuke—to their intimacy) and the photographer's handiwork (the overcast sky has been mottled with haphazard splotches and streaks). They may have one another, but they are fated to be subsumed within the encompassing disintegration.

It's useful to keep in mind that the exhibition's photos all date from decades prior to the first Russian incursion into Ukraine in 2014, let alone the full-scale invasion in 2022. However dire, this Dantean portrait of the country doesn't include the social and infrastructural toll of years of war. Nothing, we can assume, has grown more lovely. But long before armed conflict, the Soviet era's grinding ruination left a blasted landscape and demoralized citizenry. Not satisfied to merely document the wreckage, Mikhailov lavishes it with compositional and darkroom attention to discover its strange and disquieting allures. In this fallen world, it is forever dusk.

*4Columns*, February 14, 2025.

# Self-Portraits in a Complex Mirror: The Photographs of Vivian Maier

The discovery of the so-called "undiscovered genius" is the driving narrative behind the boom in what's come to be called outsider art over the past few decades. The notion that great art is being made unbeknownst to the powers-that-be by hospital patients, truck drivers, janitors, and neighborhood loners satisfies our wish to believe in a fully democratized community of artistic expression. Bodies of work by Martín Ramírez, Henry Darger, Charles A. A. Dellschau, and William Hawkins, to name just a few artists who have come to prominence recently, certainly do attest to the pervasiveness of the visionary impulse across class and racial lines.

This evidence may be tonic, especially within the context of the current art scene in which pricey educational credentials and the connections that follow seem all but essential to gaining recognition. But, of course, "outsiders" live up to their name. The support and benefits that might follow in the wake of a successful first show by a recent MFA graduate was never theirs. Their success is typically posthumous, which, as success goes, may be good for us; less good for them.

Vivian Maier spent some forty years working as a nanny in Chicago. When she died in 2009 at the age of eighty-three, she left behind well over a hundred thousand photographic negatives (of which she had printed a small number), evidence of decades spent wandering the streets of her hometown, as well as other cities and locales around the world. In 2007, Chicago photographer and historic preservationist John Maloof purchased a box of Maier's negatives at auction, and this led him to discover the rest of her sizable cache of images. Intensely private, some people who knew her were surprised to learn she took pictures.

Two years ago the Howard Greenberg Gallery presented a much-praised show of her street photography and many of these images were published in a book edited by Maloof. Since then her reputation has grown (more books; a documentary film, *Finding Vivian Maier*, premiered at the Toronto Film Festival this fall) and now this once anonymous woman with a Rolleiflex strapped around her neck is increasingly regarded as a peer of masters like Gary Winogrand and Robert Frank. It is hard not to conjecture, though, what turn her life and art might have taken if she had tried to enter the rarified precincts of the art world when she first began taking pictures. Would she have found a place and thrived? If rejected, would she have taken the judgment to heart and abandoned her photography altogether?

While these speculations are moot, the current show at Greenberg, one devoted to Maier's self-portraits, confirms without a doubt her vigorous consciousness of herself as an artist—perhaps one without a gallery or publication, but no less a visionary for such deficiencies. Maier's considerable art is not a fluke—as if she were a hobbyist whose images just happen to incorporate the aesthetic sophistication associated with professional artists. Every photograph in this show (collected in a volume published by powerHouse Books) testifies to her acute awareness of self-portraiture's long tradition, and particularly its more inventive (Man Ray, Parmigianino, Frida Kahlo) permutations.

The meta quality (the photographer is almost always seen with her camera in the act of taking the shot) and obliqueness (she's reflected in car mirrors, shop windows, or hubcaps, or seen only in shadow) that characterizes nearly all of these portraits might come across as over-determined, too earnestly artful, if not for Maier's droll approach not only to composition, but to her own facial and bodily demeanor. Maier often affects a deadpan, somewhat distracted look, her eyes blankly regarding something just outside the photo's frame. She is her own unwilling subject, just tolerating the intrusion of the camera she's holding, arms akimbo, below her chest. And then there are the hats—berets, fedoras, straw—that lend her profile a rakish air, sometimes undermined by a slightly doleful expression. Maier presents herself as someone aloof, and contentedly so.

In a photo taken at a Chicago beach in 1971, the photographer is visible in shadow at the bottom of the frame. A dark shape on the sand, the flat-brimmed fedora and clothed shoulder loom ominously; has a detective or gangster come to pay an unwelcome call? Maier goes tête-á-tête with her subject, a sunbather sporting a mass of curlers, to create an off-kilter symmetry that's enhanced as much by their similarities (neither woman's face is clearly visible, with each sporting a pronounced head adornment) as their differences (the monochromatic shadow casts a wintery specter while the summery beachgoer reclines on a striped towel in a striped swimsuit). Maier sparks narrative as well as formal drama, even as a wry wit animates the proceedings.

Parmigianino's *Self-Portrait in a Convex Mirror* may have been the inspiration for the image, offering the photographer neatly framed in an oval mirror. (There are several such reflective ovals: some of them, the back of an auto's rear-view, a VW hubcap, a bookshop's theft prevention mirror are, in fact, convex.) Taken in Anaheim, California, in 1955, this complex portrait reveals Maier as a rather young woman who is already in possession of an ambivalent mien—one guarded yet anticipatory.

The image suggests that she is shooting into a large mirror as she holds a small circular one, the kind with a stand that might be found on a dressing table; she has angled the camera to frame her face as a tondo, while some of her torso (she wears a prim white blouse) and her hand are visible. Well-lit and sharply focused, the face emerges from what could be a dark ether; her hand is a murky presence, barely registering as such, if not for being set against the shirt's luminescent white. This layering of focus with diverse qualities of light creates an uncertain, somewhat illegible background that permits her face an almost startling definition. Her boyish visage hovers amid her body, as if in consequence of the preternatural.

In a few images, Maier can be seen without her camera. In a 1960 shot, she broods purposely—chin in hand, beret appropriately tilted—in a snowy park. But in most of these self-portraits, the tool of her trade is unmistakably present, often vying with her face for prominence. The camera is carefully held—offered?—to the viewer as the object deserving our attention. The formality of her poses, her studied impassivity, lend an iconic note to several of these photos, as if she were seeking not to capture herself but to delineate some Platonic notion of "the photographer." If the potential aesthetic missteps that attend this sort of self-mythologizing are numerous, Maier appears well aware of them and equally confident of her ability to avoid stumbling.

There is no coyness in these photographs; no attempt to sell a persona. Her ambition is directly conveyed, without embarrassment or emotional hedging: you immediately understand Maier as an artist because that's how she understands herself. Decade after decade, going to work, taking care of other people's children, another walker among city crowds cloaked in an unremarkable guise, she went about her life convinced, these photographs show, of her remarkability. Maier's genius was hardly undiscovered.

*Hyperallergic*, December 13th, 2013.

# Review of *Thomas Struth*

The difference between looking and seeing—between mere perception of surfaces and an understanding of their meanings—is a division that photographic art is especially disposed to explore. Photographers have long pressed against their art's presumed documentary function, creating a subjective sense of the seen by applying the tools of their craft. This persona-driven approach was challenged by Bernd and Hilla Becher, founders of the Düsseldorf School of Photography, whose students included Thomas Ruff, Andreas Gursky, Candida Höfer, and Thomas Struth. Known for their typological studies of industrial structures, the Bechers declined to pursue the "decisive moment" and instead sought clarity and near-scientific objectivity.

By producing ordered sets of similar pictures that reveal the subtlest differences and congruities, Struth has proved his fealty to that aesthetic. But this comprehensive volume—*Thomas Struth*—of more than forty years of work, also charts an ongoing revision of the Bechers' ideas. As the black-and-white images of urban scenes in New York and Europe give way to more recent, color-rich portraits of families and crowds in museums, Struth complicates the typological impulse. The city photos are mostly devoid of people and often shot from the middle of a long street toward a single, distant point of perspective. By eschewing human incident and social detail, these rigorously symmetrical compositions direct attention to intersecting vertical and horizontal lines (building columns, signage, sidewalks); *Dey Street, Financial District, New York, 1978,* could be a surveyor's evidence for zoning purposes. As such, these streetscapes invite a double-take: the matter-of-fact surface that initially resists close reading and thematic resonance is a cunning feint, one that causes the viewer to question assumptions about what merits attention.

Struth's numerous depictions of museumgoers in Venice, Paris, Chicago, and elsewhere dramatize this notion explicitly. In *Louvre 4, Paris 1989,* Théodore Géricault's massive *The Raft of the Medusa* occupies the center of Struth's frame while several visitors assemble—left to right, from crowd to solitary figure—in a way that echoes the bodies on the raft, even as the group's placid demeanor contrasts sharply with the agonized commotion rendered by the painter. We can't see the faces of those in the audience, but much can be gleaned about the interaction between them and the art: The head of the woman on the far right casts upward to examine the apex of the composition; next to her, a man bends to peruse a guidebook or adjust a camera; the woman in a blue coat focuses on a corner of the painting; and the casual posture—hands in pocket—of the gray-jacketed man next to her connotes emotional distance from the death and dying. Struth knows that we will be drawn to our fellow spectators; we share with them a remote vantage on the frightful scene and easily identify with the visually sated lot of the museum attendees. We see ourselves, in the photo, not seeing.

*Bookforum,* February–March 2018.

# Hiroshi Sugimoto: *Seascapes*

Pilots call it "spatial-D," short for spatial disorientation—the dizziness and inability to determine where your body is in space when you're deprived of a clear visual horizon. The phenomenon can send a pilot into a tailspin; viewers of Hiroshi Sugimoto's *Seascapes* won't crash anywhere, but they will find themselves inhabiting a perplexing limbo where sea and sky meet uncertainly, their border blurred, the nature of each realm thrown into question. Sugimoto has often chosen subjects that confound predictable responses: His images of glowing white cinema screens (achieved by capturing a whole film in a single exposure), a candle's flame (again made with a long, long exposure), and American Museum of Natural History dioramas (eerily lifelike portraits of the fake animals) require us to think about what we are and aren't seeing. The blank screens in the theater series could be beckoning portals to an ever-lucent, heavenly realm, or they could be the emptiness that human expression—at least two narrative hours' worth—ultimately offers. In either case, it is light and its fundamental role in visual experience that the photographer is exploring.

In *Seascapes,* the images of bodies of water (the Aegean, Mediterranean, Black, and Tyrrhenian seas and the Indian, Arctic, and North Atlantic oceans number among the many locales) and sky have all been rectangularly framed and bisected by a line—sometimes obvious, sometimes not—that divides one from the other. Like similarly stark compositions by Mark Rothko and Ad Reinhardt, the minimalist geometry here belies subtler, less readily legible enchantments; in these unadorned seascapes, there are microworlds of energy evident only on closer inspection. In alchemical fashion, Sugimoto sets classical elements—water and air, most obviously—into relational tension. Earth is also present by implication: It's where the photographer stands. But precisely where, we can't say; he seems to be hovering above the shore. This improbable point of view, the flatness of the water (barely more than a ripple is ever visible), and the cloudless, untextured skies combine to confuse us and force an even more basic question: What are we looking at? The image of the Aegean Sea offers a gradual ascension from dark to light: Initially focusing on the frame's lower portion, the eye locates the slightest suggestion of place in the horizontal grain. What's almost recognizable as water gives way to an increasingly blurred and softly luminous zone as one element infuses the other, water rising into sky as sky descends into water.

As Edward Weston did with his abstract images of the American West, Sugimoto offers landscape photography that invites a fresh understanding of the genre. But Sugimoto amplifies the restraint and formal rigor of his forebear—these pictures can't be decoded in the way that, for instance, the vibrant patterning in one of Weston's images can be recognized as a desert sand dune. Instead, these photographs depict a site of transformation, neither earth nor air. It is a kind of no-place—an unmappable and treacherous region to which we are drawn ineluctably.

*Bookforum,* December–January 2016.

# Looking Down: The God's-Eye View of the Aerial Photograph

Two photos taken any length of time apart, when paired together, will tell a familiar story: Before and After. A photo of an altar boy taken at eight years of age set next to the police mug shot of the same boy now twenty-eight tells a readily apprehensible, if not shopworn tale. The photo of a grocery storefront on the Lower East Side in 1910 forms the first half of a sociological narrative whose second half proceeds from an image of the same building in 2002, now occupied by a sex toy shop.

It is the nature of aerial photography—because of its ability to encompass much from a seemingly omniscient perspective—to tell epic tales. The term epic is used here to describe stories that elide the role of individuals in favor of the action of large, impersonal forces. The paired images of the altar boy and the criminal evoke an arc of narrative time nuanced with the particularity of a single life; they form a biography, autobiography, or novel. The contrasting photos of the storefront certainly tell a less immediately personal tale, but it is still one marked by the activities of an identifiable community—striving old-world immigrants replaced a generation later by their unfettered, decidedly new-world children. Such storylines offer up figures who, in the manner of modern protagonists—encounter complications, struggle, and reach some sort of resolution. On the other hand, the vastly generalized information available from the "god's-eye" view—think of the famous photo of the earth as seen from the moon's surface—is too diffuse and resistant to comprehension to be compared to narrative forms that focus on the notion of individual fate. To find a narrative analog for before-and-after aerial photography, we might look back to the epic tale—say, Homer's *Iliad* or Virgil's *Aeneid*—with its huge cast of characters, myriad subplots, and irrational gods. In these narratives, the intention and agency of any one individual is subsumed within the bigger, Olympian picture—the eternal contest between creation and destruction.

In the *New York Times* on March 26th, 2000, the entire front page of the Week in Review section was taken up with two large aerial photos; they were titled, respectively, "Grozny, Dec. 16, 1999" and "Grozny, March 16, 2000." The caption below them provided the relevant context: on December 16th, Russian troops had surrounded the Chechen capital of Grozny and subjected it to "heavy artillery and aerial bombardment." By early February, the Russians had invaded the city and demolished many of the buildings left standing. The comparison between the two photos, taken about 90 days apart, is said by the *Times* to "hint at the cost of that victory."

When I first saw these pictures, I knew very little about the war in Chechnya. I know very little now. Nonetheless, I was fascinated by this pair of contrasting images, even though they provided me with no real information about, for instance, Chechen-Russian history, the role of religion and ethnicity in the region, the nature of the conflict, the combatants, the casualties; indeed, nothing tangible about the labyrinthine reality at which these two photos could merely "hint." But this hint was still revelatory. While it did not include any stories of individual struggle and loss—the stories I'd been avoiding in magazines and newspapers because I was just not ready to bone up on another conflict, another history, another tale of irreconcilable enmity—it did impress upon me the existence of powerful, recurring, and impersonal forces in the world. And this proved reassuring. Reassuring because such forces appear irresistible and ultimately unfathomable. They absolve us of the need to absorb particulars; to bear witness. To view the world principally as an arena in which these forces contend is to view life in a way that approximates the perspective of the divine. In the case of Grozny, the forces at work—the urge to settle and build a city, as well as the equally persistent need to destroy that same city—had been cleanly stripped of their human particularity by sheer altitude. I was looking down with a kind of imperturbable clarity, the uncertain knowledge of Homer's gods who never quite figure out what motivates the humans whose destinies they control.

The December photograph shows a residential area near Minutka Square. At the center of the frame, a dozen huge Socialist-style housing high-rises are arrayed inelegantly around a large traffic intersection. The massive buildings cast even larger shadows toward the upper edge of the image. In the March photograph, nearly all these buildings are reduced to rubble. Unlike the photos of Dresden in the aftermath of its firebombing, the buildings are not charred skeletons; they have been pummeled into what could be said to resemble Native American burial mounds. The shadows are gone, and everything is brightly lit; the sun has been permitted to find its way into every basement and alley. Before the bombing, there is a raised ellipse set in the middle of the intersection, which is, perhaps, some kind of public monument. This too, has been flattened, yet still it remains the most recognizable shape to survive from December. The broad avenues have been thickened with debris, and single-lane paths have been carved out—no doubt by Russian military equipment. It looks as if sheep paths that existed millennia ago have been resurrected out of the fallen city's dust. The lines call to mind another image of indigenous peoples, the Nazca Indians who left complex geometric images—visible only from a height they could never have attained—on the plains of Peru. The wiry geometry that has taken the place of streets in Grozny is available to a god's eyes as well, not to mention those with access to satellite imagery. I look down and know nothing of the lives there except: This is what people do; they build and they destroy.

In the book *Above Los Angeles,* which features photographs taken by aerial photographer Robert Cameron, an image of Playa del Rey, ca. 1925, has been juxtaposed with one of Cameron's shots of the same locale taken in the late 1980s. Over the approximately 55 years that separate the photos, much has changed. The before-and-after would seem to be a straightforward tale of urban development. Although the basic landscape of a flat plain demarcated by steep cliffs, a beach, and the ocean remains the same, the plain that was open and empty in 1925 is still so, but now purposefully—it is Los Angeles International Airport. The cliffs are studded with homes that cantilever out over the sand below. And the beach, too, has been broadened by the addition of groins. The roads that track the coastline and curve up into the cliffs are still in use, as are the bridges crossing a narrow inlet from the sea. Even a few buildings have survived Los Angeles's accelerated cycles of development and demolition. Mostly, though, there are many, many more structures. No more than two dozen buildings can be located in the 1925 photograph; several decades later, they are too numerous to count. By the 1980s, the incline of the cliffs had been softened, well-tended grass had replaced the scrub brush, and even the ocean appeared to be more carefully groomed.

This swath of arid coastline has been built over and populated, the reverse of the process evidenced in the Grozny photographs. At Playa del Rey, the timeline extends more than half a century; in Grozny, barely three months. Yet for all the apparent rationality of Playa del Rey's before-and-after narrative—the ocean is beautiful, no wonder so many people wish to live close by; the land is flat, of course you would want to land airplanes there; the beach is commodious and inviting, why not make it wider—there is, from this airborne perspective, something as inexplicable as the story the Grozny photographs tell. At this remove, these intricate human motives can only be inferred; they are no more legible than the many causes behind the flattening of a neighborhood in far-off Chechnya. While I know much more about what has happened in LA and *why* it has happened, the Olympian character of these two images undoes this knowledge. True, I know about Americans, our love of our cars, our real estate deals, our fondness for bright green lawns, for baseball fields, for convenient access to everything and everywhere, our appetite for advantage, our disinclination to leave anything—the ocean, the sky above LA—alone. If I understand all of these things to be inextricably webbed, I also understand the individual strands with felt specificity. Still, this pair of images does not conjure the individuals, their choices, desires, and, for me, the moral judgments that might attend upon such actions; instead, it offers assurance from on high: this is what people do; they build and they destroy. Seen from the birds' path or the gods' perch, the human enterprise is so large as to be very small. So detailed as to be exceedingly simple. The aerial view: it provides a peace that passeth understanding.

*Cabinet,* Summer 2003.

# David Maisel: *Proving Ground*

Throughout 2015 and 2016, the U.S. Army set off multiple clouds of deadly chlorine gas, not in some secret location in the Middle East or Afghanistan, but about an hour's drive south of Salt Lake City. The Dugway Proving Ground, established during World War II, occupies a swath of desert larger than Rhode Island. During the war, the military constructed villages that resembled German and Japanese towns in order to try out weapons, including poison gas. This activity continues to the present day. In *Proving Ground*, David Maisel's aerial and ground-level photos of Dugway—he reports that gaining access to the site took nearly a decade—lack the drama of detonations and destruction. Unlike, say, Richard Misrach's photos of a Navy bomb site in Nevada known as Bravo 20, Maisel's images do not present us with burned vehicles or spent shells. His black-and-white aerial images are decidedly abstract; each occupies a full page and shows a geometric landscape of roads and grid markers. Interspersed among these maplike images are equally clinical color photos of gleaming laboratory equipment used for biological and toxic gas experiments. But Maisel does share with Misrach, and another artist who has photographed test sites, Emmet Gowin, an investigatory impulse. All three have revealed the long-standing and ongoing disaster the military has wreaked on the American West.

The mythic stature of that region as a place of heroic doings amid majestic landscapes is undone by their chronicle of the war our military has waged against our own country. (There were one hundred aboveground nuclear detonations at the infamous Nevada Test Site alone; hundreds more were conducted belowground.) Maisel, Misrach, and Gowin offer a disturbing counterpoint to the iconic figure of John Wayne riding tall in a pristine Monument Valley.

The similarity between Maisel's uniformly square images and military maps or satellite surveillance shots appears to be intentional. The landscape is shown as if it were a target; its natural contours have been subsumed by the geographic efficiency of grid lines bulldozed across the desert to help measure the dispersal of toxins and biological agents. The photos' grainy texture is almost palpable, but their subject remains at a distant remove. As such, they feel utterly disconnected from an actual human locale, a reaction that again evokes the mindset of someone planning an attack. Among the volume's bursts of color are stills from the Army's drone footage of the chlorine gas tests, dubbed "Jack Rabbit II." Despite its sickening hue, the fluorescent green cloud roiling up from the desert floor is one of the only indications of life in these stark pages. Maisel is alert to this perverse irony as well as to the question his book's title poses: What is being proved at the Proving Ground? Perhaps nothing more than the familiar environmental indictment leveled by Walt Kelly in his comic strip *Pogo*: "We have met the enemy and he is us."

*Bookforum*, April–May 2020.

# A Boy's Own Story: A Gordon Parks Photo Essay Causes a Lifetime of Unintended Consequences

Even when a photograph of a wounded or suffering child becomes familiar, it retains the power to unsettle. The smudged face of a sharecropper's daughter, children arrayed behind barbed wire at Auschwitz, a starving Biafran child, a nine-year-old girl seared by napalm in Vietnam—these images still disturb viewers and prompt strong responses. Yet, as Susan Sontag argued in *On Photography*, it's difficult to measure their ultimate utility: "The knowledge gained through still photographs," she wrote, "will always be some kind of sentimentalism, whether cynical or humanist." That propensity for sentimentality—and its necessary appropriation of others' pain—is routinely manipulated toward political ends.

And those ends can be entirely contradictory. In 2016, a photo of a bleeding, dust-covered Syrian boy whose home had been bombed by government forces fueled worldwide calls to end the war; months later Syrian state television aired video of the boy—healthy and seemingly happy—as his father decried the use of the photo and voiced support for the regime. Something similar occurred in 1961 with Gordon Parks's images of an impoverished child in Rio de Janeiro. In the spring of that year, *Life* magazine sent the acclaimed African American photographer to Brazil to document poverty in the hillside communities known as favelas. A recent show at the Getty Center in

Los Angeles and its accompanying volume, *Gordon Parks: The Flávio Story*, reveal how images meant to serve as political propaganda sparked a genuine outpouring of support for one poor boy and his family, yet left uncertain consequences in their wake.

Throughout the 1940s and '50s, Parks had chronicled the effects of economic and social segregation on Black Americans. As an artist with an activist impulse ("I use my camera as a weapon," he once declared), he was an apt choice for *Life* editors working to advance Kennedy's Cold War agenda. Launched just after the President's inauguration, a series of special features—"Crisis in Latin America"—emphasized the threat posed by Fidel Castro and aimed to substantiate an urgent need for economic intervention. While combating poverty was a goal shared by Parks, it's unclear how aware he was of these behind-the-scenes machinations.

When Parks arrived in Rio, he teamed up with José Gallo, a local Time Inc. employee who would serve as a translator and guide. They ventured into a notorious favela, Catacumba—the catacomb—and met the da Silva family. Parks's editor had instructed him to document the life of a destitute family, and the da Silvas certainly were that. The parents, José and Nair, had eight children, and they all lived in a single room with a corrugated metal roof, a single bed, one crib, and wooden boxes for furniture. Raw sewage ran nearby; stray dogs roamed free. Twelve-year-old Flávio, the eldest child, appeared to be responsible for the care of his siblings and the household in general. Parks decided to focus on the boy's daily life, intrigued by his maturity amid burdensome circumstances. In *Flávio*, his 1978 memoir of the experience, he recalled encountering the boy hauling water up the favela's steep slope: "He was horribly thin, naked but for his ragged pants. His legs looked like sticks covered with skin and screwed into two dirty feet. He stopped for breath, coughing, his chest heaving as the water slopped over his shoulders and distended belly.... Death was all over him, in his sunken eyes and cheeks, in his jaundiced coloring and aged walk." In subsequent days, Parks witnessed Flávio overtaken by recurrent bouts of asthma; after a visit to a local health facility, he learned the boy would likely die within two years. In the magazine,

Parks portrays the household's deprivation and Flávio's caretaking with a sense of impending doom. In the most striking image, Flávio lies in bed, half covered by a ragged blanket, his swollen chest exposed, anguish on his face. The foreshortened perspective and partial exposure of the body explicitly recall Mantegna's *Dead Christ,* as does the caption, in which the child-as-father worries about his family: "I am not afraid of death.... But what will they do after?" The effect was to imbue the sick, malnourished child's suffering with meaning far beyond the sociological.

Titled "Freedom's Fearful Foe: Poverty," the photo essay (along with Parks's diary entries) appeared in *Life* on June 16, 1961, beginning with a two-page spread showing Isabel da Silva as a toddler crying in what the caption describes as her "shadowy slum world." The section concluded with another dramatic spread—the ailing, Christlike Flávio paired with a neighbor child, also shot from a foreshortened angle, wrapped in a winding sheet, surrounded by candles, awaiting burial. The compositional echoes between the two images all but declared the twelve-year-old's imminent fate.

Guilt and empathy combined to motivate readers: letters and money poured into the magazine, organizations sent food and donations directly to Brazil, and an asthma hospital in Denver offered to treat the boy for two years free of charge. By the end of the summer, the "Flávio fund" had collected over $24,000, and he was living in Denver with a Portuguese family while receiving top-notch medical care. In its July 21, 1961, issue, the magazine touted the transformation with a color cover depicting the scrubbed and smiling boy hugging a stuffed animal. A self-congratulatory cover line, "Flávio's Rescue: Americans bring him from Rio slum to be cured," introduced images surely calculated to reward readers—Flávio making friends, trying out new shoes, and warily regarding a baseball bat. The dire shot of the sick boy that previously ran juxtaposed with a child's corpse was now run next to an image of a gleeful Flávio on a playground swing. If this salvation narrative didn't fully soothe the disquieting sentiments provoked just weeks before, there were also photos of the da Silva family in their new "modern" home.

That this apparent triumph of American goodwill illustrated a microversion of what Kennedy planned to do to halt the spread of communism in Latin America—use foreign aid to gain influence throughout the region—wasn't lost on Brazilians. When the *Life* articles appeared, the country was in the midst of political upheaval sparked in part by Cold War tensions. *O Cruzeiro*, a magazine devoted to photojournalism, assigned one of its premier photographers to travel to New York to expose *its* "shadowy slum world." Like Parks, Henri Ballot had spent decades documenting victims of economic and racial oppression, particularly the indigenous peoples of Brazil. And, like Parks, when he arrived in the city, he sought out a poor family—in this case, Felix and Esther Gonzalez and their six children, Puerto Rican residents of the Lower East Side. Ballot's images mirror those of Parks. Indeed, the American's photos were included in *O Cruzeiro* as insets to demonstrate the parallels. The provocation hit home: The photo of nine-year-old Ely-Samuel asleep on a torn and filthy mattress, cockroaches crawling over his body, was later reproduced along with the photo of Flávio in bed in *Time*, *Life*'s sister publication. The article, titled "Carioca's Revenge," even accused Ballot of manipulating his images, perhaps even placing insects on the boy.

Despite both photographers' strong sense of social mission, their images served goals they didn't fully apprehend. The same can be said for their subjects, who were marshaled as proxies in a larger geopolitical duel. Flávio initially benefited from Parks's and *Life*'s intervention; his asthma cured, he became quite accustomed to middle-class suburban life. When his treatment was completed after two years, arrangements were made for him to return to Rio. But he asked Parks to adopt him so he could remain in the United States. "I would rather stay here with you," the boy pleaded. "Don't you want me?" His return home touched a nerve, prompting a nationalist response from Brazilian newspapers that claimed Flávio now had "airs of superiority." As might be expected, there was a personal toll. Time Inc.'s Rio bureau chief, who monitored the homecoming, reported that Flávio was "close to traumatic shock." Over the course of subsequent years, he struggled to assimilate the disruption he had experienced—he was expelled from the private school *Life* arranged for him to attend—but eventually settled back into his new, old life.

Parks and Flávio reunited in 1976 when the photographer was working on his memoir. In the foreword to *Flávio,* he confessed doubt about stories he'd done that altered people's lives, wondering "if it might not have been wiser to have those lives untouched, to have let them grind out their time as fate intended." Having found the da Silvas' once-new home in distressing shape, Parks registered the difficulty of redeeming an entire family, if not a vast social ill, in one fell swoop. A photo taken during that visit catches a contemplative Flávio studying a collection of Parks's images from the 1961 shoot. A twenty-seven-year-old night watchman with a family of his own, Flávio gazes at a picture of his younger brother Mario crying after being bitten by a dog. Although he had come so far from what had seemed a hopeless future, Flávio was discontented; before Parks left, he again asked for help returning to the United States. When he saw this depiction of a suffering child, or the now-iconic image of himself as a boy in bed struggling to breathe, what was his reaction after all these years? The pain of that time had been memorialized and mobilized by forces outside his control. Was he conscious of his role in distant political strategies? No one, it seems, thought to ask him.

Now seventy, Flávio attended the opening of the show at the Getty Center. Standing in the galleries, he surely took note of how profoundly the photos in *Life* had changed his life and how, in their ongoing evocation of both his pain and his joy, they were changing him still.

*Bookforum,* December–January 2020.

# Dead Man Rising: War Photography

Viewing the War Photography show currently at the Brooklyn Museum offers a test of emotional restraint as well as the inclination to aestheticize. If the number of images (over four hundred) is daunting, the sum of human pain on display registers as a body blow. Only a practiced and necessary resistance to the actuality depicted (corpses burned and dismembered, hangings, shootings, the contorted, agonized faces of the wounded) allows the viewer to move through this horror show without being overwhelmed.

I found some images easier than others to insulate myself from: those from the distant past—the Crimean War, Gettysburg, Iwo Jima—are familiar from old magazines and textbooks and so appear embalmed in the protective aura of the historical. More recent scenes from Afghanistan, Iraq, Vietnam, or Somalia were snapped in far-flung locales, places where violence seems to have been safely sequestered. Aside from my personal relation to the photos of the World Trade Center in flames, I am a wary tourist in this domain of mayhem. The show's curators acknowledge their audience's naiveté—Anne Wilkes Tucker's epigraph from Susan Sontag for the catalogue's introductory essay is an apt and telling one: "The understanding of war among people who have not experienced war is now chiefly a product of the impact of the images [of wartime photographs]."

While these virtual intimations of mortality pale in comparison to actual combat, it is still difficult to remain immune to their force. Part of their impact springs from their artfulness—the deployment of light and composition to deepen the photo's impact, its memorability. The effect, though, is twofold: to be sure, when skillfully presented the visceral detail is sharpened and the viewer braced; but that artfulness also offers an alternative response, one primarily focused on those formal properties—the way a soldier cradling a comrade resembles the *Pietá*, or the grainy finish that blends the texture of mud with the skin of a wounded man. We retreat from the fact of bloody spectacle by focusing on the blood's subtle palette.

A photo taken in 1966 by French photographer Henri Huet is efficiently described by his caption: "The body of an American paratrooper killed in action in the jungle near the Cambodian border is raised up to an evacuation helicopter, Vietnam." Although he grew up in France, Huet was born in Vietnam and returned there to cover the First Indochina War and then the US involvement. A series of powerful photos published in *Life* magazine in early 1966—the cover image showed two heavily bandaged G.I.'s, one a medic, attending to the other—is often cited as among the first graphic depictions of the war for an American audience. He continued his work in Vietnam until a helicopter carrying him and several other journalists was shot down over Laos in 1971. Everyone aboard died. Their remains weren't recovered until 1998.

In Huet's soft-focus, black-and-white photo, we see the helicopter from a vantage directly beneath; the paratrooper's body floats midway between the ground and the chopper. The bright sky obscures the cables attached to the corpse so it appears unsupported; in fact, it's easier to see the figure as diving from the helicopter rather than being lifted up. The corpse's arms hang loosely and the head falls back, but a closer look allows us to imagine the arms outstretched and head flung back in joy—the retrieval of a casualty morphing into an exultant ascension. Trees, vehicle, and Marine emerge in silhouette, the lack of interior detail enhancing the image's abstraction. The biomorphic quality of the helicopter—the torso-round cabin, the elevators in the rear like open arms—suggests a corporeal, even maternal connection between man and machine: the soldier descends or rises in either embarkation from or return to home.

Such speculative readings are, of course, routine; they are made at the image-maker's invitation. Huet's complex image affords the viewer ample opportunities to aestheticize, but does our reflex to interpret compromise an ethical and emotional response? What does it mean to attend to the pattern of light and dark, the way the sky's white glare encases the shadow-bound body, even as we dim our awareness of this lost life, a young man who bled out on the forest floor, a world away from home?

For more than a century and a half, America's wars have taken place somewhere else. Over the past decade, flag-draped caskets have returned, and families have grieved. Yet less than one percent of the nation's population has served in Iraq and Afghanistan, so this pain is well quarantined; the rest of us know about the widows and amputees because we've seen the pictures. It's nowhere near enough knowing, but if you look unguarded, it's really too much.

*Hyperallergic,* January 18, 2014.

# Night and the City: Weegee Showed New York the Spectacle of Itself

The tabloid photographer Arthur Fellig, better known as Weegee, produced many iconic New York City images, but one in particular, taken in December 1940 in the East Village, captures the quintessence of his life and career. The photo presents a slain gangster, one Lewis Sandano, face down on the pavement, partially covered by what appears to be a crumpled and bloodied sheet of butcher paper; a policeman stands beside the corpse and takes notes with businesslike aplomb. But this otherwise ordinary crime-scene image offers a wry comedic twist—dominating the foreground of the frame, hovering over the body, is a lamppost mailbox that bears the official request MAIL EARLY FOR DELIVERY BEFORE CHRISTMAS. The grisly subject, deadpan humor, and compositional showmanship (much debated at the time was whether the body had been moved to make the joke) are all trademarks of Weegee's art. His attentiveness to the viewer, the voyeur, and the witness—in this instance, the impassive cop—marks his chronicle of mayhem as distinctive and revelatory. As a freelance photographer, he prowled the streets in a Chevy with his Speed Graphic camera and police radio, arriving on the scene while the blood oozed and the flames still rose. These images came to define the sensibility of New York between the wars.

Like many of the artists who came to prominence during the Depression, Weegee arrived at Ellis Island as a child from Europe, in his case from Ukraine. He grew up on the Lower East Side. Around 1913, he dropped out of the seventh grade and, according to Christopher Bonanos's *Flash: The Making of Weegee the Famous*, had a "life-changing" experience when a street photographer took his picture. Fascinated by the technical process of producing tintypes—the complex camera, dunking the slide in an alkaline solution—he soon acquired his own kit. He began his freelance career in suitably opportunistic fashion: He would grab a kid on the street, prop them up on a pony, shoot, and then peddle the pictures to the child's mother. Bonanos reports that the horse ate all his profits, but Weegee still learned a lesson in professionalism: "He washed the children's faces, too, later saying, 'That's how I got pride in my work.'" Another lesson—this one stylistic—grew out of the experience. He printed on high-contrast paper in order to give the kids, as he described it, the "nice white, chalky faces" their immigrant parents preferred.

His first real job was at the *New York Times* drying fresh prints and negatives; the task conferred a nickname, "Squeegee Boy." It was this rather mundane origin, Bonanos reveals, rather than his so-called Ouija-like prescience about crime and catastrophe, that led to the nickname Weegee. Capitalizing on a newspaper war between the *Daily News* and the *Daily Mirror*, he sold both tabloids pictures through a photo agency. The cagey, self-promoting Weegee of legend emerges from his moment when rampant crime and competition for scoops fed a citywide fascination with increasingly morbid depictions of sin's wages. He donned a doctor's white coat to gain access to the hospital room where gangster Dutch Schultz was dying, and paid, as he bragged, "special attention to the bullet holes in his chest"; he photographed himself (via a tripod and cable release) peering into a trunk stuffed with the contorted corpse of a mobster; he snapped another dead gangster lazily sprawled on the sidewalk, the victim's bright white straw hat unbent and unblemished. "I gave them all my love and care," Weegee said. "Made 'em look like they were just taking a little rest."

He hit his stride in the late '30s, producing many of his most poignant and enduring pictures, and won his long battle for credit in the papers (his work had previously appeared without attribution). He became a name brand, a photographer who often wrote his own sardonic captions, and more and more an artist attuned to compositional nuance and human drama. A paddy wagon shot of two seated men shows them only from the waist down: "Factory Frankie," a mob insider, sports a suit and polished shoes; the other guy, a low-ranking dockworker in the organization, wears dungarees and beat-up oxfords. Although Weegee shot numerous fires, one of his most memorable among such images might be that of a mother and daughter who had escaped their burning tenement, leaving family members behind. Each woman's face contorts with agony; the mother casts her face upward, likely at the building they just fled, while her daughter—her face illuminated by the flash—regards the camera, imploring us for empathy or perhaps privacy.

Further exposing the voyeurism and anonymity of city life is a photo taken on Prince Street. A body lies in the doorway of a tenement, but Weegee shoots from afar to take in most of two buildings; from nearly every window onlookers crane to observe the spectacle. The photo appeared in *Life* magazine, and Bonanos tracked down Vito Cosenza, who was then seven and recalls, "There's a little face on the third floor, looking out. That's me." Focusing on the spectators' response to violence, Weegee foreshadowed the sense of isolation and indifference that would crystallize around the Kitty Genovese case some decades later.

While Weegee found beauty in the mess: the chance tumble of a corpse, its inelegant posture, hand outstretched toward a pistol, or the gawker, her neck straining, and eyes aglow with mortal revelation, one iconic image of his incorporates many of the formal imperatives of classical art. The photo that appeared in the *Daily News* presents two party-going Brooklynites, Charles Sodokoff and Arthur Webber, sitting in a paddy wagon. The accompanying copy read: "In Top Hats—In Trouble" and went on to describe how the "[b]oys were tippling at Astor Bar Saturday night when they decided to slide down banisters for fun (???). Cop was called and they assaulted him."

The preceding hijinks may have been unruly but Weegee's depiction of the aftermath contains formal elements that could mark a scene painted by Raphael. Both men hide their faces with identical hats, both wear satin-striped, black pants, black shoes, silk socks, and black coats. The shine on their shoes allows a call-and-response of highlights; their bodies mirror one another in nearly every aspect, even to the four fingers each man displays across the crown of his hat. A spare tire affixed to the wall seems akin to a classical archway, through which, in a Renaissance painting, we would view a distant village.

Unlike many of Weegee's subjects—gangsters or gaudy citizens of the demimonde—who faced his camera with flagrant disregard, Charles and Arthur are twinned in their shame. Their desire to hide could be attributed to the location of their arrests—the bar at the Hotel Astor, the most famous gay rendezvous in all New York. These two young men—the paper gave their ages as 28 and 32, respectively—very likely have more to hide than an encounter with the police. Even in the highly stylized composition, Weegee's tabloid sensibility is felt; the camera seems to push into the van, it's flash pressing against them, illuminating the back wall to contrast the darkness of their garb and articulate every last detail—the folds of the coats, the buttons, the crescent trace of each man's hair just above the hat. They may have cloaked their faces, but the photographer subjects everything else to meticulous inspection: they are exposed in their concealment.

The strange allure of the image resides in this revealed furtiveness. The viewer registers the men's fear—as well as their need to not appear *too* afraid. Such a perceived overreaction might prove incriminating to friends and family members opening their newspapers the next morning. After all, what's to hide—just a bit of a bar brawl. Embodying the paradox of exposure and enclosure, the symmetry intensifies the actual tightening and tensing of bodies by forcing them into such overly precise iconography. Symmetry thus reads as a kind of straitjacket, one that articulates the sensation of emotional compression surely felt by Charles and Arthur as they cringed from the camera's pursuit. Rather than serving the beautiful, an ideal of physical and moral balance, the symmetry at work is a force of restriction, of intimidation.

A paparazzi *avant la lettre*, Weegee stalked damage and distress and played it as he found it—disordered and raw. Yet in this photograph, he drew on the polite aesthetics of the academy to expose not only his subjects but, via his classical touch, something of the nature of his craft—how the hunter corners his prey.

By the early '40s the murder rate had declined, and Weegee, who was losing interest in those bodies that did turn up ("I don't waste my genius on most of them"), turned to documenting proletarian New York, broadening his audience to include the socially conscious members of the Photo League and curators at the Museum of Modern Art, who were newly aware of the artistic qualities of photojournalism. Two recent residents of an all-white block in Washington Heights—an African American mother and her one-year-old son—are photographed at their front door, its glass shattered by rocks thrown by neighbors. Bonanos correctly notes that the image could easily stand alongside work by Dorothea Lange or Walker Evans. Weegee had an intimate and unsentimental understanding of poverty. A photo of eight children sleeping in disarray on a fire escape surely recalled the summer nights of his youth, yet the merciless lighting reveals the children's dirty feet and bruises, the stains on the blankets.

Weegee might have left the corpses behind, but he could hardly abandon his antic, satiric sense of humor or his willingness to cheat when necessary. In what Bonanos dubs "one of the most famous images of the 20th century," two jewel-and-fur-draped ladies arrive at the Metropolitan Opera and confidently approach the camera. Just off to the side, a gritty, disheveled woman scowls at them. Each embodies a prescribed role: The two wear tiaras on coiffed heads while the other clutches her bags as if they are her only possessions. But maybe too much so; Weegee denied staging the confrontation, but years later, his assistant admitted that the photographer had plied the woman with booze and put her into play. Nevertheless, the photo, known as *The Critic,* propelled him into an upper tier of artists—a display at MOMA, gallery shows, a meeting with Alfred Stieglitz, and eventually *Naked City,* a book of collected photos. With his newfound recognition well beyond the grimy quarters of tabloid readers and police precincts, he had truly earned his self-made honorific, "Weegee the Famous."

Of course, Hollywood came calling, and Weegee lent his book title and some city savvy to Jules Dassin's film of the same name, which, quite unusually for the time, was shot on location on the streets of New York. He pressed producer Mark Hellinger for a role but settled for a cameo. In Los Angeles, he turned his attention to more bit parts, set photography, and portraits of movie stars. He found a fellow newsman in Stanley Kubrick, who had worked as a press photographer for *Look* magazine before becoming a filmmaker. Weegee took the set photos for *Dr. Strangelove* and trained his eye on the director, catching him framing shots and peering into camera lenses. "Once again," Bonanos comments, "the voyeur photographed the watcher—and was there ever a more acutely focused watcher than Stanley Kubrick?" Back in New York he joined a club devoted to cheesecake photos and managed to produce an image that stands with his best—a shot of Bettie Page in a bathing suit, taken from just behind her as she stands, arms akimbo, under glaring spotlights, while some half-dozen men aim their cameras at her.

The incriminatory nature of the photo extends to Weegee himself and beyond, to a voyeuristic culture. A drunken woman drafted to perform as an outcast or the mailbox message appearing above Lewis Sandano's body makes it easy for us to confront misery and murder. It was different a few years later when Weegee arrived in Williamsburg to document the demise of a gambler named Peter Mancuso, who had been shot in the head and heart. Weegee did not photograph the body but instead turned from within the circle around it to capture the varied faces of the throng—mostly children—assembled to gawk or grieve. The tumultuous bodies and intensity of emotion evoke Caravaggio, even as the scene feels utterly contemporary. We know these people. The dead man's aunt sobs open-mouthed; the kids jostle one another, some trying to gain a better view, others to greet the camera with toothy grins; the eyes of a small girl at the center of the image, almost next to the wailing aunt, are aflame with an insistent desire to *see*. Her excitement charges the frame with anticipation. Whatever fills her wide and seemingly greedy eyes isn't available to us; we must imagine it. Weegee titled his frenzied tableau *Their First Murder*. This one, he made clear, isn't about the bodies or the killers; this photo is about the thrill of looking. It's about us.

*Bookforum*, Summer 2018.

# Saul Leiter: Centennial Showcase

A city might be defined as a place whose inhabitants live in public. Whether on the sidewalk, square, or subway, we are available to be watched and scrutinized; even in our apartments, we can be spied out from the avenues, our shadows moving behind curtains. A generation of street photographers—Lee Friedlander, Helen Levitt, Garry Winogrand, and Weegee among them—made New York City their open-air studio, one in which they relied on those moments of spontaneous revelation the town so freely disburses. Saul Leiter roamed the same streets during the same period as these photographers and bore a similar affection for the city's ongoing spectacle. But when he died in 2013, he had just begun to be recognized as their peer. The release of a documentary film—*In No Great Hurry: 13 Lessons in Life with Saul Leiter*—that year and the subsequent publication of several volumes of photos advanced his reputation while also revealing his pronounced distinctiveness from the pack. Despite street photography's necessarily offhand, voyeuristic method, the photos produced by its luminaries often have a studied quality. Exhibiting a classical composition and social narrative, Winogrand's *New York World's Fair* (1964), with its row of variously animated women on a park bench, is justly iconic, an image ready-made for the museum postcard rack. Leiter, on the other hand, creates impressionistic effects that often obscure his subject, ones that are often themselves obscure. He is a poet of the interior world of public space.

At Howard Greenberg Gallery, a show marking Leiter's centennial offers a range of his work over several decades—street photography, fashion images for *Harper's Bazaar,* moody chiaroscuro nudes, and paintings bearing kinship with assorted Abstract Expressionists. In each of these categories, most especially street photography, Leiter proves an ingenious craftsman whose skill resides in cloaking a wry subversiveness within seeming naivete. His artistry doesn't announce itself. Perhaps this is why it took many years and his passing for him to gain deserved recognition. And, of course, there was his disinclination toward careerism: in *13 Lessons in Life,* he repeatedly expresses dismay at being its subject. "I'm not carried away by the greatness of Mr. Leiter," he tells director Tomas Leach.

A series of black-and-white photos titled *Shoes of the Shoeshine Man,* published in *Life* in 1951, offers only that: images of men's footwear awaiting polish on the sidewalk. Some are tattered and others well kept (such as in the example on view in the gallery), but the implied social hierarchies, while present, recede within Leiter's formalist approach, and the images take on an abstract, taxonomic quality that might call to mind the work of Bernd and Hilla Becher. Unlike their photos of sizable structures, though, Leiter's pictures deliver viewers to the unnoticed, even disdained realm of pavement level. This is where intimate things—a torn sole, frayed cuff, bare ankle—usually evade notice. Although no face is in sight, Leiter's voyeuristic intrusion cuts sharply.

Foul weather suited Leiter's desire for subjects who, rather than conversing on park benches, are burdened with heavy coats and hats, darting amid snowfall or a downpour. "There's something about raindrops," he says in the film, and he often allows the precipitation to blur his lens, or he shoots through splattered glass. The color print *Pull* (ca. 1960) depicts two figures, a woman and a man, visible through a streaked and foggy glass door (a "pull" sticker dominates the foreground). Standing in slush, their bodies are charcoal smudges that appear to deliquesce in the condensation. They inhabit an otherworldly, ever-decomposing zone rather than some familiar New York scene.

Leiter began using color in the '50s when it was dismissed by critics as not serious. He employed its eloquent possibilities in sly, unexpected ways. In another winter scene, a woman makes her way through billowing flakes, her red umbrella daubed with white. Her posture suggests she was moving quickly through the storm. We might imagine that Leiter was aiming to capture the cryptic graffiti on the facade behind her when she darted into his viewfinder. The umbrella arrives in this gray tableau as if by accident, its hue a quiet eruption. *Red Umbrella* (1958) displays a quintessential urban encounter—a swath of empty, anonymous space pierced by a random passerby, one glimpsed partially and then, by implication, only for a second. Leiter isn't looking for Henri Cartier-Bresson's "decisive moment," but rather those moments that elude us even as we experience them.

The occluded or atypical perspective is surely Leiter's trademark. He shoots people from inside moving cars, reflected in mirrored surfaces, or observed from beneath a canopy. A crowd of tourists jostles at the rear of a San Francisco cable car in an untitled shot taken from the backseat of a taxi through its windshield. Or we inspect street scenes from elevated perches, the camera's field blocked by subway trestles or window gates, the subjects arrayed like anthropological specimens below. One shot in the series *From the El* (1950s) presents two men from directly above, their faces invisible beneath hats, next to a bishops-crook lamppost; the arching light looms over these mere acolytes to their vertical master. Leiter works against compositional conventions to achieve a visual equivalent of storytelling's *in medias res*, a sense that the *before* and *after* of what the camera has recorded is of equal and perhaps greater importance.

Photography's uneasy relationship to verisimilitude has been broadly understood since well before the era of digital manipulation, yet we still continue to believe in the rough equivalence of photos to facts. Leiter questioned this connection with images that prize what can't be known, his camera often entering a scene veiled or at an oblique angle so as to register the mechanism's inadequacies. *Through Boards* (1957) is candid about this choice. (Unfortunately, it is not in the exhibition, but can be found in the thorough new monograph *Saul Leiter: The Centennial Retrospective*.) The shot was taken behind planks, perhaps from within a construction site, that blind us to all but a lustrous sliver in the center of the frame, where a shiny white automobile appears to be parked and pedestrians regard a shop window. The bottom half of the photo is almost completely black, while the top consists of two bands, one black, one rust colored; between these Rothko-like striations lies the slender domain of lived life, its fullness withheld from us, fleeting in this unknowing. This is Leiter's unheard melody. "The real world," he confides in the documentary, "has more to do with what's hidden." The paradox—that an instrument dependent on light might serve the goal of concealment—is only one of the many satisfying provocations afforded by this retrospective.

*4Columns,* January19, 2024.

# Review of *Type 42*: *Fame Is the Name of the Game*

In the spring of 2012, artist Jason Brinkerhoff found a cache of some 950 Polaroids devoted to television images from the 1960s and early '70s. The photos—the book's title takes its name from a popular Polaroid film stock, Type 42—gathered in this sampling from that collection are mostly of actresses appearing on what is probably a modest-size black-and-white television. Each actress has been shot during a close-up, and her name (whether famous or quite obscure) has been inked on the snapshot's border. Although attempts to trace the archive back to its creator have proved fruitless, a few speculations might be made: The photographer was obsessed with Polaroid photography, famous women, whom he or she very much liked to watch. The images themselves—dark-hued, grainy, out-of-focus—conjure the close quarters of an apartment lit only by the screen's glow. The compulsion evidenced by the number of photos, their careful identification, and the fidelity to a single, palpably interior motif all suggest a lonely life whose most vital relationship may have been with the faces flickering on a vacuum tube.

Dating from a pre-HD, pre-cable era, when broadcast signals depended on rabbit ear antennae, and black-and-white portable sets could turn even sitcoms into film noir, these spectral portraits are imbued with sadness and longing. They cast a gloomy spell, even though their subjects (Ursula Andress, Doris Day, Catherine Deneuve, Anita Ekberg, Jane Fonda, Virna Lisi, Sophia Loren) are the epitome of klieg-lit glamour. Along with screen legends, the anonymous artist also favored second-tier ingenues like Yvette Mimieux, who started in B pics (*Monkeys, Go Home!*; *Where the Boys Are*) and aged into made-for-TV movies. Owing to the lack of focus and overexposure, Mimieux's blond mane incandesces against the surrounding blackness, and her facial features are nearly submerged in blurring light. Yet she remains recognizable (despite the haphazardness of the image and its uncertain context, she's clearly—perhaps only to me—the shy, barefoot Eloi girl that Rod Taylor returns to the future for in *The Time Machine*); even minor fame leaves us with an indelible imprint.

That Elizabeth Taylor's iconic visage might emerge from the murk of Polaroid printing and bad reception is less surprising. The film and the scene are readily placed—an angry Liz confronting her alcoholic husband (played by Paul Newman) in *Cat on a Hot Tin Roof*. Taken at what seems to be a slight angle to the screen, the photo distorts Taylor's face and shoulder, the slight elongation of both suggesting her resistance to being swallowed by static. Taylor's not one to go gently—she holds the corner of the frame, teeth bared, eyes blazing. The subtitle of the volume, *Fame Is the Name of the Game*, is the title of a 1966 TV movie, and as such it's penned on a print showing a somnolent Jill St. John, lost, it seems, in a soft-focus dream of beautiful, caressing light. A long time ago, in a room with shades drawn, someone discovered you could live in that radiance at the turn of a dial. If the ghostly faces in this realm were indeed as evanescent as Pound's "petals on a wet, black bough," they might still be saved on Type 42, a pocket-size mercy that postponed for a while the final fade out.

*Bookforum*, April–May 2015.

# Go with the Slow: Ragnar Kjartansson's *The Visitors*

Behind a curtain in the darkened gallery space at Luhring Augustine, nine screens, each equipped with its own speaker, have been arranged into two somewhat discreet areas. Eight of the screens feature the image of a single musician—a guitarist, pianist, banjo player, cellist, and so forth—and one screen offers a view of the porch of a large house where other instrumentalists, singers, and assorted folks have gathered. Ragnar Kjartansson's video installation titled *The Visitors* documents in a single take the 64-minute-long performance of one song.

The Hudson Valley mansion where the film was made has been employed before by the Icelandic artist: In 2007's *Blossoming Trees Performance,* he documented two days on the property in which he "performed" the role of a landscape painter. More recently, in 2011, at the Carnegie in Pittsburgh, Kjartansson staged a live three-week performance (*Song*) in which three of his nieces repeatedly sang fragments from a poem by Allen Ginsberg. His work can be situated within the long tradition extending from composers of Gregorian chant to Gertrude Stein, John Cage, and Christian Marclay, all of whom employ repetition and duration to explore the sensation of passing time.

Testing the patience of an audience is only one aspect of Kjartansson's gambit. By dilating the temporal, he's also attempting to reorganize our sense of narrative. After the first, say, 20 minutes of watching *The Visitors,* the viewer either accedes to the experience or grows bored and departs. If you stay, you'll see that, on their separate screens, the musicians play introspectively, often almost immobile except for the movements required to sing and strum. Soon you'll become aware of even their tiniest movements, the slightest variations from their otherwise inward, almost stately dispositions. When the pianist lights a cigar during a lull, it feels as if the first rudiment of a story has been put in place. When the bassist leaves his room/screen to join him in a smoke, the effect approaches the dramatic. Otherwise, insignificant gestures acquire purposeful heft as they fill out the durational largesse.

Each screen is a carefully lit tableau vivant: sculptures, paintings, floral print fabrics and domestic bric-a-brac contribute to a painterly scene—a guitarist sits at a desk in a library of red leather-bound books; another guitarist perches on the edge of a bed while someone sleeps beside him; an accordionist sits half in shadow, half in light by an open window. The HD video projection shimmers with detail and depth: Vermeer or Caravaggio could have set these stages. The stillness of these scenes, the dirge-like pace of the song, as well as its repetitive lyrics (the line "Once again I fall into my feminine ways" is probably heard a few dozen times) combine to focus attention on what is typically recessive, unnoticed—the visual space between the players, the auditory space between the sung words and struck notes. As viewers, then, we find ourselves *amid* rather than *at* a performance. As our status as viewers gradually erodes, we discover that we aren't the audience; we're, well, visitors.

The musicians play the arrangement precisely and in harmony, their successful interaction facilitated by the headphones they wear. They are alone, each isolated in one room of the house (except those on the porch), yet intimately connected via technology, via their common endeavor—the performance. The house itself becomes a metaphor for this duality of alone and together, inside and outside, as we roam about its interior and then see the whole structure in the shot, presenting performers and friends on the porch and lawn. Perhaps more than a metaphor, the house is, in fact, the instrument they are all playing. Kjartansson has placed himself in perhaps the least aesthetic, most comically self-deprecating circumstance; he strums a beat-up guitar while lounging naked in a suds-filled tub. Pudgy, pale, and dreamy-eyed, he makes an improbable yet somehow charismatic frontman. Like the artist's performance of a landscape painter in *Blossoming Trees*, here he plays a role—the musician lost in tuneful reverie; at one point, he sets down the guitar and splashes the water as if it were a keyboard.

If Kjartansson is the soulful singer in the shower, privately enacting a public role, the other musicians follow suit to varying degrees; the cellist rocks in her chair as if possessed by the swelling sounds, and the accordionist's feet dance beneath her chair. No one regards the camera: they act as if they are unobserved. They portray aloneness, even as they act collectively. Is this duality—its tensions and attractions—in some way related to the repeated declaration the singers make, that they are falling into their "feminine ways"? The line comes from a poem by artist Ásdís Sif Gunnarsdóttir, Kjartansson's ex-wife. Another much-repeated line is "There are stars exploding around you, and there's nothing, nothing you can do." This, too, suggests ways to think about individual subjectivity amid larger social subjectivities. Are the negotiations between these modes what constitute feminine ways?

Walking around the divided room, circumambulating the center wall with its screens on either side, may be the ideal way to inhabit the installation. Such movement feels apt when set against the relative stillness on the screens. (The group on the porch, though, is more active. On the lawn, a cannon barrel is tamped with old rags and eventually detonated.) As the hour mark nears, Kjartansson rises from the tub and, wrapped in a towel, departs the bathroom; the other players also leave their posts, all the while playing (even the cello is borne along) and singing, congregating in one room, and then proceeding out to the porch. The entire group then ambles down the lawn to the field below the house. The camera remains stationary as they drift into the encroaching dusk, their voices growing ever dimmer. The band and sundry friends, now finally joined together, their voices meshed without mechanical aid, appear fanciful, like medieval troubadours, as their song—their very long song—finally fades. The sense of ending is unexpectedly profound. While nothing has happened, musicians merely played and sang, the overall experience pulses with momentum; paradoxically, the lack of action has made much of very little. In leaving their separate rooms and gathering for the journey outward, the musicians seem to enact an ancient and joyous ritual.

In *The Visitors,* Kjartansson tries our patience, but not without an emotional reward that is all the more stirring for rising out of the commonplace. The beauty of this immersive work catches us unaware, in part because the artist has situated us in his art. We, too, perform as we "visit" each screen, listen closely to each voice; we've fallen into this house and its ways. And when the video ends and you part the curtains to leave, you cannot help but feel the fresh excitement of setting off, in company, with real and imagined others.

*Hyperallergic,* March 16, 2013.

# Garry Winogrand in Living Color

As we know from the countless photos and films, a good deal of the first half of the 20th century took place in black and white. We are surprised when we see color pictures of, say, soldiers celebrating the end of World War II or Greta Garbo; it's as if these scenes, these people, have been untethered from their proper historical context to present a fresh notion of how the past occurred. Black-and-white photos—dependent as they are on the contrast between shadow and light—signal seriousness even when they depict flagpole sitters or Fred Astaire.

Although color became increasing available by the 1950s, photographers like Robert Frank, Lee Friedlander, Diane Arbus, and Bruce Davidson worked mostly in black-and-white, no doubt influenced by the prevailing "fine art" aesthetic expressed by Frank ("Black and white are the colors of photography") and Walker Evans, who deemed color images "vulgar." But color did emerge as the dominant style in commercial venues, and Garry Winogrand, who shot for such publications as *Collier's* and *Sports Illustrated*, took a liking to Kodachrome. Attracted to its high resolution and lifelike hues, he began carrying two cameras to immediately follow his black-and-white shot with a color version. Because color film was expensive and difficult to develop, he typically presented this work with a projector, in the manner of family slide shows.

The Brooklyn Museum displays the 425 images assembled for *Garry Winogrand: Color* in much the same "carousel" manner. In a darkened room, eight projectors rotate through a few dozen thematically or stylistically related photos, lingering on each one for several seconds.

This allows viewers to get some sense of the prolific Winogrand's working method (these were chosen from 45,000 images). The fleeting appearance mimics the photographer's seemingly indiscriminate, point-and-shoot style. For instance, as a lively parade of Coney Island beachgoers flickers past, we seem to stroll with Winogrand through the crowd, turning this way and that.

But the rapidity proves a barrier to fully enjoying these lush and potentially entrancing photos. Winogrand had a knack for discovering intimate dramas—an untitled image from Coney Island captures two tan, tattooed young men, one affectionately leaning his head against the other's shoulder. Deeper engagement with these social connections is cut short until the image cycles back minutes later. It takes a few viewings to discern the homemade tattoo that suggests affiliation with some neighborhood group ("32 St boys") or the echoing curves of shoulders, elbows, knees, and chins. In this case, a black-and-white version would deprive the image of the richly tanned skin and its associations with seaside pleasures, diminishing the air of languorous sensuality. Color plays a similar role in an untitled image from Cape Cod in 1966. This study in shapes—cylindrical mustard and ketchup dispensers arrayed like sentries around bowls of relish and onions—is enlivened by the saturated, almost electrified reds and yellows Kodachrome produces. The gleaming relish exudes pungency; so vivid are the two foremost bottles they seem to be begging for a squeeze. It's a festive summer day, the sunlight palpable on each object. This insistent realism and sense of the moment owes almost entirely to the lucent quality of the color slide.

But this formalist treatment of inanimate objects isn't Winogrand's typical mode. More frequently, he was drawn to people—their interactions, postures, and movements. His New York street photos capture the theatrical quality of pedestrian life: his subjects often appear to dramatize an element of plot or characterization in a play. In an untitled image from 1965, the photographer peers directly into the oncoming foot traffic. The two women in the immediate foreground are engaged in conversation; a Black woman speaks as her white companion listens pensively, eyes downcast. Both are likely office workers; they are well-coiffed, stylishly dressed, and sporting conspicuous necklaces.

The turn of the speaker's head, her canny, assessing glance, suggests she's imparting some confidence—perhaps a piece of news about an office scandal or a romantic liaison. The listener, in a blue dress, holds her cigarette outside of their conversational space, as if acknowledging the importance of what's being said. Around them are men in dark suits and white shirts, the unvarying uniform of the day.

Even if Winogrand hadn't shot this scene in color, thus not registering one woman's sparks and splashes of red (lipstick, handbag, and jewelry) or the near palpable nap of her friend's mauve coat, we would be struck by their emergence from the clutch of gray-clad men, like protagonists stepping out of a crowd of extras. But the vivid hues further announce and animate their forward-moving presence and bring the women into familiar visual terrain—their fashion may be outdated, but the impulse toward colorful, expressive adornment is not.

Winogrand's black-and-white photographs, despite their dynamic narratives, can sometimes carry a whiff of bygone days. Especially as the '50s and '60s recede in memory, we find ourselves enjoying period details—vintage buses, the ubiquity of men's hats, the formality of street attire in general. If a scrim of nostalgia threatens to obscure the photographer's compositional acuity and preternatural alertness to his subjects' self-possession, these Kodachrome slides dispel it handily. They deliver a contemporary jolt to long-familiar tableaux and allow us to see what Winogrand himself was seeing: a city, a world, as alive as the one you walked out into today.

*Hyperallergic*, July 16, 2019.

# Flow Charts: Edward Burtynsky's Photos of the World's Watery Parts

It's well known that landscape photographer Edward Burtynsky thinks big—big subjects, big photographs. His large-format prints (dimensions up to 60 × 80 inches are not uncommon) match the physical scope of the oil industry, quarries, and ship breaking, as well as their thematic implications. His newest series on display at Howard Greenberg and Bruce Wolkowitz Galleries takes on one of the biggest (70 percent of the earth's surface; about 60 percent of you and me) topics on the planet: water. More particularly, it is human interaction with water that draws his attention.

This theme of how people flourish within and simultaneously corrupt the environment is one Burtynsky has explored many times over the past two decades. Originally taking inspiration from American photographers Ansel Adams and Edward Weston, Burtynsky eventually turned to landscape revisionists such as Robert Adams, Joe Deal, Louis Baltz, and especially Frank Gohlke (a group often labeled the New Topographics) who were determined to keep the human element in the frame, and not present nature as pristine in its isolation.

The photos at these galleries all take aim at the way we use water—dams, stepwells, irrigation systems, sewage treatment, beaches, mining runoff, and rice terraces are some of Burtynsky's subjects as he ranges around the globe (India, Texas, Spain, China, Iceland, Arizona) to document these industrial-scale interactions. Many of these photos are necessarily aerial; it's not simply that the sheer expanse of some of these locales requires a panoramic view, but that many of their most striking imagistic qualities aren't revealed at ground level. Anyone who has flown cross-country is familiar with the circular plots (the mechanism at work is called pivot irrigation) that pattern great swaths of the Midwest and West. Burtynsky dutifully offers a pair of photos—one in Texas, the other in Arizona—that are as readily recognizable as the pizza pan or vinyl record shapes you have spied from your window seat. On the ground, one of these giant discs would appear as just a field of alfalfa.

Other god's-eye perspectives would be harder to obtain: glacial runoff in Iceland, an aquaculture farm in China, or a sewage treatment plant in London. Most likely, we haven't seen sky-high views of these, but Burtynsky's treatment amplifies our unfamiliarity. In Skeidararsandur, Iceland, the camera seems to be floating out over the middle of the glacial flow—and consequently the photo lacks any evidence of land; it's hard to tell if what we see is even a stream. The rhythmic cascade of melted ice with its metallic sheen doesn't suggest water so much as the molten product of a blast furnace or a great rumpled sheet of aluminum. The aerial view also confounds reflexive expectations. From above, the London sewage treatment plant reveals its elegant structure; the facility's geometrically arranged tanks could be a game board or an abacus.

Burtynsky generates a revelatory tension between the images' environmental content (and, indeed, their advocacy) and the aestheticizing of ecological stress, if not outright disaster. Two photos that bring us up close to the roiling brown water and sediment spewing from the Xiaolangdi Dam on the Yellow River in Henan Province, China, have a painterly quality we would recognize from the work of J.M.W. Turner. Turner depicted destructive, storm-tossed seas, while Burtynsky focuses on another, more incremental kind of damage. This dam, like almost all other such waterworks, brings benefits but at a great cost—the destruction of river communities, natural habitats, and consequent urban development. But the photos are no less alluring in their presentation of tumult and power. This doubleness—of both the art and the manufactured landscape—perhaps holds at least as much importance for him as his determination to scrupulously document global despoilment.

Burtynsky's epic-size prints are color-rich, offering granular detail. With even scant study, we can make out the faces and details of dress on some of the thousands of pilgrims assembled to bathe in the sacred waters of the Saraswati for the Hindu rite, the Kumbh Mela. The photographer's eye encompasses a mile-wide swath dense with human activity. It's hard not to feel a sense of amazement, as if the gallery wall had opened up to provide an Olympian view of a teeming scene just out of reach. The scale, visual precision, and elevated point of view, though, carry the unavoidable aura of the glossy *National Geographic* gatefold. And with that comes overtones of scientific observation, as well as more unsettling notes of imperial regard. This touristic element is not easily set aside: a totalizing impulse contends with a less generalized, more empathic subjectivity; the method and material of these photos can feel disconnected from the photographer's desire to investigate our intimate relation to the natural world.

Burtynsky, though, doesn't offer the conventional binary notion of human life in opposition to the earth's. Instead, his images present human activity as not apart from nature, but rather as integral to the planet's being: our mess is the mess that nature makes. Whether he is showing the luminescent colors produced in a phosphor tailings pond in Florida or the more ecologically benign image of an Escher-like terraced stepwell in India, Burtynsky candidly documents human effort, human beauty, and human carelessness. For instance, the photographer's vertiginous images of quarries suggest inverted cathedrals. How did they lift huge blocks of marble out of that hole? How did they lower massive machines to its bottom? The very scale of ambition and prowess on display complicates a facile response to the despoilment. Burtynsky's pictures are big because their subject—our so-called battle with nature that's in fact a battle with ourselves—is big. To be drawn into their vast yet intricate domain is to gain some felt knowledge about this conflict: that gorgeous, mesmerizing plain of glacial melt delights the eye, even as it signals impending cataclysm. The emotions and instincts that drive and complete this seduction define our species, but they also may just be what doom us.

*Hyperallergic,* November 2, 2013.

# Places in the Art: The Real Dirt on Environmental Photography

The United States is what it is, said ever-pithy Gertrude Stein, because "there is more space where nobody is than where anybody is." True when she wrote it over many decades ago, and some 150 million people later, it remains so. Next time you fly cross-country, look out the window and you'll find your visual machinery struggling to process the continuous ocean of land rolling out below you. With less pith but apt drama, Charles Olson echoed Stein: "I take SPACE to be the central fact to man born in America.... I spell it large because it comes large here. Large and without mercy." But from this landscape stretching out mercilessly before us, Americans have exacted some quotient of revenge: we have chopped, fenced, dammed, and poisoned as much of its infinite expanse as possible. It was a big job, but we're a big-headed people. Along the way, we nurtured a romance about home where buffalo roam and wide-open spaces, an Edenic myth of grandeur and nature's redemptive power. This paradise was reflected and embellished in the landscape photography of Ansel Adams, Eliot Porter, and Edward Weston, the court photographers of the modern plains and the West.

These photographers crafted an idealized vision of a Western American landscape unsullied by people and progress, untouched by the environmental catastrophe that began in the mid-19th century and continues today. They registered each nuance of paradise's beauty but neglected to include Adam and Eve, let alone the snake. Yet during the last two decades, a new breed of landscape photographer has emerged, guided by a complex and always unsettling aesthetic—the study of how people and the land get along, or don't. Their landscape photography, sometimes called the New Topographics, documents interactions as diverse as open-pit mining and backpacking, nuclear testing and tourism.

In *Measure of Emptiness,* Frank Gohlke dramatizes the raw openness of the Midwest by emphasizing its human presence. His formally elegant, high-contrast black-and-white shots of grain elevators—"the cathedrals of the prairies"—poised amid the ceaselessly flat plains of Texas and Kansas provide a sharp-edged paradigm of the man-altered landscape. Cropped to emphasize the grain elevators, whose mere 10-story height appears epic against the farmland, the photos present the landscape as a tabula rasa and the structures as human script. Indeed, the presence of these sleek towers provides the scale against which the farmlands' uncluttered vastness is calculated—the measure of emptiness. The pun here—the elevators which hold many cups, or measures, of grain are themselves often empty—complicates the dichotomy of unbounded space and containment. The space created within the walls of a grain elevator is as vacuous as the land around it; the construction mediates degrees of emptiness by shaping the space within as well as without. Yet Gohlke's photos permit these outsize intruders to fit in, and even grace the prairie.

Rife with such paradoxes, New Topographic photography rarely indulges in easy judgment on Man the Destroyer; an agile curiosity tends to override the environmentalist's didactic impulse. Gohlke has thoroughly researched grain elevators, and he supplements his photos with a detailed essay by agricultural historian John C. Hudson on their architecture and economic role. Gohlke wants not only to reveal the strange allure of these starkly functional structures but also to acknowledge how complexly they are wed to both their builders and the flatlands from which they appear to burst. Often set on the outskirts of small towns at the intersection of both roads and railways, the elevators represent a crucial juncture in the industrial food chain—the moment when gathered grain is dispersed to distant kitchens. Like the Empire State Building with its antennae on top, each grain elevator serves as regional symbol and broadcast perch, sending out amber waves rather than electronic ones. Gohlke's pristine, symmetrical compositions locate and polish the iconic stature latent in what is just a big storage bin. He writes that the essential grain elevator view is had through a car's windshield, "as the speck grows to colossal size and then shrinks to rejoin the horizon." His best shots re-create this processional approach, catching a sun-bleached spire as it looms up at the crest of some highway's lazy bend.

Mark Klett, another practitioner of the New Topographics, tracks down the scattered detritus—rock carvings, burnt-out autos, dune buggy trails, and golf courses—of human culture throughout the Southwest. Although his photos in *Revealing Territory* possess the slightly clinical feel of gathered evidence, it's softened by the offhanded, often witty compositions he favors. Klett flexed his documentary impulse more strictly while participating in the recent Rephotographic Survey Project, an effort by landscape photographers to locate the sites of many classic 19th-century shots by William Henry Jackson and Timothy O'Sullivan and rephotograph those scenes from the original vantage points. What the photos revealed was sometimes expected (delicate rock formations hacked off to serve time on country club lawns) and sometimes surprising (a site where a mining town once sat, now cleansed of any human trace). The paired images juxtapose our frenetic human clock with geology's epochal pace; they also show the ways photography, however straightforward, still manipulates and recreates the landscape it depicts. This self-consciousness remains an important part of Klett's work: his photos deliberately show unfinished edges, and he inscribes captions directly on his prints. Often his shoe or shadow sneaks into an image; gone is the illusion, fostered by Adams and Porter, of a pure photographic eye that captures nature's spectacle without making car tracks to get there.

Klett upends stock notions about the value we place on some human marks and the disdain we hold for others. Several familiar images of Native American petrography are included along with more modern contributions to rock art, like the letters *TV* inexplicably painted on a huge boulder, a big-chested female outline scratched on bare stone, or the message "U + Me" spelled out in neatly placed rocks. In a few hundred years, some archaeologist may puzzle over this haphazard scrawling with the same interpretive intensity now devoted to the work of the Navajo or Hopi. People and their stuff achieve a sly prominence through Klett's work; whether viewing a once bare valley paved over with a plush golf course or an ephemeral human shadow cast across a rock, we can never ignore our own insistent and often disquieting habitation of the landscape. Useful essays by Patricia Nelson Limerick and Thomas W. Southall delve into how this awareness plays against the myth of noble isolation amid barren space in the American West. Klett's photo of a U-Haul truck parked in Monument Valley—the definitive Western topography—accurately depicts the pioneer movement of the automobile age without suggesting that covered wagons and horses, however quaint, were any less an intrusion. To sample the sacredness and thrill of such epic landscapes, as well as to mine and litter them, people have to be there. Klett's photographs require that we meet the West's vast terrain honestly, not as awestruck nature converts but rather as co-conspirators in both its enjoyment and domestication.

How we've set up housekeeping in the great outdoors is depicted with studious precision by Peter Goin in *Stopping Time: A Rephotographic Survey of Lake Tahoe*. Updating pictures made between the 1860s and 1930s, Goin constructs new images from as close as possible to the angle of the original photo. The resultant pair often looks like a view through a lopsided stereoscope, near-mirror images that challenge you to find what's wrong with this picture. In choosing the Tahoe region, Goin sets the stage for an earnest polemic; the crystal clear, glacier-carved lake sits like a jewel among the alpine peaks of the Sierras, but this scenic splendor draws more than 18 million visitors each year to its burgeoning resort community. An environmentally correct contrast that would play a Redwood spire off against a casino's neon sign springs readily to mind. Instead, Goin delivers evidence of subtler, more mundane changes: we see that the faux quaint, cupola-peaked Ta-Ne-Va-Ho Diner and Bingo Parlor from the 1940s has become the sleeker, even tackier Crystal Bay Club and Casino, a remnant of its cupola still visible. The human landscape may not evolve at the grand tempo of geologic time, but it does proceed according to laws just as predictable. In the case of gambling joints, they will always get bigger, better lit, and more hospitable to the automobile.

The dramatic refashioning of the land required by cars can be seen in nearly every image; to ease the flow of traffic, cliffs have been blasted and mountains sliced. Yet when we compare two shots of Echo Summit—the first from the 1930s during the first stages of paved road construction, the second showing a smooth ribbon of stone and asphalt curving gracefully around the mountain—it's difficult not to credit the engineering skill, and even the aesthetics, of the builders. If these elegant constructions enable more cars, more visitors, to spoil the Tahoe area, they remain no less beautiful to contemplate. In this way, Goin troubles, rather than indulges, the knee-jerk environmental impulse.

As C. Elizabeth Raymond points out in her introduction, the Lake Tahoe region is "vigorously managed" in order to preserve a pristine appearance for consumption by tourists. This means that in some photographic pairs, the historical view features landscapes being mined or logged, photos that proudly proclaim human dominance over nature, while the contemporary picture reveals nature's deliberate restoration. In one case, a railroad track has been replaced by a bicycle path. But is this maintained nature natural? Is that even a useful question? What Goin's photos offer, besides brief excursions in time travel, is a lesson in the unerasable humanness of place; these images make clear the intertwined narratives of stone, water, and Winnebago.

In contrast to Goin's precision-driven black-and-whites, *Between Home and Heaven* features large, luscious color reproductions. With a title that posits the middle ground of a lived-in paradise, and observant prose from Merry A. Foresta, Stephen Jay Gould, and Karal Ann Marling, this catalogue for the recent show at the Smithsonian signals a coming-of-age for the New Topographics. While some of the artists who helped define the aesthetic, such as Lewis Baltz and Robert Adams, are unfortunately absent, many other significant figures—

Richard Misrach, Goin, John Pfahl, David T. Hanson, Robert Glenn Ketchum—receive generous attention. The criterion for admission is a willingness to reimagine the pastoral now that human conquest of the continent is complete.

Inevitably, such images have a political cast, but these photographers hold themselves in check, opting for a neutral, anti-dramatic style that allows the charged meanings in certain landscapes to emerge uncoaxed and unadorned. Goin's eerie shots of nuclear test bomb sites in Nevada and the South Pacific could have been taken by a government surveyor, while Deborah Bright's multiphoto view of the entire length of Antietam's Bloody Lane contrasts the calm authority of completeness with the historical record of carnage. Environmental concerns are also addressed obliquely, often within the vocabulary of form and color. For instance, Skeet McAuley presents what seems to be a typical, plush, wide-angle vista of a forest, until you find the trees' unpredictable shapes met at the top of the photo by a series of right angles—a sky-colored pipeline cuts almost invisibly through these Alaskan woods. In a photo taken in Death Valley, Karen Halverson instructively contrasts the quality and sources of light. She shoots a jeep, with its doors flung open and headlights flaring, parked facing the sunrise. The jeep's meek high beams point at a brightly polished patch of water lit by the not-yet-visible sun. Of course, the machine's no match for nature, but the jeep does adequately illuminate the dark, not yet sunlit area in which it's parked. It is precisely that technology which delivered the photographer to her sunrise, and put the camera in her hand.

This complicity in the damaged landscape raises one of the aesthetic issues central to the New Topographics: Is human handiwork always ugly? When John Pfahl serves up a Hallmark-pretty image of the cooling towers at Three Mile Island reflected in the glassy surface of the Susquehanna River, he subverts our idea about what can be beautiful while also deflating attendant political ideology. The cooling towers, looking like fancifully wound cotton spindles, make an undeniably pleasing picture when aestheticized and lifted from their fearsome reality. We can appreciate the image as we would an Adams photo of

Half-Dome at Yosemite, or maybe a postcard shot of Mount Saint Helens just before it blew. Mother Nature plays rough, too.

The final photograph in the book sums up with wry humor the dilemma not only for landscape photographers but for anyone who holds open space dear and believes that, while we have throttled the wilderness from our continent, we should still retain some vestige of pastoral values. Jim Stone's high-definition black-and-white photo admits us to a spectacular solar display over a lake in Arizona. It is a textbook picturesque landscape shot. There is swaying brush in the foreground, then the bright disc of sun on the water. On the far shore, a mountain range, which appears to be the product of some gentle celestial kneading, recedes into the distance; above, the clouds detonate softly with the sun's last rays. But wait: off in the corner sit three cast-plastic chairs mounted on wooden beams for maximum audience visibility. They are empty but nonetheless very present. Unavoidable, in fact. In America, as the 20th century winds down, there is less and less space where nobody is. The New Topographic photographers assert this when they decline to crop us—the somebodies—out. We're here, they say, and any peace made with the landscape must first acknowledge that. Meanwhile, have a seat and enjoy the view.

*Village Voice Literary Supplement,* November 1994.

# Exquisite Corpses: Lifestyles of the Dead and Buried in Funeral Photography

When other 11-year-olds suited up for Little League, I joined the casket team, a select cadre of altar boys who served funeral masses. Although delighted with perquisites like being excused from class and the dollar tips the funeral director slipped into my sleeve, I was excited most by my day laborer's familiarity with the mystery and power of death. Almost once a week I found myself in a black cassock, poised rigid beside a coffin, dizzily inhaling incense as sporadic sobs from a grieving family tore through the priest's reading of the Lazarus story. Stoic child amid others' pain, I earnestly played my bit part in a pageant of last things, sensing how ancient rites sought to transcend not only the drama of a single loss, but that of death itself.

It was clear to me even then that while religious ritual and social custom make an elaborate show of honoring the dead, they chiefly, and sensibly, seek to comfort and instruct the living. The dead, after all, are no longer paying customers. Only survivors can pride themselves on erecting a stylish monument, take solace in a particularly apt epitaph, or feel their spirits brightened by flowers blossoming on a grave. Although palpable tokens of a world beyond, funeral trappings are built, bought, and kept up by the tenants of this one. The investment and effort reflect our need to impose sense upon the raw uncertainty of death. A wake, the Kaddish, or a mausoleum reveal themselves as emblems of human order, both chronological and moral; they serve us as the final periods in life's governing grammar.

Traditionally, our sentences come to rest beneath a patch of grass and a piece of stone wedged among the teeming dead in some boneyard, grand or small. When we pass a cemetery—whether well-mowed suburban hills or iron-fenced parcels of jagged teeth and bent trees in the city—mortal thoughts trouble our transit. Rarely do we wonder how the place came to be where it is or look the way it does. Four generations of David Charles Sloane's family have designed, landscaped, and managed cemeteries, so when he tells that story in *The Last Great Necessity: Cemeteries in American History,* he does so with a professional's equanimity and expertise. In his exploration of the evolving design, economics, and social role of the American cemetery, Sloane handily demonstrates the cemetery's vital connection to popular culture, one he believes to be at least as strong as its more obvious tie to religious custom.

In colonial America, death was a domestic affair. The last breath and the preparation of the body took place at home; family members dug the grave in the backyard or the churchyard down the street, and the whole town attended the funeral. But as cities grew, so did the population of the deceased; by 1800, there were over 100,000 corpses interred in downtown Manhattan's Trinity churchyard. Increasingly formalized customs replaced quainter ones like the burial of suicides at crossroads. Also, many urban cemeteries had risen several yards closer to heaven because the limited space was reused. Since so many corpses lay rotting in crowded communities, citizens worried about "miasmatic transmission," especially during the 1822 yellow fever epidemic. Public health officials began to advocate intervention in what was once the most intimate of family rites.

Designed to provide ample burial space for generations in an ornamentally landscaped garden far from urban congestion, Mount Auburn Cemetery, just outside Cambridge, MA, initiated what was called the rural cemetery movement. Mount Auburn and distinguished successors like Green-Wood in Brooklyn retained some communal spirit. These cemeteries were voluntary, nonsectarian organizations of families who sought to provide picturesque, inspirational burial grounds for their kin. Of Mount Auburn, Emily Dickinson wrote in 1846 that "it seems as if nature had formed the spot with a distinct idea of its being a resting place for her children." Indeed, such cemeteries proved popular enough to cause a reverse migration; as the living moved into cities, the dead were moved out. They also provided a "didactic landscape," where "visitors were thought to enter the cemetery in a state of anxiety and ambition and to leave calm and contemplative." And visitors did come. So many thousands enjoyed Sunday strolls in Green-Wood that the design became a touchstone for the architects of Central Park. An "island of peace," the rural cemetery provided an apparent counterpoint to the bustling mercantile life of the 19th century; still, in their economic hierarchies, expressed by increasingly grand monuments and segregation of the dead by race, these garden graveyards accurately reflected a less than serene civic culture.

Soon, the cities engulfed their cemeteries, which fell out of fashion and were succeeded by the lawn park and memorial park designs. Suburban and spacious, these new cemeteries demanded that monuments, headstones, and floral arrangements all conform to a master aesthetic plan. This streamlining for efficiency also characterized the process of dying and mortuary preparation. By the turn of the century, most people died in hospitals, and all subsequent details were increasingly turned over to funeral professionals; standardized routines replaced personal choice and involvement in death's rituals. Gradually, the sacred and ritualistic elements of death were siphoned away. Our technological epoch substituted the more palatable superstition that death was a "collective process," one fully embraceable by rational thought.

But individual idiosyncrasies persist and even thrive. Witness the photographs by Lucinda Bunnen and Virginia Warren Smith collected in *Scoring in Heaven: Gravestones and Cemetery Art of the American Sunbelt States*. Just as the graveyards of southern Europe sport livelier, more expressive monuments, so do America's southern cemeteries. Northern Protestantism and southwestern Hispanic-inflected Catholicism might bear on the contrast, or perhaps the warmer climes encourage the work of outdoor artists. Whatever the reason, these photographers have caught a lushly sentimental decorative spirit not easy to find in the sober, manicured cemeteries of New England. To buttoned-down tastes, these images—pampers and apple juice bottles strewn on an infant's grave—will appear excessive, if not weird. Yet this plaintively sharp evidence of a keening heart speaks undeniable truth about the absoluteness of death's devastation.

The photos have been grouped loosely by content—Hands, Ribbons and Roses, Boots and Saddles, Feathers and Shoes—so each section shows variations on a theme, confirming the folk artists' craft as they adapt, for instance, the use of toy bunnies or stopped clocks to their specific occasion. It's an unselfconsciously inventive art whose purity of articulation can be arresting: an oval wedding picture, bride and groom's eyes locked in standard loving regard, set on a heart-shaped granite stone. The emotionalism is as unashamed as the trope is moving: it marks a spouse's loss by invoking the vow "till death do us part." The monument echoes, however dimly, a distant past when death, then both frequent and intimately managed, maintained a vigorous presence in all the rituals of the living. (The AIDS epidemic has had a similar effect, intensifying our daily lives with intimations of mortality.) Not all the *memento mori* are so nakedly heartfelt; others defuse grief through humor. There's the pink telephone, receiver off the hook, and accompanying note, "Jesus Called," or the headstone engraved with a man bowling a strike and the message "Scoring in Heaven." Many bear regional emblems of the deceased's hobby or job: cowboy boots, oil rigs, banjos, trucks, and beloved cars. By and large, these are working people who cannot account for themselves with expensive sculpture or mausoleums; their stories get told through searing, enigmatic detail. On the marker for a 24-year-old Vietnam vet, two pints of whiskey have been laid. Graffiti scratched into the polished stone reads "Outlaws Forever," "We Love You Brother," and "Vengeance Is Best Served Cold." Biker? Killed in a fight? Driving drunk? Whichever, no happy tale, no moral lesson here. This death refuses to be sanitized and robbed of its terror. It is what it is—a loss, tragic and unredeemed.

Death's tyrannical finality can be found on frightening display in Dr. Stanley Burns's collection of 19th- and early 20th-century memorial photographs and daguerreotypes, *Sleeping Beauty: Memorial Photography in America*. Almost every one of its stunning reproductions inspires shivers and achingly vivid pathos. An epigram from La Rochefoucauld—"One can no more look steadily at Death than at the sun"—hardly prepares you for this frank confrontation with the dead themselves. Pictured in a wide variety of poses and backgrounds are lifeless adolescent girls, old men, gunslingers, clergymen, whole families, and children, many children. An atlas of death's various faces, this collection delivers us to the juncture in the previous century when a new technology found immediate application in a mourning tradition. Keeping a lock of hair, some nail clippings of the deceased, or making a death mask as a memento count among our oldest funeral rites. Photography offered a more precisely evocative keepsake and was widely employed (and according to a recent Ann Landers column, remains so) to preserve one last and lasting image.

These photos undo the mortuary business's slick veneer of euphemism; those photographed haven't gone on, left us, or found their rest. Simply, they're quite dead, still here, and don't generally appear rested so much as lost in thought. As modern viewers, we react with horror to the gruesome portrait of a malnourished child, a skeletal face, her half-open eyes fixed on some distant point. Shocking to us because of its unmediated depiction of not only death, but the even more fearsome act of dying, such an image would have been commonplace when the photo was taken in 1848. As Burns points out in his observant notes, the child mortality rate during the 19th century ran from 30 to 50 per cent. Most everyone lost siblings growing up, lost children later as parents. All of these pictures of infants and children, freed from their status as macabre curiosities, become testaments of ineffable sweetness. If we recall that this photograph would have been a treasured remembrance, the powerful, enveloping love of her parents seems to wash over the girl's aged, emaciated face, to confirm that her dying was no deformation, but simply part of the brief life she shared with her family. This may not be—may never have been—the truth about death; it is, however, the necessary truth about grief. The dead do not require transcendence, whereas the living crave it.

Memorial photos developed their own styles and variations. The wife or brother posed contemplating a husband or sister, the religious iconography suggested by the composition of mother cradling her dead child, or the sleeping beauty, a young girl laid out in an elegant dress on an elaborate canopy bed—one Tiny Alice with sausage curls clutched a wide-eyed doll—sound the faith that death, like sleep, is merely transient. Again, this is folk artistry that cuts deeply while it reassures. When Poe described the rural cemetery as an "interval of tranquility," he might also have included memorial photos. Initially, perhaps intentionally, disturbing, they repay close attention with a sense of human poignancy. Even in their honest commemoration of the dead, these silvery, luminescent prints promise, if not resurrection, at least one triumph over the void; they shed some small grace on the living.

When we are alive, the flesh houses us; when we die, our survivors, in turn, will house that flesh. In image or stone, they commemorate a life by marking out a piece of turf, some mantel space. Even shrunk to that little measure, we are not simply commended to an urn or cemetery, but rather to the memory of others. But funeral architecture and ornament serve that memory as a catalyst, and as a point of instructive contrast; recollected vigor is inevitably brought up short when set against a gravestone's mute finality. Renaissance poets had a phrase that capsulized this lesson: *Respice finem*, regard thy end. If our sense of ending has been banished to an unacknowledged, shadowy realm by technology's bright promise, these artifacts and rites of death allow our mortality some frank and necessary survival in the daylight world.

*Village Voice Literary Supplement*, December 1991.

## Acknowledgements

The editors of these essays and reviews improved them in every case. I am grateful to Eric Banks, Natalie Haddad, Jeffrey Kastner, Jeremy Lybarger, M. Mark, Ben Metcalf, David McNeill, Michael Miller, Sina Najafi, Nicole Rudick, Polly Shulman, Rob Spillman, Margaret Sundell, Jennifer Szalai, Ania Szremski, and Hrag Vartanian.

"For Keeps: The Christian Sanderson Museum." *Tin House*, Winter 2003; reprinted in *Cooking and Stealing: The Tin House Nonfiction Reader*, edited by Charles D'Ambrosio. Bloomsbury, 2004.

"Peep Show: This Museum Wants to Sex You Up." *Tin House*, Spring 2003.

"Diamonds in the Rough: On Havelock Ellis's Studies in the Psychology of Sex." *Tin House*, Winter 2012.

"Weird Séance: Tony Oursler's Compendium of the Paranormal Reveals a Twilight World." *Bookforum*, Summer 2017.

"Some Trick: A New Volume Surveys the Art of Magic." *Bookforum*, Summer 2019.

"Frédéric Bruly Bouabré: World Unbound." *Bookforum*, June–August 2022.

"Enumeration Sensation: Umberto Eco's Book of Lists." *Bookforum*, December–January 2010.

"Past Forward: Joe Brainard Made His Memories Yours." *Bookforum*, April 2012.

"Art House: On 'John Ashbery Collects.'" *The Paris Review Daily*, October 22, 2013.

"Soon There Was Nothing Left: A Posthumous Volume from John Ashbery Troubles the Line between Finished and Incomplete." Poetry Foundation, June 2021.

"Unpopular Mechanics: Photographers Search Archives to Uncover Hidden Story of Post-War America." *Bookforum*, April–May 2017.

"Quote Unquote; Or, You Can Say That Again." *Village Voice Literary Supplement*, June 1993.

"On the Record: The Talk Writers Talk." *Bookforum*, February–March 2007.

"String Theory: The Elusive Art of Harry Smith." *Bookforum*, February–March 2016.

"Top Secret: Images from the Stasi Archives." *Bookforum*, December–January 2014.

"The Lost Generator: Gertrude Stein Builds a Better Reader." *Village Voice Literary Supplement*, November 1988; reprinted in *The Best of the Village Voice Literary Supplement*, edited by Joy Press. Riverhead, 2001.

"Collected Letters: Ed Ruscha Draws Language the Way It Feels." *Bookforum*, March 2015.

"John Yau's Letters for Anna May Wong." Paper delivered at the Louisville Conference on Literature and Culture, February 2024.

"Review of *One Long Black Sentence* by Renee Gladman & Fred Moten." *Bookforum*, September–November 2020.

"Post Modern: Ray Johnson's Contrarian Sensibility Inspired Mail Art." *Bookforum*, Summer 2014.

"Correspondence School: The Changing Face of Letter Writing Manuals." *Village Voice Literary Supplement*, October 1994.

"Tour of Duty: A Baedeker's Dozen." *Village Voice Literary Supplement*, February 1994.

"The Criminal Within: A Genre of How-to Manuals Indulges Our Darkest Fantasies." *Harper's Magazine*, March 1999.

"In a Word: Jackson Mac Low Restlessly Reinvents the Line." *Paris Review Daily*, March 1, 2017.

"The Bookness of Not-Books." *Paris Review Daily*, June 22, 2017.

"Nonsense and Sensibility: The Absurd Humor of Glen Baxter." *Bookforum*, April–May 2016.

"Review of *Bruce Nauman: The True Artist* by Peter Plagens." *New York Times* Book Review, December 5, 2014.

"Made Men of Letters: Our Thing about the Cosa Nostra." *Harper's Magazine*, October 1997.

"Lost Highways: Finding Our Way Home with the *National Geographic Road Atlas*." *Village Voice Literary Supplement*, July 1998.

"Off the Map: The Way of Some Worlds." *Tin House*, Spring 2005.

"Blue Is the Color of Blockade: Boris Mikhailov." *4Columns*, February 14, 2025.

"Self Portraits in a Complex Mirror: The Photographs of Vivian Maier." *Hyperallergic*, December 21, 2013.

"Review of *Thomas Struth*." *Bookforum*, February 2018.

"Review of *Seascapes* by Hiroshi Sugimoto." *Bookforum*, December–January 2016.

"Looking Down: The God's-eye View of the Aerial Photograph." *Cabinet*, Summer 2003.

"Review of *Proving Ground* by David Maisel." *Bookforum*, April–May 2020.

"A Boy's Own Story: A Gordon Parks Photo Essay Causes a Lifetime of Unintended Consequences." *Bookforum*, December–January 2020.

"Dead Man Rising: War Photography." *Hyperallergic*, January 18, 2014.

"Night and the City: Weegee Showed New York the Spectacle of Itself," *Bookforum*, Summer 2018.

"Saul Leiter: Centennial Showcase." *4Columns*, January 19, 2024.

"Review of *Type 42: Fame Is the Name of the Game*." *Bookforum*, April 2015.

"Go with the Slow: Ragnar Kjartansson's The Visitors." *Hyperallergic*, March 16, 2013.

"Gary Winogrand in Living Color." *Hyperallergic*, July 16, 2019.

"Flow Charts: Edward Burtynsky's Photos of the World's Watery Parts." *Hyperallergic*, November 2, 2013.

"Places in the Art: The Real Dirt on Environmental Photography." *Village Voice Literary Supplement*, November 1992.

"Exquisite Corpses: Lifestyles of the Dead and Buried in Funeral Photography." *Village Voice Literary Supplement*, December 1991.

## About the Author

**Albert Mobilio** is the author of four books of poetry: *Same Faces* (2020), *Touch Wood* (2011), *Me with Animal Towering* (2002), and *The Geographics* (1995). A book of fiction, *Games and Stunts,* appeared in 2016. His essays and reviews have appeared in *Artforum, Paris Review Daily, Harper's Magazine, The New York Times Book Review, BOMB, The Village Voice, Cabinet, 4Columns, Hyperallergic,* and *Tin House*. In 1998, he received the National Book Critics Circle Nona Balakian Award for Excellence in Reviewing. In 2000, he received a Whiting Award. He was a MacDowell Fellow in 2015 and was awarded an Andy Warhol Arts Writers Grant in 2017. A former editor at *Bookforum,* he is an associate professor of literary studies at Eugene Lang College at the New School.

www.ingramcontent.com/pod-product-compliance
Lightning Source LLC
LaVergne TN
LVHW091112080826
845145LV00008B/1890
* 9 7 8 1 9 6 8 4 2 2 0 1 1 *